LIVE WIRE

Live Wire

Long-Winded Short Stories

KELLY RIPA

DEYST.

An Imprint of WILLIAM MORROW

HarperCollins books may be purchased for educational, business, or sales promotional use. For information, please email the Special Markets Department at SPsales@harpercollins.com.

FIRST EDITION

Designed by Renata De Oliveira

Library of Congress Cataloging-in-Publication Data
has been applied for.

ISBN 978-0-06-307330-2

22 23 24 25 26   LSC   10 9 8 7 6 5 4 3 2 1

FOR MARK,

the keeper of the spark

CONTENTS

LIVE WIRE

"Allow myself to introduce myself."

—AUSTIN POWERS

A PROTRACTED INTRODUCTION

"Please, please. I need to push. I'm begging you. . . . I need to push."

I know what you're thinking. And you would be wrong. No, I wasn't in labor. Just stay with me, and it will all make sense, I promise.

"Can I just get a minute? Maybe we should push the announcement. Don't you think I should push?" The question was one posed by me, to my editor, to my agents, my PR team, my manager, Mark, and anyone else who would listen. "I mean, what difference does a day make?"

The answers came universally and swiftly, "No. We don't push. We stay the course. We announce tomorrow, 9:00 a.m." Never one to trust the experts, especially ones I'm paying, I pushed back, "Really? You don't think the Prince Harry of it all will suck the wind out of any announcement?" You see, I was set to announce my book on the same day that Prince Harry was announcing that he was going to be publishing his very important and revealing memoir. We wouldn't be publishing at the same time, but we were going to be telling the world about our impending books on the same day. This seemed wrongheaded to me.

Hosting a talk show for the past twenty-plus years and interviewing many, many authors has made me skeptical about publicizing my publicity. No, I'm not clever enough to come up with that on my own. My dear friend and former publicist, Stan Rosenfield, coined that phrase to mean when called upon to promote oneself, one must never promote oneself. That's what people like me are for, but here I am. Paging Stan!

So, it already felt gross to put out a press release announcing my book. But since I was being gross already, I thought, if a press release falls in the forest and nobody, you know, whatever the rest of that stupid phrase is . . . But did I want my little quiet announcement overshadowed by THAT BIG GIANT GLOBAL ANNOUNCEMENT? 'Twas a royal pain in my arse. We would have to let Prince Harry go first.

But none of my love for things having to do with the British royal family negates the fact that I've spent the past year and a half of my life, and I mean almost every day, writing this collection of essays. A year and a half of my life! I had to have my desk chair at first reupholstered, then eventually replaced, due to the overuse. I also had microneedling on my rear end, which had taken on the shape of my chair from chronic sitting. How I suffered to bring you this future award-winning work of art!

Also, I'm not a writer. Not in the sense of writing for a profession, but I've written plenty of forewords for other people's books, not to mention cover quotes, speeches for other people's book tours, and my fair share of talks for New York's 92nd Street Y. I've also written some scripts that you've never heard of, but let me state, for the record, that I have no expertise in the world of books, or publishing. As a matter of fact, I don't have any expertise in most of the crafts in which I've earned a living for the past thirty-plus years. Some people are gifted. Some people have ghostwriters. And some people are me.

I'm also incredibly risk averse, and frequently prone to regret. So, I was about to call this whole thing off, even though I was 99 percent done, due to the chatter of the press release ratcheting up.

Personally, I think my very perceptive editor was on to me and sensed I might pull the plug on this entire thing. And she was not wrong, as the idea had crossed my mind several times. It's crossing my mind now, even after the announcement. In fact, I wish you would put this book down right now and walk away. Go ahead, I'll wait.

It's a funny thing to write a book, especially one of personal essays, which I thought would be easier, and frothier, than writing a memoir, which seems like a nightmare of an idea. But once I got started, I realized right away that organizing life events in a series of short stories with a beginning, middle, and end was way more complicated, and rife with land mines than I anticipated. I thought it would be an easy, breezy, funny jog down memory lane. But some of the memories weren't easy, breezy, or funny. Some made me depressed. Some made me angry. Some left me stunned at myself, for accepting such unacceptable treatment, for such a long time.

Writing a book is a lot. Like, A LOT. Now that it's done, that I've done it, I feel I owe it to you, and to me, to be as honest as I possibly can without violating any of the myriad NDAs and confidentiality agreements I had to sign with my current employer. There were several times in this process when I regretted the decision to do this at all because (a) I don't know what I am doing, (b) just because I like to read books doesn't qualify me to write one, (c) so many of my friends have done this and have encouraged me to do the same that I fear I just caved into their peer pressure, and (d) I am too old to fall victim to peer pressure.

But, and there is always a but . . .

What I realized in my recollections is that often things that appear easy are really quite difficult. And while nobody's life is perfect, there were times when I was called upon to make mine appear

3

as close as possible. I did my job day after day, making it look fun and easy when at times, and let me be really real here, it was none of those things. But as a woman, I stood up and did the job I had to do. Playing a character is what all women do, but playing yourself on television is the hardest role I've ever had, especially when I started before I even knew who I really was.

Maybe that's why I decided to call the book *Live Wire*. Because *Becoming* by Michelle Obama was already taken. And my editor thought *Uneducated* was too derivative.

Because I'm a fatalist, when things started to feel comfortable, I started looking for signs that I should stop, pull out (tee-hee). I checked fortune cookies, read horoscopes, and asked Audrey Slater (my stylist who seems to know things), but the most prophetic input that I received came from two surprising and very unlikely sources. And although I hate to name-drop in the introduction, I fear I must.

Mega-bestselling author James Patterson and former president Bill Clinton (perhaps you've heard of them?) were on our show to discuss their thriller, *The President's Daughter*, a follow-up to their best seller, *The President Is Missing*. When we went to commercial break, Ryan Seacrest, my colleague and longtime friend, piped up with "You know, Kellyripa here is writing a book," enthusiastically, pointing toward me, so they would know who he was talking about. AS IF!

As if either of these men would be the least bit interested in my little womanifesto.

Mr. Patterson and President Clinton both smiled congenially. "We know," they said at once. Oh no. My blabbermouth had infected everyone I work with. I have been obsessing about this book hoping someone might love me enough to step in and say, "ARE

YOU CRAZY? DON'T RUIN YOUR LIFE BY WRITING A BOOK. YOU'VE LASTED THIS LONG. WHY NOW?" You know, like they did when I tried to run the New York City Marathon. But instead, I'd been subjecting everyone to the story of my stories. Including poor Ed Connolly Jr., the producer in charge of this segment, and possibly the nicest man on earth, who had clearly been regaling these two literary titans with tales of my upcoming publication.

Out of an abundance of politeness, James Patterson then asked, "Are you writing a memoir?"

"No, no, it's not a memoir, it's a collection of essays. Kind of funny, kind of tough stories about my life and childhood and work and you know, that sort of thing," I stated, in the staccato of a person who has just found out how truly uninteresting she is. Not to mention how insecure I am chatting about writing with two well-published authors. Not just flash in the pan authors, mind you, but one author who is a former president of the United Sates and Rhodes Scholar and another who has written 114 *New York Times* best sellers, but more importantly wrote the "I want to be a Toys "R" Us kid" jingle as an ad executive. I know when I'm outmatched.

Consternation fell across both men's faces, as they spoke in tandem, "Why wouldn't you just write a memoir? It's so much easier than a book of essays. Yeah, a book of essays, finding the in and out. Oh my. Who's your cowriter?" The sweat came from my feet, and like a geyser, moved all the way up my body to the top of my head. *Hopefully, it's just menopause*, I thought to myself, but I knew that was a lie.

"Oh, um, I am just writing it myself . . . I don't have a cowriter or anything." A look of shock landed on both their faces that was hard to describe, although Patterson's was more one of concern, and Clinton's was more amusement. I was left to wonder why this stupid commercial break was so long.

So obviously, that was a pretty big sign that I should just give back my advance and give up on my dreams of retirement or best sellers. But I didn't. Still, the process has been a little bumpy. You should know that by now, you've gotten this far in. It's not too late to quit. Put it down. I'll wait.

I WENT INTO WORK ON THAT TUESDAY, JULY 20, 2021, DREADING the inevitable. I would announce that I was releasing my first book. A collection of personal essays. A not memoir. I hoped that my tiny announcement was not totally swallowed whole by the GIGAN-TIC ANNOUNCEMENT from Prince Harry the previous day. I also made sure to preorder his tome, because we promised each other we would preorder each other's books. I'm kidding, calm down, or you're definitely not going to make it through the first essay.

Having just removed my PPE, because nowadays working in a television studio is like working in a surgical unit, I was touching up my high-definition makeup, when *Live!* executive producer, Michael Gelman, came into my dressing room. He immediately struck an impossible yoga pose. His signature squat, in a wide, second position, with his knees quietly tucked behind his shoulder blades. (I know, it doesn't make sense.) There is something about the door jamb of my dressing room that compels Gelman into a yoga position usually found in the *Kama Sutra*. Have you ever seen a grown man in a sports coat and skinny jeans doing a solo reverse cowgirl? Certain things cannot be unseen.

Just then, I heard a thunderous crack, and assumed Gelman's pants had finally succumbed to the pressure. But it was the boy wonder, Ryan Seacrest, bounding out of his dressing lair, squirting something that looked like a urine sample into his hot water. "Hey, we are definitely getting preempted. No doubt. They haven't even blasted off yet. Are you watching?" What I was watching in front of me was far more intriguing than yet another billionaire space launch, I have to be honest. Give me *Kama Sutra* Gelman and Seacrest the Urine Sampler over Blue Origin Bezos shooting into space any day of the week. Unless, of course, I'm asked to join in on the space launch. In that case, it's bye-bye G-man, hello G-force! For a naturally risk-averse person, I sure do love the idea of going into space. And not just substratosphere. I want the full O. As in orbit. Especially now that they're letting anyone apply, even without a mastery of math and physics. I mean, one no longer needs to be an astronaut to go, but I would rather travel with an astronaut or two on board, just in case there's intergalactic fuckery.

"Hey, um, are we preempted?" Clearly, if our little television show was getting kicked off the air, I wouldn't have to announce my book! Then, I could give the money back.

Twenty-plus years of doing this show, and I'm still shocked that there is no sense of urgency backstage on *Live!* As Frank, our stage manager, gave us the thirty-second warning, I spied Lauren Travaglione, my long-suffering, one-woman, joint chief of staff. She was on the phone with someone, and nervously chewing on her thumb cuticle. The only sign that the shit is hitting the fan is that thumb cuticle. I usually start my day by reading my horoscope, followed by Lauren's thumb, to judge just how awful things might get. I heard Lauren's voice elevate, "I need to know right now! We've got ten seconds!" I looked toward the thumb—uh-oh . . . that fucker was raw.

We began to walk into the studio, since the show open had begun. I looked back toward Lauren, who said, "Hold off until tomorrow!" Then, her thumb gave me the finger.

We sat at our host chat desk, inside the studio, which, before the pandemic, would have been filled with about three hundred enthusiastic audience members. Now, however, our six in-studio producers were forced to be the members of the audience, albeit exceedingly disinterested ones.

We all sat in nervous awe, waiting for the Blue Origin rocket to launch. We carried on like the show was not preempted, because it wasn't in a handful of markets in America and three in Canada.

"Hey, can we take a shot of Blue Origin to see if it took off yet?" Ryan asked with his characteristic enthusiasm. That was when our director, Brian Chapman, took the feed from the network to the studio floor, and our audience at home.

Immediately, I was spellbound. Right there, on live national television, and on computer and TV screens across the globe, sat the Blue Origin rocket, which was clearly shaped like a large penis with a rather bulbous head.

My eyes darted around the room, looking to see if anyone was seeing what I was seeing. Was this a joke? Was the control room pranking us by showing us an old clip from *Austin Powers*? Was Jeff Bezos influenced by all those "back massagers" he sold, then stuffed into boxes to deliver to his clients? Wasn't anyone paying attention? Was my book announcement preempted by a vibrator?

DOESN'T ANYONE ELSE THINK THAT LOOKS LIKE A PHALLUS?

I heard all six of our producers and three camera people burst out laughing, then, "Excuse me, Kellyripa, what was that?" Ryan giggled.

What? What'd I say? Wait, did I say that out LOUD?! (See? I'm a live one.)

As unreal as the entire shot looked, I couldn't help but hold my breath watching mission Blue Origin ascend above the clouds.

Even though it wasn't my first penis of the morning, I was still in awe.

Then, just like at home, after a mere three minutes, the bulbous head of the shuttle came floating back down to Earth, attached to three mega parachutes. What I'm certain was anything but, sure looked like a soft landing to me.

Speaking of soft, my book announcement went from getting upstaged by a prince to being eclipsed by the king of dildo memes.

All of this is a roundabout way of saying: This book was hard for me to write. It was hard for me to announce. I kept getting blocked. Prince Harry. Mark. My kids. Bezos's cock rocket. But, because I am me and because I never take the easy way out, I didn't write a memoir. I kept going and wrote these essays, myself, because I figured that my life, as I've lived it, as I see it, is hard, too. But it's easier if we share it.

So, strap one on, folks. I apologize in advance. Actually no, I don't.

XO

Kelly

"Keep in mind that I'm an artist, and I'm sensitive about my shit."

—ERYKAH BADU

CHAPTER ONE
MUCH ADO ABOUT IMPOSTER SYNDROME

Mark and I had found ourselves in that familiar territory of trying to find something to talk about during one of our least favorite activities; sitting in traffic on the Long Island Expressway. (Still unsure about the placement of the semicolon, and so are you.)

We were coming home from a holiday weekend on Long Island. And what long weekend would be complete without snarling standstills on the LIE on the way back to New York City to suck the three days of fun—and by fun I mean shitty weather at the beach—right out of you?

In case you're wondering, "Long Island" is how entertainment-industry types and those with enough money and good fortune refer to the Hamptons because it allegedly sounds more relatable and less asshole-ish than, say, Southampton. Even though, everyone knows you're not sitting in traffic to go to Levittown.

As we grew increasingly hypnotized by the parade of red brake lights that greeted our gaze as soon as we pulled out of our neighborhood on Long Island, we also grew increasingly passive-aggressive in our mindless chatter.

We huffed. We puffed. We wondered where exactly all these people in the other cars were going, though obviously they were also returning to The City just like us.

We/I wondered aloud if we should have left earlier, like say, after lunch.

We/he wondered if lunch would have happened sooner had I not insisted on taking a double Soul Cycle class.

We/I reminded him that I had taken a double class with the instructor Trammel Logan, and Trammel hardly ever taught out here, and a Trammel double is like an anybody else quadruple, and in the grand scheme of things it was ninety minutes, far shorter than the twelve hours he spent riding his "actual" bike this weekend.

And so forth and so on it went, following our usual patterns, checking off our usual boxes.

Waiting until dinnertime on Sunday night to leave, assuring we spent the maximum amount of bumper-to-bumper SUV time as possible.

Check.

Waiting until we had no choice but to stop at the McDonald's drive-through so we could feed our kids dinner, as Waze declared our Sunday night commute would take no less than three and a half hours.

Check.

Me reminding Mark of how many other food options we would've had at the VERY superior Jersey shore.

Check.

Mark hissing out something about funnel cake not being dinner.

Check.

Me prattling off a list of women I knew, none of whom had jobs to get to in the morning, FYI, who were taking helicopters back to the city to shorten their commutes.

Check.

Mark reminding me that every single person I had just named was an asshole.

Check.

And a miserable person, helicopter or no helicopter.

Check.

And then asking if I would prefer being married to their husbands.

Checkmate.

Me reminding Mark that just because one complains about the Sunday evening gridlock does not mean one wants to be married to some miserable asshole's more miserable husband.

Then, he threw down my least favorite gauntlet and exclaimed that I had three healthy kids and a husband who loved me, and I should be grateful.

Now, why do you suppose a girl can't have three healthy kids, a loving husband, AND a shorter commute? I'm so tired of my healthy kids being thrown in my face as a way to make me yield!

So, I decided to punish him for this infraction. I gave him the silent treatment for at least an hour, or as Waze told us, four feet.

It was there, in that deafening silence that I achieved clarity. It suddenly occurred to me that I wasn't punishing Mark with my silence, but rather rewarding him with it.

Mark LOVES when I'm silent.

But just as I was about to end my self-imposed gag order, Mark beat me to it and uttered my second least favorite phrase. I suppose it was his rudimentary form of small talk, short on content, and actual words, placing all the conversational burden on my shoulders, or mouth as it were.

"So . . . what else?" he asked, while scratching the back of his head, which told me two things.

Number one: He didn't want an answer to "so what else?" And two: He was just using idle chatter to try and keep himself awake.

13

A move he had clearly stolen from my talk show playbook. He suppressed a yawn because apparently the triple espresso he drank before we got on the road is never going to kick in for the rest of our lives together.

"Would you like me to drive?" I offered, knowing full well he would say no, but maybe would accept later on if he really started feeling it.

"No, thank you, baby doll, but maybe later on if I really start feeling it," he said as I mouthed the words along with him, still hypnotized by the parade of red lights. He then took my hand, and, using it like a puppet or a head scratcher, began to rub his head.

I wondered if it felt different or better to use my hand, like when someone else shampoos your hair. I shampoo my own hair almost every day and feel absolutely nothing. But place my head in a salon sink and let any random stranger wash my hair, and I want to bequeath them everything I own in my will.

But because Mark robbed me of the opportunity of breaking the silence first, I'd semirecommitted to the silent treatment, and refused to ask him if it felt better with my disengaged-inanimate hand being raked across his mink-like hair.

I turned on the radio in time to hear the end of "Deja Vu" by Beyoncé featuring Jay-Z. As the song faded, I wondered if Jay-Z and Beyoncé ever sat in traffic. I wondered if Jay-Z ever used Beyonce's hand as a head scratcher. I wondered what songs they listened to on the radio. My mind tends to wander in moments of extreme frustration/boredom.

"HAVE YOU GUYS EVER HEARD OF IMPOSTER SYNDROME?" Lola screamed from the back seat of our SUV. She was watching a movie playing on the screens in the back of the car, wearing headphones with the volume on full blast.

Mark and I both jumped out of our skin with the unexpected noise explosion.

"Turn the volume down, turn it down!" I screamed back, while gesturing for her to take off her headphones since she clearly couldn't hear me. Lola and Joaquin were both watching something that Joaquin found extremely funny. He was giggling in his booster seat. Michael, who was reading a comic book instead of watching the movie, answered Lola's question.

"Imposter syndrome is when you don't believe you're good at something other people think you're good at. Or like when you don't believe you can do the things you're supposed to do. Or something like that. Right? Mom, is that right?" I listened to Michael's definition rather spellbound. "Mom? Right?" I didn't answer because I honestly had no idea. I had never heard that phrase before, much less that there was a syndrome, but there was no way I was about to admit that in front of those kids, who would no doubt use it against me at a later date. I was certainly concerned, however, and prayed the syndrome wasn't contagious and something they could pick up in school and bring home to us.

I turned to Sleeping Beauty to see if he might weigh in. "Babe? Anything to add?" Mark's eyes darted from the rearview mirror, to me, to the road, back to the mirror.

"Um, yeah, buddy. That's it. It's very common. It's basically feeling like a phony. I feel that way at work all the time. Walking onto a new set or working with new actors and a new director . . . I always feel like they're going to figure out that I shouldn't be there." I stared at Mark, shocked by his revelation on the LIE. The SUV lurched forward another six feet, almost as if to concur.

"Yeah, me too. Sometimes in math class, when everyone is answering the questions, I have no idea what's going on," Michael added enthusiastically, then Lola screamed, "SAME!" Mark and I side-eyed each other, fully preparing to blame our kid's mathematical deficiencies on the other's side of the family. Joaquin howled from the back seat, "Impossibledom!" What on earth were they watching?

The kids seemed to be satisfied with Mark's answer and went back to the movie. Michael put away his comic book and donned his own pair of headphones to join the feature presentation, already in progress. I glanced back to take in the serenity of an unforced sibling simpatico. My three littles, enraptured by the movie, no doubt starring either Hillary Duff or Lindsay Lohan. Their wide eyes glued to the individual video monitors that pulled down from the ceiling of the SUV and came standard with the model. I suppose I should have been telling them to turn off the screens and read a book? Although, I'm always extremely nauseated reading in a car, so maybe I shouldn't have. Still, I felt like a bad mother for not making them engage in some game of "name the states and capitals."

I felt like an even worse mom for letting Joaquin watch the same movie as his siblings, or any movie for that matter. I was certain I made Michael wait until he was older to have TV time, although I can't really say for sure. The only thing I'm certain about is that Mark has never had these internal conflicts or ever felt guilty about anything.

We had been in traffic for so long the movie ended, prompting the kids to ask for another. They debated about which DVD should come after *The Parent Trap*. (Lohan, I knew it!)

Of course, my friends who have young kids presently have no idea how we did it. They think we were primitive with the level of technology we had available to distract our children. Their kids don't have to agree on a movie, they have separate devices with sep-arate screens for separate viewing. They bring their devices into the restaurant and sit quietly enraptured by *Peppa Pig* or *Paw Patrol*, whatever those are. Maybe they have a point. Mark and I didn't get to sit down and eat together in a restaurant for at least six years. When our kids were young, we would take turns walking them around outside the restaurant when they got bored. There were no iPads to whip out and plop on the table. There was no Xbox or EarPods or iPhone on the plane. We just hoped whatever movie the airline was showing would be family friendly, meaning not too vio-lent. But at least we had the SUV and those miraculous pull-down video screens and a bag full of McDinner for when we were stuck in four hours of traffic on the LIE. And before you judge: you've done it, too. (Miraculous use of the colon, I'm assuming placed by my editor.)

What I want to know is, how did our parents do it? When we were snarled in traffic on the Garden State Parkway, we just sat there. We didn't cry, or else my father would come back there and "Give us something to cry about, Goddammit." There were no gad-gets to occupy our minds. There wasn't a movie theater in the back of the car. Sure, we had the Eagles' *Their Greatest Hits* 8-track tape, which played on a loop, so at least we had music, but we certainly didn't have personal arcades in our laps. Fortunately, my parents also had me at the ready, willing, and able to insert myself, literally, between their two front seats. Delicately yet precariously perched on the center console. Diligently and relentlessly asking my mom and dad if we were, in fact, "there yet." And being one of the fore-most self-declared authorities on traffic jams, always helpfully pointing out other, lesser used "lanes" as a way to circumvent the congestion. Dad, never one to relinquish the power of the driver's seat, especially to an eight-year-old, swiftly barked something about the "hazard lane," and batted me away, discarding me to the back seat of my parents' black 1974 Pontiac Bonneville. Relegating me to the place usually reserved for children. Fortunately for all of us, my folks found those pesky safety belts that suddenly came standard with all Pontiac cars unsightly, referring to them as "eyesores," and pushed them deep down into the farthest crevices of the plum velour interior. Apparently Mom's fear of You Know What* applied to safety belts as well.

The lack of child safety apparatus allowed for my efficient and immediate return to the commander's deck, or center console. It was from there, on high, I silently forged a path to the Jersey Shore—Ocean City, New Jersey, to be precise; Gillian's Wonderland Pier to be even more precise. I would stop at nothing to get a slice from Mack and Manco's Pizza, and a Bob's lemonade. Using nothing more than my telekinetic abilities, common with most children of the 1970s, to move the cars in front of us out of the way. I especially focused on the cars with Pennsylvania license plates, because they were the worst drivers. (Everyone says so behind your backs PA drivers, so get over it!)

I would imagine I was in an X-wing starfighter, like Luke Skywalker, blasting off at light speed, leaving all those Pennsylvania drivers clogging every lane in my dust. Darth Vader, following close behind in his Bonneville, enraged that I had used the force to escape the back seat yet again.

I glanced down at Waze and noticed it sneakily added twenty

---

*When my mother refers to You Know What, she is exclusively talking about Cancer. Unless she is talking about sex.

additional minutes to our commute when we weren't looking. "We could have been to Bermuda twice by now," I said to the dashboard, wondering if Jay and Bey ever went to Bermuda.

"I think the kids might need math tutors," Mark responded, instead of acknowledging that we could have, in fact, been back and forth to Bermuda by now.

"Yeah, I'll ask around tomorrow, assuming we'll be home by tomorrow," I said, because the passive-aggressiveness is strong in this one. But then I needed clarification on that earlier discussion.

"Babe, you know that syndrome you were talking about with the kids. What's it called again?" Mark glanced at me, probably shocked that I stopped suggesting alternative routes . . . to Bermuda.

"Imposter syndrome?" he asked.

"Correct. That. Is that a real thing?" I was dubious that there could have been some kind of mental or emotional syndrome I hadn't already diagnosed myself with, so I had to assume that it was some trendy new thing.

"Of course, it's a real thing. Don't you ever feel that way? Like you're going to be found out? That they're going to figure out that you're not capable? That they're going to find out that you don't deserve the job?" I was startled by his serious tone, and intrigued by who "they" were, but I had no idea what he meant.

"No. I mean no, never. I usually feel overly capable, if anything. When I first started working on the soap, I had no idea what I was doing, and I was the worst actor, but I had no feelings of inadequacy whatsoever. I just knew I would figure it out on the fly. I think learning from experience is the best and most efficient way to learn. I know that if someone showed me how, I could land a plane. Or fly one. And not to bring it up again, but I could certainly fly a helicopter. I believe that I have an untapped ability to paint. Houses, yes, but also frescos, and probably some contemporary shit, too. I mean, look, I know I never have painted, but I've watched that Bob Ross show on PBS, and I got it. After every Winter Olympics, I'm reminded that I could definitely become a competitive figure skater. I remember as a very young child teaching myself to ice skate right there in the living room of my parents' house. Back then my routine had a high degree of difficulty due to the thick, plush green carpet impeding my compulsory moves. Don't get me wrong, I know I'm not going to win a gold for Team USA immediately, but if I put my mind to it and found the right trainer, I could be a competitor."

Mark was now staring at me like I had suggested we have another baby.

"Have you ever ice-skated on actual ice?" he asked incredulously.

"No, of course not, but you're missing the point. I know I could if I tried. I think. Don't you remember when we watched the Olympics last winter? How fast did I learn Sasha Cohen's routine?" Now Mark snapped his head so swiftly, the SUV swerved ever so slightly into the right lane, causing the usual outsized reaction only a New Yorker could muster; the guy in the Volvo next to us laid on the horn with all the gusto of a person whose car was stuck in the path of an oncoming train. I gave him a thumbs-up with my middle thumb.

Mark was now sputtering, "Routine? What routine? You moved all the furniture in the living room and slid around the hardwood floor in your socks screaming, 'Triple cow'!" Proof I was dealing with an amateur.

"First of all, it's called a triple salchow, and any pro athlete will tell you that it's way harder to do in socks. I could barely get off my edges to complete my spins!"

It appeared that Mark was finally beginning to blow his stack. "WHAT EDGES? You were in socks on the floor. You didn't spin! You just kept saying the word 'triple'! Saying the word 'triple' and actually spinning three times in the air are two different things!" DUH.

"That's why I said I needed to hire a proper coach. That's the point! Same with the Summer Olympics. My floor routine would definitely be way more competitive if I had proper coaching."

The traffic finally started to move. I looked for signs of an accident but found none, which should have been a relief, but after a four-hour road crawl, at least give me a discarded shattered taillight or a police flare or something! Come on LIE.

"Floor routine? A Physique 57 class is not a floor routine." Apparently Mark wasn't finished discarding my accomplishments, but I ignored his slight.

"The point is, I believe that if I see something, I can do that thing. Ride a bull. Lasso a calf. Barrel race . . ."

I realized, of course, I was looking at a billboard advertising a rodeo coming to Madison Square Garden at the entrance of the Midtown Tunnel. Right underneath it was the billboard for Cellino & Barnes, the infamous New York City injury attorneys, "800-888-8888. Don't wait, call 8!" "I could have just as easily been an attorney, not in the legal sense of course, but practically. I've been sued and won, and if that doesn't make me an attorney, then nothing will. I've read countless court filings. I've taken legal action against the tabloids, if you recall. I've read enough legal nonsense to know that NDAs never hold up in court, and handwriting experts are bullshit. I've also watched a shit-ton of Court TV. I could be a great pro hac vice if we ever make the move to LA."

Now Mark was laughing, "Except you didn't go to law school

so you'd be a no hac vice." He could try to kill my dreams with his fancy talk about legality all he wanted. Any good theoretical attorney will tell you, laws were made to bend.

"You'll at least grant me that I'm for all practical purposes a doctor. The amount of well-baby visits and throat cultures and ear infections and emergency room visits I've attended? I'm a pediatrician. I'm certainly a homeopath." As we headed downtown to SoHo, Mark stopped at the first of 800 red lights, to cap off our four-and-a-half-hour commute. He looked at me and sighed. "No. You are not a doctor. But you are a mom, so I'd say you are, medically speaking, extremely capable." Ah, even the smallest victory is still a win!

"So, circling back to you Mark. It makes me sad that you ever feel like you're an imposter. I'm not sure how someone who works in the industry as much as you do can possibly feel like a phony. Although, if you think about it, that's the entire job of an actor. You are always embodying other people, so it would make sense that you might feel odd at the start of a new project. It's a very vulnerable position to be in. Right? I bet most actors feel the same way."

Mark yawned loudly, shaking his head in disagreement, too exhausted to realize I had just cured his feelings of inadequacy. "I should've studied psychology. But I guess I don't need to, since I am, as it turns out, a therapist. But that's more of a hobby."

How could one of us be so lacking in self-confidence, while the other seemed riddled with it. "I wonder who came up with the term 'imposter syndrome'?" I said more rhetorically, than as an actual question.

"No idea." Mark yawned back.

"I wonder if they have a name for what I have. I wonder if there's a word for someone who believes they can do anything and everything. A person who only needs to see it once, then can essentially do it. Whatever it is. Do you think they have a word for that?"

I looked to Mark, his face awash in the red glow from the stop lights of Nolita.

"I think what you have is called asshole syndrome."

Addendum:

Mark believes the term "imposter syndrome" was introduced by someone other than Lola, and disputes some of the order of events in this chapter. He also insists there was in fact an accident on the LIE that evening. Mark also has a hard time recalling where he places his wallet and keys on a daily basis, so who are you going to believe?

A second addendum:

I realized over the course of writing this book that I do in fact have imposter syndrome. I actually have the textbook definition of it.

Im·pos·ter · syn·drome

NOUN

The persistent inability to believe that one's success has been legitimately achieved as a result of one's own efforts or skills. Doubting one's own abilities, leading to one feeling like a fraud.

Writing this book has caused me to have imposter syndrome. I suppose it just took something this emotionally revealing to cause it.

"There's dead.
And there's dead-to-
me dead."

—KELLY RIPA

CHAPTER TWO
THE GARDEN STATE

I was born and raised in the Garden State. South Jersey, to be exact.

Yes, there's a North and a South Jersey. Just like the Carolinas, only minus all the blessings of the hearts and Cracker Barrels. Just like the Dakotas, minus all the snow and "you betchas."

Okay fine, I suppose, technically, we are one state. But we have two very separate vibes in New Jersey.

What's the difference between the two parts of this fine state? Well, first of all, we keep it simple in the South. We are from South Jersey. The northerners tend to say they are from Northern New Jersey. Well, ooh la la, Northern New Jersey! You must be from Bergen County—that one just across the bridge from New York City. Fawncy. Insert martini emoji.

I don't think any resident of the Garden State would dispute that there is a North and a South. The one caveat being nobody can decide or pinpoint the dividing line between our two imaginary states. Over the years I have heard of several petitions to officially divide this already tiny state in two. As far as I can decipher and based on my own childhood experiences, Trenton is the dividing line. If my dad, who is from Camden, has to travel to Trenton, he says he's going up north. My girlfriend Gretchen Randolph, who lives in Franklin Lakes, would say she is going to Trenton in South Jersey. See what I mean? Trenton is the de facto Jersey Mason-Dixon Line, at least in these pages.

As far as other differences?

Well, we in South Jersey have the best tomatoes, corn, peaches, hoagies, and custard. (That's heroes, and soft serve ice cream, for those of you not from South Jersey.) In fact, my father can grow heirloom tomatoes on any fence anywhere with nothing but seeds, water, and dirt. However, we just call them tomatoes, because heirloom tomatoes are tomatoes for people who shop in Whole Foods.

We are the home of Hammonton, South Jersey, aka THE BLUEBERRY CAPITAL OF THE WORLD! Thank you very much. We also have Philadelphia as our backyard. Northern New Jersey has oil refineries and 30 percent higher taxes, so naturally they think they're better than everyone else.

I suppose they also have that obnoxious banner that stretches across the overpass outside the Lincoln Tunnel, in Union, that screams, "WELCOME TO NORTHERN NEW JERSEY, EM-BROIDERY CAPITAL OF THE WORLD SINCE 1872." I mean, what are they overcompensating for? How is embroidery trumping BLUEBERRIES? I just said, we are THE BLUEBERRY CAPITAL OF THE WORLD, but you don't see us crowing about it. Well, I mean, I just did, but keep in mind, the publishers are paying me by the word.

They say the people of North Jersey curse more than the gentle folks of South Jersey. That is simply impossible for me to believe, so on this one, I'd say it is most definitely a draw. As a matter of fact, the state, in its entirety, loves a good four-letter moment, or series of moments. The shared usage of colorful language, for both of the Jerseys is what, I believe, has kept our delicate union together. Perhaps we are all descendants of pirates? However, the South Jersey accent is so—how shall I put this—unique, that I'd go so far as to say that some people might not actually realize they are being cursed at by someone from South Jersey when it actually occurs.

I have to thank *Mare of Easttown* for shedding a light on the South Jersey accent. Even though the show was set in Pennsylvania, lots of places have this regional accent. I call it "Delaware Valley–ese." Delaware, Philly, South Jersey, you get the idea. Most films and television shows botch it completely, either having the characters sound like they're from Brooklyn or with a strange Southern twang. *Mare of Easttown* is the closest to the real thing I've ever heard, and I gotta say, it filled me with great pride every time I watched, or at least both times I watched.

Both North and South Jersey have water ice, only in South Jersey it's pronounced "wooder oice." Both places have phones, only in South Jersey it's pronounced "phewns." Most of the residents in the area live in homes, only in South Jersey it's pronounced "hewms." Most citizens of the state love a good bagel, only in South Jersey it's pronounced "beggle." I'm told I still pronounce it that way, but I honestly don't hear it. That's the other thing about the accent, nobody who has it hears it. So, don't bother crowing to your friend from South Jersey if you're reading this, because they won't know what the *hack* you're talking about.

Maybe the battle between the Jerseys has nothing to do with the North and the South, and more to do with the statewide identity crisis. New Jersey is one tiny state wedged between two mega, historical metropolises. The people of the North identify with, or wish they were, New Yorkers. The people of the South all think they are Rocky Balboa, and are, therefore, from Philadelphia. These two big cities suck up all the air and all the history and all the attention. Jersey just sits there, like the awkward third wheel, hoping that those other two bullies won't notice them enough to kick them off the lunch table.

And why shouldn't New Jersey have an identity crisis? We don't even have our own sports teams! What do we do in the fall if we want to go to a football game? We, in South Jersey, root for the Philadelphia Eagles (pronounced: "Philedalphieh Iggles"). While, upstate New Jersey, naturally has a choice of two, count them, two New York football teams. Which, by the way, play their games in New Jersey. Greedy bastards. New Jersey can't have a single football team, but New York gets two?

There's no baseball team in New Jersey, either. We've learned to be satisfied to root, root, root for the other states' home team. Yep, South Jersey has the Phillies, which, there is no way for me to type that pronunciation, so maybe just listen to the audiobook. And North Jersey has, yet again, two teams to root for based out of New York. At least those jokers play in New York City.

We did once have a basketball team. Maybe you've heard of them? The New Jersey Nets? Yep, they play in Brooklyn now, because, evidently, New York has a small penis, and needs two basketball teams as well. So, North Jersey, once again, has their pick of teams. South Jersey gets the Philadelphia 76ers. They are way cooler anyway. I know what you're probably NOT thinking. What about the Jersey Devils? What about them? That's hockey. What, are we supposed to be thrilled that they threw us a bone with Canada's favorite sport? And by the way, South Jersey roots for the Philadelphia Flyers, and North Jersey roots for the New York Rangers or the Islanders, so I'm not sure who is rooting for the Devils.

This is why Jersey can't have nice things, I suppose.

What we, as a state, need to do, or should at least try to do, is focus on our similarities. We need to focus on our shared passions and try to bridge the divide between the North and the South. Our love of the Jersey Shore and amusement parks. Our love of boisterous conversations and heated disagreements. Our love of lifelong grudges that we take to the grave. Our love of family-style dining at any and all restaurants, and, of course, our love of funnel cakes. And forget what you've heard about the bonobo apes in the Congo, because the humans from New Jersey invented food-based conflict resolution. Got into a fight with your sister? Go over for some cake and coffee (pronounced: "cakencoffee") to work it out. Got into a fight with the lady at the dry cleaner? Bring her an Entenmann's (pronounced: "bringeranentenmanns") so she doesn't ruin all your dad's shirts. Got into an argument with the choir director at church? Bring her a Frappuccino (pronounced: "bringerafrap") so she sings nice at your grampa's memorial service. Got into a fight with the Little League coach? Well, fuck him, cause he always lets his own kid bat cleanup, and his own kid sucks. This behavior is statewide. And effective. Trust.

When people from New Jersey see one another out of state, they cannot help but congregate together, and talk about how much better everything is in New Jersey. North Jersey, South Jersey, it doesn't matter. Jersey pride is strong and endures multiple time zone changes.

I'VE MET PEOPLE FROM NEW JERSEY IN ITALY, FRANCE, GREECE, Canada, Bahamas, Croatia, Corsica, UK, Nevis, Turks and Caicos, Mexico and, of course, Florida, the New Jersey of the actual South.

The conversation usually goes like this, and is always screamed, at a decibel level not usually employed in the foreign country in question: "Hey, yo! Kelly Ripa, WE'RE FROM JERSEY! WHAT THE HELL ARE YOU DOING HERE?" (As if I only live inside the television set?) Then, again screaming, "WHAT DO YOU THINK OF ROME? CAUSE, I'LL TELL YOU WHAT, THE PIZZA AIN'T AS GOOD AS SAL'S, AM I RIGHT?" This is usually when I suggest we keep our voices down inside the Sistine Chapel. That suggestion always results in another five-decibel increase in volume. "YOU KNOW I'M RIGHT. SAL'S ALL THE WAY." Then, while pulling a total stranger unusually close inside the Sistine Chapel, I will whisper, "I'm more of a Mack and Manco person myself." Right away, I regret my confession. (Oh GOD, I am heartily sorry for having offended THEE . . .).

"EHHHOHHHHH! MACK WENT TO JAIL! DIDN'TCHA KNOW? IT'S CALLED MANCO AND MANCO NOW! DID YOU HEAR THAT HUN? KELLY RIPA LIKES MACK AND MANCO PIZZA BETTER THAN SAL'S! I TOLD HER THAT MACK WENT TO JAIL, AND IT'S JUST MANCO AND MANCO NOW!"

"KELLY FREAKIN' RIPA! I KNEW THAT WAS YOU WHEN I SAW MARK! [Suddenly whispering] We didn't want to bother him. We know he's on vacation. WE'RE FROM NEW JERSEY, TOO! COULD YOU BELIEVE THIS? WHAT ARE YOU DOING HERE?"

What I wanted to say was, "What am I doing here? I'm trying to find an escape hatch!" But what I whispered was, "Can you believe it? Here we are!"

Then, "NO HUN, MANCO ALSO WENT TO JAIL, I THINK TAX FRAUD, SO NOW IT'S JUST PLAIN MANCO. CAN I GETTA PICTURE?" (I detest all my sins because of thy just punishments . . .)

It's then that Vatican security comes over and aggressively shushes us. Being quieted down by Vatican security is a uniquely humiliating experience because you know God knows, you know? I need to act fast. This is going to sound like a humble brag, and I don't mean it to, but I've learned how to apologize in four languages, including English, for this very reason. "*Mi dispiace*," I say effortlessly, because I spend an inordinate amount of time apologizing in Italy.

We took a vacation to Nice, France, once, back in 2011. I remember specifically, because Hurricane Irene was expected to make landfall in New York City on the day we took off. We were the last flight out before the airports were shut down. The storm hit South Jersey and the barrier islands around Atlantic City particularly hard, but Irene was downgraded to a tropical storm by the time she reached New York.

We arrived at our hotel late in the evening, and I quickly called my family back home in New Jersey to make sure they were safe, and thank God, they were. Then we turned on CNN to see how our beloved, adopted home city was fairing. We didn't see much coverage about the storm in New York, as it was upstaged by even more hot air. There, on a loop, was New Jersey's then governor Chris Christie's press conference. In characteristic Jersey bombastic bluster he was yelling at people to "STAY THE HELL OFF THE BEACH!" As we drifted off to sleep, our first night in the South of France, we were lulled into slumber with the dulcet tones of Governor Christie's dire warnings. Ooh la la! The next morning, we woke to the bright, blazing, crystal blue skies and seas. The New Jersey governor was still shouting at us in our beds. We dragged our severely jet-lagged children down to the hotel restaurant to have a late breakfast, because we are Americans, therefore, we cannot skip a buffet.

As I perused the endless line of French fare with the kids, trying to figure out what was an actual yogurt, while also searching to bring Mark back something buttery and flaky, I heard an unmistakable language, in an unbelievable volume.

"YO, KEL! KEL!" Kel? The familiar? Was it possible someone I knew was at this hotel in Nice? The question gave me pause, then, "KELLY RIPA!" Nope. There's no way I knew this person, so I kept perusing, and pretended I didn't speak English. Unfortunately, my honest children exposed my charade. "Mommy, the man is calling you." Thanks, guys.

"KELLY RIPA! I'M FROM JERSEY, TOO! WHAT IN THE WORLD ARE YOU DOING HERE? CAN YOU BE-LIEVE THEY CALL THIS A BUFFET? WHERE'S THE TAYLOR PORK ROLL? HEY, DID YOU SEE YOUR GOV-ERNOR ON TV LAST NIGHT? YELLIN' AT EVERYONE TO STAY THE HELL OFF THE BEACH?"

Wait, why is he my governor? I haven't lived in New Jersey since 1989! "Yep, I sure did. Saw it on the news," I whispered, while still assembling a platter for Mark and the kids like the badass multi-tasker I am. As expected, my whisper led to an increase in his volume by 25 percent, "IS THAT WHY YOU'RE HERE? CAUSE THE BEACHES ARE CLOSED?"

I couldn't help it. "Don't we all hop on a flight to the South of France the minute the Jersey Shore is closed? You got me."

See what I mean? How could I possibly think that the beaches in the South of France might offer something more beautiful than the beaches of New Jersey? Only in the cases of natural disasters. Don't get me wrong, I love the Jersey Shore as much as Snooki and JWOWW. But that morning, I just wanted to feed my hungry kids a Go-GURT.

Not too long ago, we were with most of the family in Greece, for a summer vacation. I'm talking, in-laws, nieces, kids, everyone. We heard about this hidden and idyllic spot, on a very remote Ionian island, where the locals go to watch the sunset. This area is famous for their sunsets, not just because of their beauty, but also, for their duration. During the summer season, I believe it takes almost two hours to fully experience the sun's vanishing, and even then, the colors in the sky linger like an after show, as if painted by Zeus himself. Streaks of pinks, blues, and oranges painted across the infinite sky, mirrored precisely, on the turquoise and quiescent waters. The area itself was in the middle of a tiny hamlet. Only fifty people live in this particular village year-round. It is accessible by either water taxi to a cab then a short climb, or by a treacherous hike to the short climb. I thought it would be wise to take the taxi, so naturally, we hiked. We were off to an inauspicious start when our small rental boat crashed on some rocks. We smashed onto the rocky beach, with as much noise and havoc as possible, assuring everyone knew the American tourists had arrived. I, naturally, saw this as a sign that the Greek gods were trying to warn us against hiking, however, my own Mexican god of obstinance, Mark, would not be daunted. Nor would any of his kids, or nieces, give up the chance to climb the side of a cliff, in search of a sunny vista and an ice cream. Up we climbed, sometimes on all fours, as the earth beneath us shifted. We climbed up granite, stone, and shifting pebbles. There was only one path, so people had to pass one another going up, as well as coming down. There were many signs written in Greek along the way, which probably warned us to turn back and save ourselves, but since none of us read Greek, it was literally Greek to us. And before you ask, no, there was no Wi-Fi, so I couldn't Duo Lingo or Babble it.

After about a forty-minute climb, in what felt like high noon heat, we arrived at the base of the little village. It was 7:30 p.m. We were hot and thirsty, but otherwise alive, so I couldn't blame Mark for forcing me to fall to my death as I had planned. As we began to walk the final hill, toward the sunset viewing area, and hopefully toward a bar so we could buy some water, I heard something. A sound so familiar, but it couldn't be. I quickly realized that I was suffering from extreme dehydration.

Maybe it's just goats, I thought to myself. But then one of the goats started screaming, "HOLY SHIT! THAT'S MARK CON-SUELOS, HEY! WE'RE FROM NEW JERSEY!" I decided I was clearly hallucinating as goats don't speak Jersey. I kept climbing, past a three table taverna, and once again, heard that uniquely deafening volume. "KELLY RIPA! HOOOOO! HOLD UP, SISTER. I ALREADY YELLED AT MARK, BUT I DON'T THINK HE HEARD ME!" What I should have said was, "Babe, they can hear you on Mount Olympus," but I held it in, just in case I really was hallucinating. There was an ancient stone wall separating us, but the woman from the taverna stood up and thrusted her camera toward her husband, who said, "KELLY RIPA. YOU GOTTA TAKE A PICTURE WITH DAWN. WE'RE FROM NEW JERSEY! WE SAW MARK, AND SHE WAS YELLIN' AT HIM, BUT I DON'T THINK HE HEARD US."

It was in this moment I began to wonder if they would let me have a sip of their drinks. "YEA, I REALLY WANTED MARK'S PICTURE, BUT YOU'RE FINE, TOO. WHAT ARE YOU DOING HERE?" I should have said, "Oh I'm here in case Mark can't hear whoever wants his picture," but what I actually said was, "What part of Jersey are you from?" This question seemed to silence them, which made me consider if they were Garden State imposters. And by the way, who pretends to be from New Jersey?

"WE USED TO LIVE IN JERSEY CITY, BUT WE LIVE IN FLORIDA NOW. MOVED TWENTY YEARS AGO." I should have known.

We took our picture, Dawn and me, when it suddenly dawned on me. Ha! Maybe the reason people from New Jersey find one another, all over the globe, is because we have a certain confidence. Or maybe it's our no-nonsense, tell it like it is, directness. A toughness, yes, but also a warmness toward others that's unmatched. It didn't matter to the couple in Italy, or the guy in Nice, or Dawn at the taverna, if I was from South or North Jersey. All that mattered to them was that we were all from the same place. A place with better pork roll, and better pizza, than almost anywhere. We had all come from a place that is much maligned, but arguably better than everywhere else. Or at least we have better produce, and malls, and embroidery, and nobody can take that away from us. Sure, sometimes we have short fuses and loud voices and sound like we are Mare from Easttown. But we're not from Easttown. We're from New Jersey. The Garden State. The greatest state on earth.

"Keep an eye on that boy, he has potential."

—MARK WALDEN

CHAPTER THREE
SCENES FROM A REAL MARRIAGE

I've never slept with a fifty-year-old man. Actually, I suppose I will have by the time this book comes out. Wait, now that I think about it, by the time this book comes out, I'll probably be sleeping with a man nearly in his mid-fifties (fifty-two is close enough). Mark, of course, has slept with a fifty-year-old woman plenty of times. I'm assuming I'm the only fifty-year-old, but you know what they say about assuming . . .

I turned fifty on October 2, 2020, smack dab in the middle of the coronavirus pandemic. The very same day it was announced that the Trumps had been diagnosed with COVID-19. Comparatively, Oprah had a surprise party with John Travolta, Stevie Wonder, and Tina Turner when she turned fifty. Some talk show hosts have all the luck.

Mark is a full six months younger than I am and never resists the opportunity to call me a cougar. That's months, folks, not years. He was born on March 30, 1971, in Zaragoza, Spain (pronounced: "Theragotha, Thpain"). So, therefore, he believes, and still says out loud, that I am not only a cougar but also an international cradle robber.

Mark's a funny guy, as is very clear by his hilarious observations mentioned previously. But that is not why I fell for him. Oh no. I knew I was in love with him from the time I saw his head shot. Sounds shallow, you say? Oh, yes. I was 100 percent shallow. I based my love/lust for this man, this stranger, purely on his incredible looks. But then I met him in person and knew that we would be together for the rest of our lives, or at least until the publication of this book. I don't take anything for granted.

I should point out that I am not a romantic and had never believed in love at first sight, and yet, here my dream man was standing in front of me. He was twenty-three years old at the time (the age of our oldest son as I write this). I was twenty-four, so I doubted my instincts for maybe one second. I thought I couldn't be with someone younger than me, as it went against the laws of . . . of . . . whatever those laws are. Also, I certainly didn't want to do that thing, and be that girl who falls in love with her costar. IT NEVER ENDS WELL. Trust me. Actors who fall in love on set are always causing drama off set when the romance goes tits up. Which it always does. I'd seen that movie too many times to go into that theater.

And yet, there he was, utterly dazzling. Take your breath away kinda dazzling. I mean who knows, maybe he's not everyone's type, but I have yet to meet the person who has not been swept away by Mark's charms. At least I was swept away. But I reminded myself that I was a very busy professional actress. I was also in a dead-end relationship with someone I didn't care about, so life was good and uncomplicated. Just the way I liked it.

Plus, my theoretical husband for the rest of my life might have a girlfriend.

All I knew was that he wasn't supposed to be in the rehearsal hall that day. In case you're wondering, the rehearsal hall was the all-purpose room the actors and directors used to mark out the blocking of the daily episodes of *All My Children*. The room had two industrial-sized plastic folding tables where the director and his technical director would sit, and numerous metal folding chairs. The stage on the right side of the room held a wall of mirrors, in which the actors used to look at themselves while carrying on conversations with other actors. Behind the director was a large wall of windows overlooking the West Side Highway, the Hudson River, and North Jersey, which is the inferior Jersey. (See the previous chapter on my beloved Garden State.) It was also where the actors received their fan mail and daily schedules in little cubbyholes, as if we were toddlers in preschool. The coffee urns were kept on a makeshift craft service table on the left side of the room, just past the door. The offerings were decaf, regular, and hot water for tea, as well as a singular plastic tray of dry bagels. I always had my pick of the bagels because I was one of three actors who ate carbs—the other two were in their seventies. I was sensible though, always choosing fat-free cream cheese. Remember the nineties?

No, Mark wasn't supposed to be in the rehearsal hall that day. As I sauntered in to get my coffee with half-and-half, and my bagel with sensible fat-free cream cheese, my future husband suddenly ambushed me! And by ambush, I mean he was in the rehearsal hall walking through the procedure of an actual screen test. He was brand new and had never screen-tested for anything before. And there he was. He was wearing the same sweater he had on in the headshot I had already fallen in love with, but he was even more dazzling in the flesh. He was standing with Judy Bligh Wilson, our show's casting director. She had found my future husband somewhere at an acting showcase in Florida. Judy was smiling and saying words, but I heard nothing except the sound of the sunshine coming out of future hubs's face when he smiled at me. I felt a white-hot pulse of energy through my entire body, and immediately started sweating. This was not the adorable dewy kind of glisten they apply to models in magazines and movies. I'm talking man sweat. Olympic marathon runner sweat. Comedian dying on stage flop sweat. Just moisture everywhere. Then, I realized that I was beet red, and the toothpaste was starting to melt away.

What toothpaste you ask? Well, I don't want to brag, but I looked like absolute shit that day. I had my hair set in giant-size Velcro rollers, because the larger your hair was during the nineties, the greater your likelihood of getting an Emmy nom. The makeup department was slammed with wall-to-wall actors that day, too. With a cast of forty, our makeup crew was always slammed, but my scenes were at the end of the day, so my skin was waiting its turn and at that time makeup free. Thus, allowing my future husband to see every blemish and freckle. I also had my period, so I distinctly remember my puffy face having a rather large cyst on the chin that I had tried and failed to extract, then tried and failed to burn off with prescription medicine as well as salicylic acid. Eventually I gave up hope and just tried and failed to hide it with toothpaste. Why I didn't call a dermatologist is still a question I ask myself to this day.

So, to recap, on the day my future husband first laid eyes on me, I had a fist-sized pimple slathered in Colgate barking on my chin, achy-breaky helmet hair still in its pre-pageant form, and was wearing a green leotard, which one day he would slide me into when I pass out during sex and need to be taken to a hospital in an ambulance. (We'll get to that story, too.) Along with my green leotard, I had paired ripped jeans, a black leather belt, and cowboy boots because, clearly, I was searching for an identity, and that seemed to be the best costume for the day (cue *Grey Gardens*).

As I stared at my future husband, my eyes burning because looking at him is like looking directly into the sun, I was shaken to my core when I heard an awful high-pitched screech, like the sound of nails on a chalkboard, the sound of a thousand air horns simultaneously compressing. It's a familiar sound. It is the sound of my own voice.

Noooooooooooo! Stop it. Do not say anything, I tell myself. It's too late.

I began to do the very thing I detest most—I started to tap dance for his approval. And five, six, seven, eight. "Hi! It's so nice to meet you. You sure you want to work here? Look at me . . . I used to be beautiful like you when I started working here and just look at what they've done to me." *Ha-ha, ha-ha*. And scene.

Future hubs was nothing if not polite, and he smiled warmly as Judy tried (in vain) to save us both from myself. "Well, I better show Mark around. You two will see each other tomorrow. Kelly here will be your scene partner in the screen test." *Who's Kelly?* I thought to myself, and decided, at once, a man like that needed to work with and marry a woman as glamorous as the one who played Andromeda on *Battlestar Galactica*. I then wondered if I had enough time to legally change my name by the screen test tomorrow.

That night I had a dream. I dreamed of the man called Mark, a man from Florida. A man wearing the same sweater as the real Mark was wearing in his head shot. That man had the same bright smile, dark skin, thick hair, and warm eyes. In my dream, he was taking us to Rome with our little girl in tow. He had elegant hands and long fingers wearing a thin platinum wedding band.

Thank god the flight attendant from my dream never turned off the overhead alarm or I never would have heard the actual alarm clock and probably would have slept right through my workday. As it was, I had no time to shower or wash my hair that morning. All I could do was brush my teeth, wash my face, and put on extra deodorant. There was no time for coffee or a cigarette or even a light perusing of the screen test script. *This poor guy*, I thought to myself.

From my apartment, I ran the six short blocks and three long ones as fast as I could. I made it to the studio at 320 West 66th with enough time to realize that putting on extra deodorant did not mask the stench of my unprofessionalism. I also heard my character's name being called to the rehearsal hall. The actors of *All My Children* were never referred to by their real names when in the building. We were always called by our character names. It was very empowering.

I ran up the emergency staircase (as this felt like an emergency) and into the third-floor rehearsal hall. Waiting for me were all ten of the actors screen-testing for the role of Mateo Santos, as well as our director, Conal O'Brien, who seemed very irritated at my tardy and overall unkempt appearance. "Sorry," I muttered to Conal while simultaneously scanning the room for the man named Mark. I didn't care about the other nine guys, not at all. It was only my future husband I was looking for. And then, BOOM, there he was. Coffee in his beautiful hand with long, elegant fingers. Just like in my dream. Same sweater from the dream. I began to wonder if that was his only sweater, being as he was from Florida and really didn't need more than one. Just as I started to sashay on over to the father of my unborn children, Conal began prattling on about something, and I remembered that I was not at a speed dating event. I was at work.

Conal gave a general overview of how the test would work—which was basically me walking and talking around the guy testing for the role. The screen-testing process of soaps is fascinating. The female character is always doing the walking and talking around the male character who is usually posing, preening, squinting, and shirtless. Sometimes they kiss. Sometimes he has to lift her, but usually it's the female character doing all the emotional heavy lifting. Yay feminism.

As I began the process of walking and talking around my centrally posed, silent scene partner number one, I could feel myself really start to perform far more than I normally would. The idea that future hubs was watching me was electrifying, and I looked into the mirror to check his reaction. Sadly, however, all he was doing was writing down the blocking in his script like he was not even on the date!

My screen test with Mark was all business. His total indifference/professionalism was like catnip to me. I envisioned the two of us walking the red carpet as he went to collect the first of his dozen Emmys.

After everyone was done with the blocking portion of the day, there was always a break for hair and makeup touch-ups before the camera tests up on the studio floor. Normally this is the time when some smart-ass actor would try to dazzle me with his résumé and attempt to pick me up. Well guess what? Today, I'll be doing the sexual harassing, so step aside fellas.

I made a beeline for the actor named Mark, aka future hubs. He was talking to another actor when I made my approach.

"Hi! Remember me from yesterday? With the hair and um, skin?" I was tap dancing again. And I was powerless to stop. "I just have to tell you! I had a dream about you last night." Skidoo! Both Mark, and the actor he was standing with, also named Mark, were now staring at me like I was from another planet. A normal person probably would have read their perplexed social cues and beat a hasty retreat to hair and makeup, but the Marks weren't dealing with a normal person. The Marks were dealing with me, and I was just getting warmed up. A five, six, seven, eight . . .

"We were on a plane to Rome, and we had a baby with us! A daughter, our daughter! So funny right? She was wearing red footie pajamas." Whoopee! Mark, future hubs, seemed acutely aware that the entire room had fallen silent and was listening to this manic unraveling. Lesser Mark and the others seemed gobsmacked by my overtures. Looking back now this all seems wildly inappropriate, but in the moment, the nineties, it seemed like the right and appropriate thing to do. It felt like what I had to do.

Finally, Mark began to speak, and I braced myself for the inevitable conclusion that he, too, had the same dream. He would tell me it was kismet, that he was sent to New York City by some divine higher celestial force so powerful that he would stop at nothing until he found me. "Have you ever been to Rome?" Mark purred.

"No, never. No. Not even ever." Damn. Why can't I ever say something like a normal person?

Then my future lover cooed, "We used to live in Italy. Rome is beautiful." And just like that he walked away, leaving me with lesser Mark. I turned to lesser Mark who looked half hopeful, half horrified that I might tell him that I dreamed of him as well, but before he could open his mouth I said, "Who the fuck is *we*?"

This is the stuff that dreams are made of.

WE ALWAYS TELL PEOPLE WHO INQUIRE THE STORY OF HOW WE MET, MUCH to the embarrassment and horror of our three children, which is also why we tell it. People invariably come around to that question. I suppose that's because we are both in our fifties and have been married for over twenty-five years, to each other, and working in a business not known for its successful marriages. Or maybe it's because we still appear happy. Or, because, as we have been told, we look like the couple on top of a wedding cake. Whatever that means. I can always tell if Mark is interested in developing a friendship with the person asking this particular question of how we met by his answer. If Mark responds with, "We met at work," he is not interested. But, if Mark says, "Kelly, tell them how we met," I know that we will be couples dating soon.

I once read in a book, I can't remember the title, that the more interesting question to ask a couple is how they stay together, not how they met.

Obviously, there is a much larger conversation to be had than the one you, dear reader, will find in this fun, frothy future best seller. (I've read *The Secret*.) However, I'm willing to give you the broad strokes if you're into it. I mean, it's your money.

How have we stayed married for so long? Hmmmmmm. As I'm typing this, I'm going to paint you a picture. I'm looking at him right now. He looks like a movie star. He's wearing green swim trunks that I bought for him, and a white, cotton button-down shirt that I did not. Black Ray-Ban sunglasses. His black hair is windswept, and his skin is dark brown, tan even for him. He has almost no body fat, like an Olympic athlete. This would all be irritating if he thought about his looks or spent time on his appearance, but the reality is, he woke up like this. He has never had Botox. So, I guess that it is irritating/borderline infuriating. I mean, don't get me wrong, he works out and he eats healthy, sort of, but honestly not nearly enough to yield this kind of a result. He is puffing on a cigar, his only remaining vice. Of course, his teeth never stain from them and are a bright, vibrant white. Also, he never has bad breath. Ever. Even in the morning. How is that possible?

He's on the phone, as usual, handling something important. He is pacing back and forth, not in a worried way, but in a way that says, "I am handling whatever this is so the people in my life don't have to." Or maybe he's on the phone with one of his field officers because he is secretly in the CIA. That thought has crossed my mind many times. There was an old family rumor that my beloved father-in-law, Saul Antonio (Tony) Consuelos was in the CIA. Okay, maybe I started that rumor, but he was in special operations command, and had the highest-level security clearance a civilian in the military could have. He also bears a striking resemblance to Saddam Hussein, and alternately, Frida Kahlo. This is just a visual detail, rather than a way for me to prove my theory.

Perhaps Mark is on the phone with his secret family. Because, admit it, at one point or another you've thought your spouse might have another family stashed somewhere. Never considered this? Haven't you ever seen Oprah or specials on the ID channel? It happens. This is always in the back of my mind—that Mark has an extra family somewhere. Maybe two. I am probably being ridiculous when I say this. Although, if anyone could get away with having a secret family, it's Mark. The man is crazy organized, hyper-focused, has all these skills that just pop up out of nowhere. Mark has to be using them for nefarious/sinister means. If that's even his real name . . .

Mark has also been living in Vancouver for the past four years, and before that, he was living in New Mexico and Los Angeles and Montreal and Toronto and well . . . he gets around. So, maybe I'm not being so ridiculous . . . hmmm?

Now that I have painted this picture for you, and now that

you have a strong visual sense of the man I am married to, you can probably understand why I keep him around. He's extremely pleasant to look at. And he does manage to take care of many things in a calm, cool, and collected way. I should mention that my husband is very intelligent and thinks outside the box. He is also one of the hardest workers I know. He is an extremely protective husband and father. He is demonstrative with his affection, not just with me, but with our children, too. And nobody makes me laugh harder. So, maybe that's why I like him. But also, that face and that body. Wow. Not bad for a simple girl from South Jersey with minimal everything.

Mostly, I believe we have stayed married this long because we have mastered the dark art of compromise. Thinking back, I'd say we were both terrified when we eloped, but too stubborn to admit to each other that we had made a mistake. Perhaps we were waiting for one of us to call the other's bluff, but like compromise, we had also mastered the darker art of obstinance.

I snapped a photo of him in the cab on the way home from JFK. It was the day after our fateful trip to Vegas, where we took the ultimate gamble. The look on his face is one of complete misery. I took another photo of him sitting on the sofa in my apartment, because we kept separate apartments at first. Again, the look on his face is of a man figuring out how to get out of the mess he'd gotten himself into. He took a picture of me on the plane as well. I was reading an unauthorized biography about Grace Kelly, as one does, and I, too, look, how should I put this . . . not thrilled. Of course, we took these pictures with a disposable camera that needed two weeks to be developed, because we were married during the Cretaceous period. By the time we got the photos back from Duane Reade, we had moved on from the generalized uneasiness of "Oops, we rushed into this thing," to the blatant hostility of, "This marriage is all your fault." It should be noted that all of our feelings were certainly wrapped up in the secrecy of what we had done. Absolutely nobody knew that we had run off and eloped. And then got matching tattoos. Dial a cliché.

People elope all the time. Sometimes it's called a destination wedding, designed for a small group, to prevent a wedding from growing out of control. Sometimes people elope before a big wedding, so they have something that is just for them as a couple, before the bridesmaids make it all about themselves. And sometimes people have a day off from work and frequent-flier miles to burn, and figure what the heck?

We were definitely that last option.

The truth is, we broke up right before we eloped. I've told this story before so forgive me if you've heard it. I've told it on the *Comments by Celebs* podcast. I've told it to my friend Bruce Bozzi during his *Lunch with Bruce* radio show. Most recently I've told it to Marlo Thomas and Phil Donahue for their book called *What Makes a Marriage Last*, which is like a manual for long-term relationships.

Mark broke up with me five days before we got married. I had never really been dumped, so the sensation was new for me. It was part rage, part indignation, part I'll show you what you lost. What's that you asked? Why did he break up with me? Good question! Thank you for asking!

Mark says he broke up with me because he thought I went home to New Jersey to see my ex-boyfriend. He was wrong. I lured him back with a hot little outfit—one he describes as "the jacket and pencil skirt with the thingy around your neck." See that? He glazed over the declaration of being wrong by complimenting my outfit, which was comprised of a turquoise Claude Montana jacket, a black miniskirt from Betsey Johnson, and a Henri Bendel scarf that I tied around my firm, young neck. I understood the power of messaging through fashion before that was even a thing. Or maybe I wasn't cognitively aware, but I knew I wanted him to see me and regret his poor decision making.

I had never felt such agony. It wasn't my ego that was hurt, it was much deeper. I felt like I was watching my future slip away. And I was being called a liar and a cheat, neither of which I was. It was the ultimate betrayal. Sure, when we met and fell for each other, we were technically seeing other people. Maybe he felt like we were getting too close, too quickly and that scared him? I'm not sure, but in that moment, he felt the need to vilify me so he could end our relationship, and I was devastated by the behavior of this man I was convinced was my husband.

I was left with no choice but to absolutely make him regret dumping me.

For my first act, I was going to have to get out of the stupid joint appearance we had scheduled over at *Live! With Regis and Kathie Lee.* (Coincidence? I think not.) Apparently, they were shooting their annual Mother's Day special, and it was one woman's very special wish to meet Hayley and Mateo from *All My Children* and to have a brand-new La-Z-Boy chair. What she really needed was a brand-new bucket list, but who was I to judge? We were supposed to surprise her by rolling out the chair, but I decided that Mateo could do the rolling by himself. I called one of my very favorite people, Sally Schoneboom, the then head of ABC daytime publicity. I wish I could have just explained the circumstances as they were, but nobody knew we were dating, much less broken up! We were very professional on set, or at least we thought we were. Neither one of us ever wanted the producers to think we couldn't do our jobs effectively. I mean, what if we broke up? Like we just did? I'm not entirely sure why we were so secretive. We weren't working for NASA or the FBI. But that was our play.

In any case, I got Sally on the phone and explained that I was no longer available to do the morning show. She told me in no uncertain terms, that it was too late to cancel. That Mark had already tried to pull out, and that she certainly expected me to be there, in the studio, bright-eyed and bushy-tailed.

Well, this gave me no choice but to show up looking absolutely gorgeous. Or at least in a killer new outfit. I hit the big three. Barneys, Bendel, and Bergdorf. I sensibly spent my next two paychecks selecting the perfect revenge outfit. Hell hath no fury like a woman falsely accused of cheating who possesses a charge card. I was careful not to eat anything that might give me a pimple, which at that time in my life was basically all food. I spent the night practicing how I would ignore Mark. There's dead, and then there's DEAD TO ME DEAD, which is way more terminal than actual death. I paced the floor of my one-bedroom, two-bathroom apartment. You heard that right, TWO BATHS! All the while thinking of him in his studio with a spiral staircase, leading to a loft bed. That lit up. At this point I'm fairly certain that I started talking to myself. "I mean, please. Who do you think you are? A light-up bed? Who has a bed that lights up? A loser, that's who! You know what? I'm glad you dumped me. I'd rather be single and lonely than with a smoking-hot guy with good skin, thick hair, and a light-up bed. Into which you've probably already lured some other girl from another network. And you'll impress her with your adult-ness, and sexiness, and smartness, and talent-ness. And then she'll fall in love with you, only for you to dump her on some trumped-up charge of infidelity." Then I made the sensible decision to spend the next five hours sobbing into my pillow, making sure my already moonlike face was as puffy as possible for my furniture moving segment on *Live! With Regis and Kathie Lee*.

At some point I must have fallen asleep, because I opened my eyes only to realize that they were in fact swollen shut. Parts of my face were stuck to my pillowcase, I assume from a combination of tears and snot. I stumbled my way to the master bath, because I had two bathrooms. Not sure if I mentioned that. I attempted to assess the damage, and it became painfully clear that I was going to have to pull a full *Mommy Dearest*. (If you know, you know. If you don't know, you simply must buy the movie starring Faye Dunaway immediately. Don't bother with renting. You'll just wind up renting it eighteen times, and then buying it.)

I had no choice. I needed to reduce the swelling the old-fashioned way—with a sink full of ice and witch hazel. I felt my way to the kitchen and opened the freezer. I pawed around until I found two full ice cube trays, which is exactly twenty-four ice cubes, not nearly enough, but I had to make it work. I then opened the medicine chest hoping to find the bottle of witch hazel I never purchased. Instead, I found rubbing alcohol, a Maybelline charcoal black eyebrow pencil that *All My Children* makeup artist Paul Gebbia had supposedly used on Madonna in the film *A League of Their Own*. He knew how much I loved Madonna, so he gave me that pencil. Basically, her DNA was ground into my eyebrows by the sheer force of my application.

I decided rubbing alcohol and witch hazel were the same. Spoiler alert! They are not the same. This was before Google and

WebMD made not knowing things passé. I poured the entire bottle of rubbing alcohol into the sink of twenty-four ice cubes, cupped my hands, just like Faye Dunaway does in *Mommy Dearest*, and plunged my red, swollen, moon face into the alcohol ice. It was then that the similarities between me and Faye as Joan Crawford abruptly and violently ended.

Did you know that witch hazel is a natural plant-based astringent, excellent for treating inflammation? While rubbing alcohol, is in fact chemical based, and extremely hazardous to humans and bacteria alike. The immediate, fiery burn of the alcohol searing my already inflamed-balloon face was temporarily overpowered by the 99 percent pure alcohol vapors that scorched my #lungseyeskidneysbladderliverspleen. If I could've screamed, I would've. But, in a dizzying display of pure self-loathing, combined with wanton stupidity, I added water and tried it again. Eyes closed, of course. This time I held my breath, but the burn combined with the not breathing, made me unable to last longer than five seconds. And by five seconds I mean .5 seconds. I felt like my face was actually on fire, with actual flames. I turned my shower on all the way cold and jumped in for relief.

As the alcohol vapors washed away, I started to breathe again. Carefully standing so only my head was under the freezing shower spray. I stood there thinking about how much I had asked of my skin over the years. I started thinking about my mom's fear that I would inherit the cystic acne that was so common on my dad's side of the family. She constantly searched for remedies. Not in a dermatologist's office, mind you, but she did search. Her methodology was unconventional to say the least. Mom decided that the best way to prevent acne was to burn off the top layer of skin, as frequently as possible. An epidermis-ectomy if you will. What's that you ask? How did she do this? Mom did it the scientific way, of course. Carefully using a washcloth, soaked in scalding hot water, enriched with chlorine tablets. After step one of the chemical peel process was finished, the spa day was then completed with a fifteen-minute sun session, I was seated no farther than six inches away from the dreaded sun lamp of the seventies and eighties. Me prophylactically baking the chlorine facial into my pre-acne skin, the lamp laughing its ass off, knowing in thirty years I'd be diagnosed with my first skin cancer.

Meanwhile, back in the cold shower, I turned off the water and stepped out in front of the mirror for the reckoning. Forcing my eyes open to assess the horror, I was shocked to see that even after a self-inflicted chemical poisoning, I looked, almost . . . good. And even more importantly, I felt good. Not exhausted. Not weak. Not burned or poisoned. I felt confident. It had to be adrenaline. Or my age. Or the sheer will to make Mark regret leaving me. Somehow, even staying awake crying all night and then dousing myself with toxic chemicals didn't quench my thirst for revenge.

Upon my arrival at the studio, I was immediately taken by the segment producer upstairs to the production office. There, she explained to me that Mark and I needed to be hidden away in the office, so as to not ruin the surprise. Then she pointed to Mark, who was sitting on a folding chair. She said with a huge smile, "I know you two already know each other . . ." Mark and I remained absolutely stone-faced. He even had the audacity to look disgusted by my arrival. Which meant my costume was working! I could tell the producer sensed the tension as she made a hasty retreat, calling over her shoulder that she'd be back to retrieve us within the hour. WITHIN THE HOUR? Why had we been told to be there so early? For maximum awkwardness, I suppose.

I decided to aggressively ignore Mark, who, I noticed, was casually holding a coffee from this new really expensive coffee place from Seattle that had just opened, called Starbucks. I had a look around the room, so I didn't have to see him ignore me as well.

The production office was quite a dump. (Actually, it still is, even after its alleged renovation.) There was garbage and old newspapers everywhere. Can you imagine? Aside from the walls lined with color-coded cue cards representing the days of the week with celebrities' names and segments on them, there was no other evidence that we were in a professional work space. It could have been an abandoned school, or a hoarder's house. If only the iPhone had existed back then. Actually, if the iPhone existed back then, I can say with total certainty that Mark and I would not be together today. We would have been too distracted by all the distractions. We would have been looking at social media. He would have been hate-reading Twitter. I'd have been hate-viewing Instagram. We'd both have been hate-perusing our news feeds. He'd have been watching Quibi. Just kidding. He'd have been playing Words with Friends. I'd have been playing Bejeweled. No better still, I'd have been shopping on Net-a-Porter. Who knows . . . maybe we'd have been swiping right, or left? Whichever one you do on dating apps. The point is, THERE WERE NO DATING APPS, OR APPS OF ANY KIND! There was no way to be distracted! It was torture.

After about ten minutes of the most ear-shattering silence, our segment producer peeked her head back into the secret hoarder's habitat to see if we needed anything. I saw Mark's head snap up from my peripheral side-eye. He asked the producer if there was a place he could go smoke a cigarette, and added "Kel? You wanna come?" Kel. He called me Kel. Like he used to when we were LOVERS.

The next conversation happened in my head, in silence, and in a split second.

Okay, I can either tell him to fuck off, but that's probably too aggressive and gives him way too much power. OR I could simply and politely offer a no thank you. OR I could go with him and strike up a casual "So how have you been since you've made the biggest mistake of your life?" OR I could go and have a cigarette while simultaneously ignoring him, and double simultaneously let him have another look at my adorable lewk. OR . . .

"Kel? You coming?" he asked again, using the very friendly Kel.

"Sure," I said coolly. I grabbed my cross-body bag, like a boss, and sashayed past him. We were taken into a garage/loading dock area that looked like it had the same inferior desecrater as the production office upstairs. It might have been the dirtiest garage I'd ever seen.

Mark offered me a cigarette, which I did not want, but accepted because I knew he liked the way I smoked. (I KNOW! BUT THIS WAS A DIFFERENT TIME. PEOPLE USED TO SMOKE.) He struck a match and I leaned in, holding my enormous wig-like hair back with one hand, and lit up. I took a long drag, which burned, and let the smoke languish out of my lips slowly like a French girl. I was careful not to look at Mark. He attempted to make small talk, and I answered with singular words: "Yes." "No." "Maybe." "Huh." "Hmmm." I was careful not to tell him how good he looked and how great he smelled and how heartbroken I was. I didn't tell him how much I missed us sitting next to each other, just reading books. I certainly didn't tell him I got my very own Pavarotti CD, so that in case he ever came to my place again he could hear "Nessun Dorma." I just looked toward the street counting the minutes until I could leave and crawl back into bed and cry some more, which was very unlike me.

I can't recall being on the show at all that day. I just remember leaving and starting to walk home with Mark hot on my heels. See? If I had a smartphone, I would have called an Uber and would have been gone in a New York minute. He asked if we could talk. I coolly ignored him, sort of, asking him what he could possibly want to talk about. He said he wanted to explain his point of view on the night he made the biggest mistake of his life. Okay, maybe I added the "biggest mistake" part. I told him I was busy and had things to do. I lied. See? If I had a smartphone, I would have called my committee of girlfriends and I would have had actual things to do. But he called my bluff and told me I had nothing to do because I, like he, had the rest of the day off from work.

"I have other things besides work, you know," I said. He stopped me and pulled me into a one-sided embrace. "Oh yeah? Like what?" he said in an inappropriately seductive way. Damn. "Stuff . . . I have things to do that are really none of your concern." For reasons still unclear to me, I made a left turn and headed toward Central Park. Where did I think I was going? Mark must have read my mind because he then said, "Where are you going?"

"None of your business" was my cool reply.

"Can I walk with you at least?" Mark asked. "Can you slow down?"

Men always have a hard time keeping up, don't they?

I eventually relented and agreed to sit with him on a park

bench across from the baseball fields, but mostly because my feet hurt.

He told me he was sorry. He told me that he loved and missed me. He told me he hadn't been able to sleep since we broke up. He told me he was unwilling to go another day without us waking up together. He told me he was foolish and jealous and unnecessarily paranoid. He asked for my forgiveness, and since I didn't have a smartphone and couldn't run it by my support committee, I forgave him.

He asked me to go to his apartment with him because he had something he wanted to show me, which was code for you know what. No, not cancer. The other you know what—SEX.

Just in case our parents or children are reading this, or god forbid listening to it, I'll spare you the details, but he really showed me something.

Afterward we went down the street to Mike's Pizza on the corner of Twenty-Fourth and Second. We ordered a large margarita pie and a sensible garden salad. Then we stopped on the way home and picked up a bottle of Ruffino Chianti. We spread out on Mark's small futon and ate like two people who had twenty-five-year-old metabolisms. We talked about our favorite pizza, his being pizza in actual Italy, mine being from the Italy of America, South Jersey.

We ate the entire pizza. We drank most of the wine. We moved the salad around on our paper plates with our plastic forks. We kissed and cuddled. Then we talked about whether or not either of us ever thought about marriage. We had not. "We have tomorrow and Thursday off. Why don't we fly to Vegas and get married?" Mark stated more than asked.

"Why don't you ask me when you're serious?" I stated back. Then it got serious.

"I am serious. Will you marry me?"

Still uncertain if he was kidding, and not wanting to get my hopes up, I answered Mark's question with a pragmatic one of my own. "How will we get there?" We both laughed at my question. Then, Mark got serious again. He asked me if I had anything at home that would pass for a wedding dress. It was the mid-nineties, so everything I owned looked like some version of a dress a person might wear to a wedding, a funeral, or a logger's convention. I told Mark I had something that could pass. He told me to go get anything I would need for a clandestine getaway, and that he would take care of everything else. (Because he always takes care of everything.)

I went home and grabbed the only option that would suffice, a floor-length, mauve, A-line dress that I had bought at the Barneys warehouse sale in 1993. (Moment of silence for Barneys.) A hundred and ninety-nine dollars for a dress I didn't need seemed exorbitant, but it felt like buying a piece of history, so I went for it. Three years later, I finally removed the tags and folded it into my travel bag.

We touched down in Vegas at 10:00 a.m. West Coast time.

We were pretty jazzed because Ricki Lake was on our flight, which we both took as a good sign. Would God really put national treasure and current reigning queen of the daytime talk show and John Waters's favorite muse, Ricki Lake, on our flight if we weren't supposed to get married? We hopped in a cab and hightailed it to the county clerk's office. It was then I turned to Mark and told him I only planned on getting married once, which was a complete lie. The truth was, I actually never planned on getting married ever. The only husband I saw worthy of my affection was a fat-free Entenmann's cake. Yet here we were racing toward sealing the deal. I needed him to know if at anytime he got cold feet, we could call the whole thing off, and just be lovers. So, that's exactly what I said. "That's a beautiful thing," said the cabdriver. "How can you say no to that?"

People gamble in Vegas all the time. That city in the desert grew from the tears of broken dreams, lost fortunes, quickie weddings, and even *quickier* divorces. It wasn't supposed to work out. We weren't supposed to work out. On paper, couples like us usually do not work out. As I reread these words I think, these two people should NOT have made it. They were immature. They met on the set of a soap opera. She rambled on like a crazy person, convinced immediately that they were destined for one another, talking about dreams and babies and Rome. They were dating other people when they started seeing each other. They kept their relationship a secret from everyone. They broke up for a dumb reason and got back together five days later and then got married? As I said before, in the photos from that flight, and the days right after our secret wedding, we both looked like we were smelling something bad, and it was the other person. Does this sound like a couple that will go the distance?

But for some reason, we did.

I mean for now, we have.

As I've said before, I do not take things for granted.

I feel the need to tell you, as I'm writing this chapter it is my twenty-fifth wedding anniversary. The #silveranniversary. I always joke that every anniversary is the diamond anniversary. But it's true. Every single year of marriage should be treated like a milestone. Not because spouses need to give one another diamonds, but because they need to acknowledge and appreciate that what they are pulling off is not for wimps. I'm using the word "marriage" here, but I'm really talking about all long-term partnerships, because not everyone gets married. That, however, doesn't mean unmarried, long-term couples are magically immune to the challenges of keeping the thing going. Marriage is work, and making a long-term marriage last takes a special kind of patience, understanding, and work ethic. It also requires bravery. Any two people in a long-term relationship will tell you that it's not for the faint of heart. Marriage is for warriors. Sometimes you might have to go to war. Not just WITH each other, but sometimes you have to go to war FOR each other. Sometimes you might be called on to be a one-person UN peace accord. Sometimes your relationship will feel like an endless roller-coaster ride. One that excites you and makes you feel queasy. Sometimes you will be bored. Sometimes you will be content. Sometimes you will be scared. Sometimes you will feel as if you are speaking completely different languages. Sometimes you will want to quit. Sometimes you will NEED to quit.

But, before you throw in the towel, look at your person. Look at the person you chose. Try to see them with the same eyes as when you first saw them. Try to imagine what brought you together in the first place. I know in the thick of whatever it is a couple might be in the thick of, it's easier said than done. But try.

Think of the roots of two individuals growing deep. Sometimes those roots grow in different directions, so that each individual can survive and thrive untangled. And that's okay, because sometimes the best marriages are the ones that end. But every once in a while, the roots of the individuals become entangled and begin to grow together, in a way that makes the couple stronger.

The roots, stronger. The power of this grown unity allows for a certain resistance to the elements—whatever form the resistance may take. You bear witness to one another during the best and the worst of times. With the gnarled and complicated beauty of a shared history.

"Every parent is
basically
Oscar the Grouch:
cranky, unshowered,
and living in
a trash can."

—@COPYMAMA

CHAPTER FOUR

DON'T LET YOUR HUSBAND PICK YOUR DEATH CLOTHES

Public Service Announcement: If you are related to me in any way, I strongly suggest you skip this chapter. You have been warned.

This story is told in present tense because the trauma resides presently in my mind, and will for all eternity.

I AM FASCINATED BY STORIES OF TWO-YEAR-OLDS VALIANTLY CALL-ing the paramedics because their mother—as it's generally the mother—suffers a medical emergency and is rendered unconscious. I read these stories in newspapers and online articles, part enraptured, part incredulous. How is it that a two-year-old not only knows to call 911, but how to describe what has happened, administer help to their mom at the instruction of the operator, and direct an ambulance to their house? My kids are grown now, but I'm certain that at no time in their lives have they known their address well enough to give it to a 911 operator. I bet if you asked them for my address today, they could only give you a vague area. I mean sure, they know how to get here when they have laundry they want me to wash, but the zip code? Forget it.

Actually, I still have to check my address on my license for my zip code because on forms I will often write 08009, my childhood zip code in South Jersey. But the point is, I at least knew my child-hood home address—complete with zip code. Is it my failure as a parent that I never walked my kids through what they should do if

I fell unconscious? I just assumed that would never happen to me. Plus, I was always busy trying to get them to learn the alphabet and how to identify a red fish over a blue fish. So, my question is, When the mother of the kid from the newspaper is reading him or her *Green Eggs and Ham*, did she slip in, "Sam I am, if Mom should fall down, hard on the ground, don't you just frown. Run, run, run, run and call 911"? Huh, maybe I should've written a kids' book instead of this one. Remind me to call my agent.

The point I'm trying to make is that there are parents out there who actually prepare their children for what to do in case of an emergency. Those are good parents, I guess. I thought that as long as my kids didn't get strep throat often and had cookies for the class bake sale, I was killing it in the parenting department. Don't get me wrong, my kids are lovely, talented, hardworking, and smart. But I think that comes down to the nature/nurture thing. I don't think my kids would've noticed I needed help until they were hungry or needed money, and even then, I'm certain they would call Postmates first and then 911. Even my spouse can't be counted on for making the right call when it comes to 911.

The year was 1997 and Mark and I were new parents to our six-month-old son. Michael was a beautiful baby with huge brown eyes, a head full of dark brown hair, he was the spitting image of Mark. The holidays were approaching, and we were so excited to experience the thrill of placing our first child on a scary-looking stranger's lap and watching him scream in terror, a tradition for the ages. It was an unseasonably warm winter for the Northeast—wet and chilly, but more like an endless fall. At the time, we lived in a two-bedroom rental on Sixtieth and Amsterdam Avenue on the Upper West Side. This neighborhood, for those of you who don't live in New York City, is the mildewed, itchy, cable-knit sweater of

Manhattan. We lived on the fourteenth floor above the Olympic Flame Diner, which kindly provided most of our meals when my mother-in-law wasn't visiting and making delicious Italian feasts. Mark and I had a rare day off from the soap opera where we both worked, *All My Children*. Perhaps you're familiar? We met on set (see the previous story). It was a Wednesday; I remember this only because it was a day off that was essentially useless. We couldn't turn it into a three-day weekend on either side. We couldn't go see Mark's folks in Florida, for example. I suppose we could have gone to see my folks in New Jersey, but that's not really a fun jaunt as much as it's a matrimonial errand involving renting a car and sitting in traffic. The point is, a Wednesday off is not a day off at all, it's more of a midweek pause.

Michael was such a good baby, but not a very good sleeper. Of course, we did everything wrong as first-time parents. We didn't sleep train him. I nursed him on demand. Since it was winter, this midweek day off with a non-sleeping baby was kind of a big blah. But then, Michael did something miraculous. He took a nap on his own. No ritual. No fussing. He nursed, fell asleep, and stayed asleep. Usually, the post-nursing removal from the breast would immediately wake him or trigger a sucking reaction that would start him feeding all over again. Or, on the rare occasion that he'd stay asleep during the unlatching, he would wake up the second I placed him in his crib. Then, I would have to stand over the crib and rub his back in a rhythmic motion for what felt like hours. When he seemed to finally be sleeping, I would slowly remove my hand one finger at a time until both hand and arm were hovering over his body, suspended next to his mobile like a strange, lactating ninja. Then I would turn to sneak out of his nursery and my knee would inevitably crack. His head would pop up like a jack-in-the-box, and the entire process would start all over again. As they sang in *Chicago*, it was heaven in two and a half rooms.

But not that day. Not on that random Wednesday with nowhere to go. Not on that drizzly, chilly, boring Wednesday off from work with nothing to do but each other. That's right. It was time for some sex. Middle of the day, unplanned sex. I hadn't even showered or brushed my hair. And I was still wearing Mark's old threadbare T-shirt that I used for nursing because it was so comfortable and smelled of milk and baby.

I'm not going to pretend it was a chore, I loved/love having sex with Mark. He should teach a class in lovemaking. I'm convinced that the divorce rate would plummet if he taught other men how to be mindful lovers. I do feel guilty when I'm sitting with a group of girlfriends who are in miserable marriages or are single and dating fifty-year-olds who don't know what the clitoris is, much less where it's located. How is that possible? I blame the American school system and luckily my husband went to school in Europe, well nursery school. But sex in the days, weeks, and months after having a baby proved uncomfortable. I felt awkward and fearful most of the time. Not about my vagina, as I had a C-section. That looked totally normal. But the rest of me felt as if I was wearing a sequined dress inside out. I naturally kept this to myself. Why bother my doctor with details like that? I began having anxiety about having sex, something I had always enjoyed. My body never felt ready. There was no Google back then, and none of my other friends had kids yet, so I couldn't ask them. My ob-gyn seemed as confused as I was because the anatomy of women's bodies, I'm convinced, is not taught in medical school. Even when the female reproductive system is the entire specialty, there seems to be a general cluelessness about vaginas and how they tick. If men had vaginas and uteruses, there would be no mystery. There would certainly be a cure for periods, yeast infections, ectopic pregnancies, and menopause. Certainly, abortions would be available everywhere books are sold. Think about how many drugs have been created for seventy-year-old men who can't get an erection. I know, this has all been debated before, but it bears repeating because when it comes to women's sexual health, I feel like we are still living in the time of the Salem witch trials. What nobody prepared me for, not the books, not the doctor, not my mom, was that breastfeeding can cause dryness. Everywhere moisture is required. (Whisper voice.) Use your imagination, don't make me get specific. My mom gets a pass because she had me in 1970 and according to her, women were told during that time that breastfeeding caused senility, and more importantly "damaged" one's breasts. I didn't ask my mother-in-law because, well you know, separation of church and state.

But here we were on a Wednesday with a sleeping baby in the next room and nowhere to be. I know what Mark is thinking before he thinks it. "Hey, you wanna go to bed since the baby is sleeping?" Mark says while pawing at his/my nursing shirt. "Like take a nap?" I say hopefully, because I'm so utterly tired my skin hurts and very insecure about my naked body, which I think still looks pregnant and yet oddly like a shar-pei puppy's face. I tell myself that I should be over those feelings by now, but the reality is that most days I feel like these two guys are sucking the life out of me. One always wants me to feed him and the other one always wants to eat. I'm just wrung out in every sense of the word.

But here we were on this workless Wednesday, sleeping baby afternoon and I'm backing into the bedroom and Mark is kissing me hard on the mouth and neck and he takes off his clothes while doing so and he's perfect. I am still in our nursing shirt, and he places his hand underneath and touches my skin. For a second I feel like I'm in my old body. He's good at making me feel that way. He tries to take the shirt off, but I back away and slither under the sheets because I refuse to get undressed in front of him in the harsh light of midday flooding through our bedroom window. At least not yet. I remove my T-shirt, bra, and panties (I know it's a controversial word) under the sheets. Mark slides in next to me and we both start kissing and giggling because we cannot believe we are pulling this off. Sex in the middle of the day, like unemployed actors do all the time! And with a sleeping baby in the next room, no less?! We both shhh each other because the last thing we want to do is wake the baby and squander this incredible opportunity. As Mark looks at me and smiles and rolls on top of me, I still can't believe that we are married. Just like in my dream, from the day we first met. We are married with a baby—a boy baby, but a real one that is ours.

We look into each other's eyes and move together silently, never taking our eyes off each other as we roll over. I feel more and more like the old me with every moment, like I'm coming back into my body after months of feeling alien. "You're so beautiful," Mark lies, and I don't care, because I feel so good. I'm getting very into this stolen afternoon of ours and now feel free enough to be naked and on top of Mark. "You're the beautiful one," I say, and Mark smiles and closes his eyes. Then I scream, "OW!"

Mark's eyes snap open, "What's wrong?"

"OWOWOWOW!" I jump up. Then nothing.

I realize I must have fallen and hit my head because I hear language and numbers, sounds that are familiar, and yet not. I hear Mark, he sounds strange. His deep voice suddenly high-pitched and loud. I am alternately hot and cold, then both at the same time.

I am shivering in a pool of my own sweat. I think I should get up now. Then, there is silence again.

I wake up to the noise of a walkie-talkie. And the sound of shoes being worn in the apartment. We are a strict "no shoes in the house" establishment, so I begin to panic at the germs being brought in that will certainly harm my baby. "Twenty-seven-year-old female, nonambulatory. Passed out while having sexual intercourse. No history of drug use. No alcohol." *Poor thing*, I think as I drift off again. I just wish all these people would stop talking. Who plays with walkie-talkies anyway?

"Kelly? Are you in any pain? Can you tell us where it hurts?"

Who me? Now I'm awake and trying to stand on the floor, which seems to be rolling. "No, Kelly, try not to move, hon, can you tell us what hurts?"

I panic. The baby! "Where's my baby?" I scream as hot tears stream down my face, and I suddenly recognize that I'm in the hallway of my apartment building. "He's with Robyn, honey," I hear Mark's voice call from somewhere behind me. "She ran over from work to stay with him, he's still sleeping, can you believe it?" Robyn from work, from *All My Children*. That's right, we have a day off. I try to focus on something, anything, as we stop to wait for the elevator. I search around for something, and that's when I see my feet sticking out from under the paramedic's blanket. They are not clad in slippers, or cozy socks. Oh no. I am wearing bright red Manolo Blahniks. Fuck me pumps, if you will. I must be dreaming, no, not dreaming, as this is a nightmare. I just need to pull myself awake so I can tell Mark. I move my leg in an effort to jolt myself from my sleep, but all that does is reveal another part of my outfit—a pair of Mark's oversized Juventus warm-up pants with side snaps. The kind soccer players wear. This nightmare is turning ugly. As I continue to attempt to sit up, I spy two other things of note. The first being that I'm belted into the gurney, which seems extreme, even in a nightmare. The second is that I'm wearing a Capezio forest-green French-cut leotard. Do I always dress this badly in my dreams? We all pile into the elevator as the gurney bounces off the hallway, the side of the elevator, and the elevator door simultaneously. I feel a cold breeze blow up from the elevator shaft and see the excruciating look on Mark's face. And that's when it hits me. I am awake. This is real! I try to free myself from the gurney and a cacophonous group reassurance begins, which has the complete reverse affect/effect, yes, I mean both, on me. Between the echo chamber of the elevator, the walkie-talkie that will not cease, and the sound of the blood pressure cuff attached to my left arm that automatically inflates every couple of minutes, I go into full fight-or-flight mode. Actually, both at the same time.

"Baby, just try not to move," Mark implores. The elevator doors open to, of course, a packed lobby waiting for an elevator that was obviously stuck on the fourteenth floor. I lock eyes with at least two neighbors I know. And by know, I mean I have no idea what their names are or on which floor they live, but I've seen them and know that they are gossipy busybodies. I quickly move to pull the sheet over my face. One of the EMTs grabs it out of my hand and pulls it back down. I try again, but he informs me that a sheet over the face means I am deceased, therefore, triggering a different response protocol and more paperwork. I think, *I don't give a shit about your paperwork, my reputation in this building is at stake.* I am wheeled through the lobby, past several more busybodies and out the front door helpfully being held open by our super because, as usual, our doorman is nowhere to be found. Then, I am hoisted into the back of the ambulance, a first for me. The EMTs grunt too dramatically as they put me down like I am the heaviest person they've ever put in the ambulance. It is nothing like the ones we use at work. For one thing, this ambulance has wheels. The lighting, however, is every bit as grim as the lighting on set. I try once again to sneak the sheet over my face, but the EMT is not having it, and I decide I hate him.

"Kelly, can you tell us what happened?"

What am I supposed to say? Am I supposed to tell a complete stranger that I was having S-E-X with my husband and felt a pain like a knife penetrate my internal organs? I had a hard time telling my ob-gyn that I thought I was pregnant.

"Well, um, we were . . . in bed? And I felt a sharp pain."

He asks me to point to the area where I felt the pain and I do. He turns to Mark and seems to pick up a conversation that they must have been having in the apartment. "Yeah, and then she shouted, 'OW!' and jumped up and fell to the floor and passed out. Twice. Then I got her dressed." I lock eyes on Mark wondering how on earth he wedged me into a ballet leotard and why? I have singular tops. T-shirts. Sweaters. And why the heels? Then suddenly, reality sets in. I feel fine. Why am I in this harshly lit ambulance on a workless Wednesday when I feel perfectly fine?

"You know, I really feel much better, is there any way we can turn this thing around. I'm awfully sorry for the trouble . . . I feel fine actually."

Then Mark asks me the dumbest question he has ever asked me. "On a scale of one to ten, ten being the worst, how much pain are you in?" Really? I've been in labor and my pain level only gets to go up to a ten? Because I've experienced at least a ninety-nine on the Consuelos pain spectrum. Mark, of course, would die at a three. I tell him less than one and he seems satisfied with that number. Unfortunately for us, the wheels are literally in motion and there is no backing out of this 911 call now. There is, we're told again, a protocol that must be followed. Again, with the protocol? Why is there never a protocol on *General Hospital*? As we make our way across town to New York-Presbyterian, keeping in mind that we lived directly across the street from St. Luke's Roosevelt Hospital, we land in every pothole. That must be protocol, too.

When we finally arrive, and my entire insides are shaken, we pull up to a jam-packed emergency entrance and are wheeled immediately into an examination room. We sail past people who look like they're in bad shape, with actual emergencies. As I am triaged, I notice a flurry of activity around our room. This level of attention feels far more than necessary considering there is nothing wrong with me. I'm asked the same questions by different people over and over again. Doctors, nurses, technicians, cafeteria workers, janitors. What happened? Where? How long? Are you in pain now? Some women would just walk by the room, glance in and giggle. My outfit was that bad.

Suddenly, in walks Shaun Biggers, my ob-gyn. "What are you doing here?" I'm shocked to actually see her in the hospital emergency room. It's like seeing your teacher in the mall during the summer.

"Well, I'm on call and when I heard a woman passed out while having sex with her husband, I had to run over here along with everybody else and see what was UP with the guy?" I didn't really hear anything else she said after she mentioned "hearing" that a woman passed out while having sex with her husband.

"Where did you hear that?" I begged her to tell me. In my head, I am blaming my busybody neighbors.

"Well, there's always an announcement over the PA system letting the ER know what's coming." It is then that I realize the entirety of the emergency room task force and anyone sitting close to the PA system has heard that a woman passed out while having sex with her husband. And that woman is me. Dressed like a street walker who enjoys a game of pickup soccer now and then. Fabulous.

"I feel fine actually. I feel silly being here. I have no idea what happened, but whatever it was, it came and went. I really feel awful taking this room away from someone who needs it."

Dr. Biggers waves me off with "Trust me, the EMTs do a visual assessment and stated that you could not have dressed yourself. That's how serious your initial condition must have been." I stare at Mark again realizing that I now have to set clothes aside "in case of an emergency." And definitely in case of my untimely death. You think I'm going to leave my coffin wardrobe up to this guy?

"Babe, I'm good at taking clothes off not putting them on." Ah my prince speaks from the shadows of the room. Mark is very squeamish in hospitals and fainted when I was given an epidural during Michael's birth, so I already know he is staying low to the ground just in case. Of course, he prefers the term "passed out." Dr. Biggers begins to examine me as I repeat one more time for the people in the nosebleed section that I WAS HAVING SEX with my husband when suddenly I felt a pain so sharp, so white hot in my lower left abdomen that I screamed, apparently passed out, and when I came to, I was poorly dressed. THE END.

Dr. Biggers determines I need an ultrasound. I have decided that this random Wednesday off from work sucks. Then came the magic wand wearing the extra-large condom. If you know, you know. They always put that strange, warmed gel lubricant on as if that's a treat, and then say the nebulous phrase "a little pressure," which is code for "Brace yourself! Here comes the medium-sized zucchini and no, I'm not going to take you to dinner or kiss you first." Well, this is not the action I thought I would be getting today.

"Ah you see that there?" Dr. Biggers is now pointing at the screen.

"No." Honestly no. I can never see what doctors tell me to look at. Even when I was many months pregnant, I had a hard time differentiating between an elbow and a foot, or a head and a butt.

Mark rises out of the chair in the corner, a look of sheer confusion on his face. Mark must be a mind reader because he nervously asks, "What are we looking at?"

The doctor answers, "Do you see that cloudiness right there?" Again, I absolutely do not see what she is talking about. We are told that there's fluid that is indicative of an ovarian cyst that must have ruptured. Mark takes a seat as his legs buckle and puts his head between his knees. A physician's assistant and a nurse rush into the room to make sure that the man who caused his wife to pass out during sex is okay. They recline him in the chair and check his pulse. They put his feet up and gingerly place a pillow under his head as well as his knees. A second nurse runs in with a ziplock bag of ice and places it on the back of Mark's neck. Dr. Biggers rolls her eyes. "You gonna make it, Mark?" This is why I love my doctor— she sounds as irritated as I feel. This always happens when Mark faints/passes out. Women from the four corners of the universe come running. And yes sometimes men, too. I don't mean to imply that he walks around fainting constantly because he doesn't. But there seems to be a direct correlation between me having any sort of medical issue, be it childbirth or random ovarian cyst, and Mark suddenly needing medical attention of his own. Many years later we will be diagnosed with codependency, but this is before we/I had therapy. Dr. Biggers tells me that she sees two more ovarian cysts and there's nothing we can do about them but wait, and Mark is so squeamish he asks for apple juice. The second nurse runs out of the room, on a juice quest.

"Really? I just have to wait and hope they don't rupture? Why can't we remove these things?" I ask, incredulously. I'm told that ovarian cysts are common and they usually resolve themselves. They would only need to be treated if I were to experience menstrual irregularities, irregular bowel movements, or pain during intercourse. OH, YOU MEAN LIKE PASSING OUT DURING SEX? Somehow this feels like a losing bet. The nurse swiftly returns with both apple and orange juice as well as animal crackers, saltines, and a strawberry Jell-O. Mark digs in like it's Thanksgiving! My eyes shift between the fuzzy images on the screen, the remnants of my ovarian tormentor, and Mark happily snacking away. *Sex can be so traumatic*, I think, and yet one of us is completely undaunted. There he is, happily munching on the saltines now and ordering a second apple juice. Mark could be at a movie, or a spa. Instead, I'm flat on my back wondering when the other two cysts will burst. When I'm holding my son? When I'm alone in the shower? At work? I already had so many reservations about getting back in the sexual saddle, between my insecurities about my post-baby body and feeling alien to myself. Now, I have to be afraid that if I let my guard down again, these lurking malicious intruders might explode? I wonder if I will ever do IT again. What happens if I can't?

Dr. Biggers asks me if I have any other questions or concerns. "No," I lie. Mark puts down his juice box and asks when we can resume sexual activity. Of course, this is at the top of his prayer list. I try to psychically will my beloved ob-gyn to say something along the lines of "NEVER!" Or "Whenever Kelly feels that she has her pre-pregnancy body back," or "When Michael goes to college." But because I haven't mastered the art of psychic conversations or self-advocacy, she says, "Oh, there's no reason not to resume sexual activity as long as you're not in any pain." And with that, Mark slurps up the last of his apple juice happy as a clam.

There is a moment I consider faking a second rupture, or intense nonspecific pain, but I've never been someone to cry wolf. I think it's important never to fake illness or orgasm. However, the problem with the latter is that I have no idea how I will pull that off. I have no desire, and actually an escalating fear of intimacy with my partner, the love of my life. Dr. Biggers tells me she would like to do a follow-up in six weeks just to make sure there has been no additional activity. *Oh, there will be activity*, I think. Knowing Mark, probably tonight or maybe even as soon as we get home. "Should we wait six weeks before we resume sexual activity?" I didn't actually say that because I'm a coward. I turn and look and see Mark standing there with his juice box and I know this sounds nuts, but I swear he is wearing what appears to be a halo. I'm almost in tears at this simple act of kindness. Mark said out loud what I only asked in my head.

I stare at this man. He looks at me and smiles. He was the one listening to my psychic conversation. He is bearing witness to the difficulty I'm having finding my way back to being his wife and lover while also being a new mother and working full-time. He is so young, and I often worry that I've asked too much of him. What twenty-seven-year-old wants to be married? And now we are married with a child, which ratchets up the stress by about two million percent, and apparently my age by forty years. And here he is standing with the resolve of a man twice his age and yet still half of mine, and with the wisdom of someone who has a PhD in women's studies.

The doctor leaves the room to start my discharge papers and follow-up instructions and Mark pulls me into his chest for a hug, the kind of hug I've come to expect from him. His hugs are warm and strong and protective. He kisses my head and I start to cry. "Hey, shhh babe. It's okay. It's going to be okay. You've asked a lot of your body. Let's just be gentle with it. When you're ready, I'll be ready. I'm not going anywhere." Now I'm ugly crying. Mark is rubbing my hair and kissing me over and over again. A million little kisses. Sobbing into his chest is the release I didn't know I needed. His shirt is soon soaked with my tears, my body is wracked with sobs, and my mind is wracked with guilt. I have such guilt that I'm not a good enough mother. That I go to work and leave my son. That I'm not a good enough wife. That I lack Mark's abilities in the bedroom, everywhere.

"Hey, baby, let's get you home to see our son." Mark knows what I need better than I do, sometimes. I wipe my face on his shirt and he reaches over with his long arms and grabs me a tissue. The scratchy hospital kind. I blow my nose and wipe my face. I catch a glimpse of myself in the paper towel dispenser and am repelled by my appearance. Mark, again the psychic, walks over, tucks my hair behind my ears, caresses my cheek, and kisses me softly on the lips. I kiss him back. He tastes like apple juice and animal crackers. He is rubbing my lower back because he knows exactly how to touch me, where and when. And that's when I feel it. A stirring inside. Like when we were in bed kissing and giggling, before the gurney and the ER. When he reached his hand up our nursing shirt. When he removed his clothes. When I first saw him. I tell him I want to go home, but I say it in a way that lets him know that I want to pick up right where we left off. Not six weeks from now, but today.

"Mom, I am
a rich man."

—CHER

CHAPTER FIVE

HAVE YOU CALLED YOUR MOTHER?

"MOM! Good news, I've decided to go see a therapist," I told my mom excitedly, on the eve of my thirty-ninth birthday. I wasn't really telling her as much as I was asking her permission, which is probably one of the main reasons I needed therapy in the first place. The idea of talking to a mental health professional about my feelings was not something I should have to ask a parent's authorization for, right? I mean I am a grown woman after all. I have been living on my own since 1990. I wasn't asking my mother to pay for said therapy. Yet, as a thirty-nine-year-old mother of three, I still wanted my mom's permission. No, not wanted. I needed her permission.

"Well . . . I'm sure you'll spend a fortune trashing me . . ." was my mom's sing-songy response. "I mean, that's all those so-called doctors are there for. Take the money and trash the mom. Because it's always the mom. Please, never the fathers. Only the mothers. And ask about the past. And your feelings about that. How do you feel about that? But it's your money, girlfriend, so do what you want." Ah, permission would elude me again today. Actually, maybe Mom was angry? She had relegated me to the "girlfriend" zone, never a good sign.

"Mom, I'm not going to therapy to talk about you at all," I lied. "I'm going to talk about how I can learn to be a better advocate for myself at work." Well, that part was true. But I was also going to discuss all the things that made me who I am, good and bad. And that involves my mother, of course. When a person grows up believing nearly everything causes—you know what—it can be immobilizing. For the record, "you know what" is how my mother referred to cancer. Still does. Cancer was like the fifth member of the Ripa family, it was discussed so often by my mother, and everything could cause it. My whole childhood existence was built around doing and not doing things to avoid it. Turns out, like usual, Mom was right about most of it. Maybe it was subconscious fear running the show. As such, I found that I suffered from a bit of emotional and professional paralysis. I'm not sure if that's the clinical term, but that's how I would categorize myself.

Also, I was desperate to form a better line of communication with my mother. I have always wanted to have the kind of mother-daughter relationships that I saw as a kid, on television and in movies. Well, not Disney movies, and certainly not *Carrie*, but you know what I mean. The kind with fictional daughters who could tell their mothers anything, and with mothers who loved their daughters without hesitation or condition. They never lost their cool or exchanged harsh words. What can I say, I've always gravitated toward fantasy films?

I wish I could define the exact nature of our mother-daughter dynamic. I wish I could just write it here and have it be solved, but that's not the reality of any family dynamic. They're always nuanced and layered, and in ours, any problems are usually my fault. As far as I can tell, our simultaneously complex and simple seesaw seems to mirror most families. Like all mother-child relationships, it's sometimes hard to know who is who. It was/is constantly evolving, includes a lot of talk of cancer, and is complicated. All I know is that I didn't have a clear idea of how much my mother sacrificed for me until I had my own kids, or how much of an ingrate I had been, until I had to withstand the ingrates I had given birth to myself.

AS A KID, I WOULD GO TO GREAT LENGTHS TO RUN AWAY FROM home with as much fanfare and theatrics as possible. *They'll be sorry when I'm gone,* I'd tell myself in front of a mirror as I practiced crying on command. I packed a small satchel and said my goodbyes at the front door. My mother would always remind me that I was not permitted to cross the street. Then, she would move in for the kill, carefully reminding me to stay alert when it got dark, because at night is when the Jersey Devil would come out to hunt for children to eat. Damn. Let me tell you, it is hard to run away from home when you're not allowed to cross the street. I could only turn left. And then left again. And then again. So basically, every time I ran away from home, I was back in under twenty minutes. And scared silly. I clearly made my point.

Part of my drive to run away was that once I was allowed to cross the street, it would be to someplace exotic where my real family lived. See, I was convinced for a time that I was adopted. That my real family was somewhere out there, looking for me. Perhaps I was a long-lost member of the Kennedys of Massachusetts. Or the Rockefellers of New York City. Or, better still, Sonny and Cher of Hollywood! Yes! Now THAT was more like it. How I lived for *The Sonny and Cher Show.* I loved watching my mom and dad sing and dance on stage dressed like elegant hippies. In my fantasy, when they were running off stage at the end of the show, they were going to go look for me. But then, I'd be snapped back to reality as they would always cart out their alleged child Chastity, at the end of the show, wearing a costume custom made for them by Bob Mackie. A bespoke-glittery confection, which was the child version of what

Cher, my real mother, was wearing. The only person who looked as out of place in their environment as I did in mine, was Chastity Bono. This kid also looked kidnapped, and sometimes appeared to be starring in a hostage video, instead of the greatest variety show of all time.

I used to imagine that I was the one being lifted into the air by Cher and placed delicately on her protruding hip bone. That those impossibly long, slender arms would carefully hold me in place on that toned, tan waist. Perhaps I would play with some of the golden fringe that was adorning my birth mom's collarbone and watch in awe as she would toss her long, jet-black silky hair over her shoulder, while simultaneously licking her glossy lips. I would envision myself doing the same to the delight of the crowd, an improv moment, of which the people in the studio audience couldn't get enough.

Chaz Bono has since transitioned into the man he always was, but this was the early seventies. To me, we were two little blond girls, and the one in Beverly Hills, California, the child of Hollywood royalty, was perpetrating a fraud against the little blond girl in Camden County, New Jersey. I had been kidnapped, and Chastity Bono had stolen my life. Clearly, I felt comfortable in this life of fantasy. Real life was not cutting it.

"He can't sing at all. She's the talent, but he's the drive. So, I guess they need each other." Thus chirped my female captor, aka my "mother."

"Mom, don't you think Aunt Shirley resembles Cher? I wonder if maybe they're related." I was laying the groundwork, slowly revealing to these Ripas that I was on to them. It never occurred to me at that time, that my aunt Shirley was my mother's sister-in-law, so even if they were related, Cher and I would still be biological strangers. I didn't let these ideas linger too long, as I was soon mesmerized once again by Cher's costume change. She was now in a white, midriff-baring beaded and bejeweled Bob Mackie original. I thought of Cher's belly button as a tight, bottomless almond. Or like the slot on a pay phone where the quarter goes. (Google it.) I imagined that if a person were small enough, they might be able to crawl into her navel, and make it to the other side of the world. That just sounded appealing to my childhood mind. How I loved her belly button, it gave me another reason to love Cher. It was nothing like my own, which looked like a thumb. Maybe, I got all of the belly button for both of us? Because if we're being honest, mine is the one that most resembles a button. A large, thumb-shaped button. Of course, this difference did nothing to dissuade me from my belief that Cher was my mother.

"Mom? How come my belly button doesn't look like Cher's?" What I really wanted to ask was, "Hey lady, why doesn't my belly button look like my mom's?"

"The doctor said you have a herniated navel" was the lady's clinical response, and that was that. A herniated navel? What did that even mean? I wondered if I could die from it, but decided swiftly that had to be out of the question. Let's not forget, this is the same woman who was concerned I would get you know what (cancer) if I stood too close to the television. So, there was no way she'd let me wander around with a terminal belly button.

MEANWHILE, BACK ON THE PHONE ON THE EVE OF MY BIRTHDAY, "Hey Mom? Do you think I should try to have my herniated navel fixed?" I decided it would be a good idea to get off the topic of therapy, which seemed to be leading nowhere fast. "I mean my belly button is way more prominent now than it used to be. Especially after Joaquin was born, you know because of that diastasis recti situation?" My large abdominal muscles had separated after delivering baby number three, and I developed a second hernia. So, even though it was a common condition, it was at times unsightly and painful. (And still is because I've done nothing about it. Joaquin is now in college.)

"Well, I took you to the doctor when you were little. Remember? You were always going on about your outie and refused to wear a bathing suit, even as a little kid. I mean you were always very . . . determined. Very headstrong and difficult." I decided not to engage in a discussion on the perils of categorizing a child as headstrong and difficult because said child (me) was too embarrassed to put on swimwear. Instead, I offered a neutral "uh-huh."

"You know what that doctor said? Remember? I told you how humiliating it was? He asked me if I was there because the navel bothered me or because it bothered you. So, we got out of there. I wasn't having him think we were there for me. I just wanted you to feel comfortable in your bathing suit. You were so small for your age, I just assumed you would grow, and it would pull in on its own. Dr. Litz was known for his terrible navels. I think he played it safe."

The great thing about talking to Mom on the phone is her ability to distract from any difficult conversation by filibuster. Back to my desire to improve our communication.

"Dr. Litz and Dr. Bacall also said you had colic. So, Dad and I would take turns walking you around all night. We each took an hour at a time, but the second we put you down, you would start screaming and crying. If the doctor had just said, 'Let her cry it out a couple of nights,' we would have done that, but we were following the doctor's orders. Obviously if it was colic, walking you around wouldn't have made a difference. Those doctors knew nothing about navels or colic. We didn't make the same mistake with your sister. Your dad and I laugh whenever we think about it. And that's how you got the nickname Tiny Tears. To this day you're an insomniac. You literally never slept. You were such a night owl when you were young. You really should think about taking half a Xanax at night. It'll put you out like a baby."

See what I mean? Filibuster.

"YOU WANT TO WATCH *MARY HARTMAN, MARY HARTMAN* OR *DARK Shadows*?" Mom asked me around 2:00 a.m. Every night we would watch TV late into the wee hours, or at least until my dad left for work at New Jersey Transit, around 4:00 a.m. In hindsight, I probably developed my poor sleep habits during these years. I assume most four- and five-year-olds are not up watching TV at that hour.

I really didn't like my viewing options, but anything after midnight meant we were dealing with syndicated reruns, so we took what we could get. *Dark Shadows* was about vampires, was in black-and-white, and absolutely terrified me. *Mary Hartman, Mary Hartman* was just plain weird. It was like a soap opera that I couldn't possibly understand. Mary, the lead character, dressed like Holly Hobbie, and also scared me, but I had no idea why. Every character seemed to be on quaaludes. Not that I knew what those were, but my mom was convinced our neighbor was on them. Anyway, I always chose the quaaludes over the vampires. I mean I was a little kid, but I wasn't an idiot. Then one night, without any warning, Mary Hartman disappeared. In her place was, you guessed it, *Dark Shadows*. I watched in frozen terror. My "mother" sat completely oblivious, happily digging around in her bowl of popcorn, searching for the half-popped kernels and burned bits. After what seemed like hours, Dad left for work, and Mom finally declared it bedtime. She tucked me in next to my younger sister, Linda. After a lengthy debate, I convinced her to keep the light on in the closet. She also left the closet door slightly ajar, open just enough for me to see the dark portal cut into the ceiling of the closet, which led to a crawl space. Just big enough for a vampire to fit through. Or at least big enough for a vampire bat to fly through and then take his vampire form in the closet. I stared at that space careful not to take my eyes off it. As hot as it was in our room, I pulled the sheets up around my neck and head, as far as I could, and sunk low into my pillow.

Mom did not want to lose her TV viewing buddy when school rolled around in September, so she made sure to enroll me in the afternoon kindergarten class. I had never gone to preschool, so this would be my public school debut. Afternoon kindergarten started at noon, and the teacher was Miss Probst. I had heard from my cousin, who was only three months older than me, but a whole grade ahead, that Miss Probst was mean. As I nervously climbed aboard the school bus that first day, I saw all the kids wearing laminated owl name tags, just like the one I had. I was kind of sad because my very best friend, Scotty Silber, was in the morning kindergarten class. He was getting off the bus as I was getting on. I touched his name tag, which was a pretty blue bird. He told me they were the Early Birds. I wanted to be an Early Bird. That schedule didn't suit my mother, so it didn't suit me.

"ARE YOU EVEN LISTENING TO ME? HELLLOOOOO?"

At some point I must have stopped paying attention, tuning out the filibustering. "No, I'm here. I'm listening." I lied to my mother. "I'm just picking up the kids from school and it's loud." "Well, did you hear what I just said? I'm trying to remember, but you had to be ten or twelve years old when I asked the doctors about your navel again. You know, because it was not going to repair on its own."

I wasn't sure what I was supposed to say, so I once again offered a neutral "uh-huh." I had been trying to not have such a quick temper with my mom. It was a real personality flaw, how quickly I got annoyed with her, and I knew I needed to fix it. This was part of my decision to go to therapy, too. But the only tool I had seemed to be the neutral "uh-huh," and it wasn't working. I was trapped in this conversation, and I couldn't get out.

"I mean, if it was Beauty, what would you do?" My mom does not refer to my kids by their names. I don't think she likes their names. She will never admit that, but I think it's true. So, instead, she gives them nicknames. Lola's nickname is Beauty. Michael and Joaquin are Mikey Jo and the Wrestler Guy or WG for short. "Well? What would you do?" She repeated.

"Um, I don't know, I'd take her to a doctor to fix it if it bothered her," I said.

"You would not. You would think she was perfect the way she was, at least I hope you would. Plus, I didn't want those doctors thinking it was my idea to fix your belly button."

I took a deep breath. "Well Mom, now you're talking about two different things. It's one thing to think your kid is perfect the way she is. That's normal. That's all parents. But you're talking about being afraid of . . . afraid of . . . wait, what were you afraid of?"

Mom did not like this question. "I wasn't afraid! What are you talking about? I didn't want those doctors thinking I was forcing you to have your belly button fixed. Are you kidding me? What would you have done?"

Oh no, here it comes. I was going to explode. "I WOULD HAVE FOUND ANOTHER DOCTOR FOR FUCK'S SAKE!" I shouted into the phone, and just like that, for some reason, Mom hung up on me. See what I mean? Bad communication skills. That was a totally unacceptable thing to say to my mother. To anyone! This, and a thousand other reasons, is why I needed therapy.

Suddenly, I was in the worst mood, but then I saw Joaquin's joyful face as he came out of the school with the rest of his class. He was six, and cuddly and sweet. He jumped into my arms and showed off his art project, which looked like a LEGO glued to a piece of construction paper. We waited for his sister's class to be dismissed next, and he told me about his art.

I heard her before I saw her—the unmistakable deep, bold, melodic laughter. Then Lola bounded toward me surrounded by her gaggle of friends, all of them clamoring for the same thing. A sleepover. Me giving my normal answer, "Not during the school week." Then, I braced myself for the collective begging and the exhaustion I would feel explaining that I didn't negotiate with eight-year-olds. But the begging never happened. It's as if they knew I needed a break. I then wondered how I would respond if Lola were to ever shout profanities into the phone at me. Little did I know what was coming a short decade later.

Sitting in bumper-to-bumper traffic in the back of a cab, I thought of the hours of my life I wouldn't get back commuting to and from SoHo, picking up my kids from school. Joaquin took a book from his backpack that he checked out of the school library. It was a *Super Friends* comic, and he asked me to read it to him, but Lola grabbed it to read to her brother instead. I closed my eyes and listened to Lola's sweet little voice telling Joaquin about Superman flying next to Wonder Woman's invisible plane. I soaked it in. The ease of the moment. The chaos that somehow felt comfortable.

I WALKED THROUGH THE DOOR PRECISELY TWENTY MINUTES AFTER running away from home. My own personal record. I'm not even sure anyone knew I was gone. I really had no destination, as by then I had given up trying to get to Beverly Hills to find my parents, Sonny and Cher. Plus, Mom told me they were getting divorced anyway. I wasn't exactly sure what that meant, but the way Mom went on about it, I was fairly certain it had something to do with you-know-what. For now, I was stuck.

PERSPECTIVE IS INVALUABLE. WHAT I DIDN'T REALIZE, EVEN WHEN I was raising my own kids, because I was too close to the page to see the full chapters, was that my mom gave me her undivided attention constantly. I needed that. I was that kind of kid. I have three kids and had a lot of help along the way, but I now see how difficult it must have been for her to essentially raise her daughters alone. Even though my parents were married, my dad worked extremely hard. He worked double shifts driving buses for New Jersey Transit to provide for us. And he did. But that meant that we were home alone with our mom a lot. And she gave herself to us. She also went without so that her daughters could have dance classes, piano lessons, and all the other things that kids clamor for that their friends have. We got all of those things. I now know how lucky I am. In these past few years, when so many have lost their parents, I feel even luckier to still have mine (everyone, knock on any nearby wood, or my mother will fear the worst). So, thank you Mom, for all of the sacrifice. You never got enough credit. I'm giving it to you now.

And thank you Cher, for just being Cher.

"*Good things happen to those who hustle.*"

—ANAÏS NIN

CHAPTER SIX
WHAT'S A BABY NURSE?

This question was one I posed to one of my very favorite people, *Live!* producer Jan Schillay when she was pregnant with her first son, Luke. Jan had the kind of pregnancy that I could have only dreamed of. The kind of pregnancy that seemed to only happen in movies, or to movie stars. She looked radiant, and unless she turned sideways, you'd never even know she was pregnant. She carried that baby like she was hiding a small ball under her shirt. As her pregnancy progressed, the bigger the ball became, the smaller the rest of her looked. I don't think she ever wore maternity clothes. Maybe she just unbuttoned her jeans, but that was about it. Comparatively, I gained nearly sixty-eight pounds with my first two kids, only Joaquin sparing me with forty-eight pounds probably because I had no idea I was pregnant with him, and I thought my body had decided not to lose the Lola baby weight. Of course, he was the same size as my other babies, almost a whopping nine pounds. And I was in maternity clothes the moment I peed on the stick, until just around their first or second birthdays. With each pregnancy, I started lying about my due date, making it sooner and sooner since everyone I met felt the need to exclaim that I HAD TO BE ABOUT READY TO POP! Jan, on the other hand, was nearing the end of her third trimester, glowing like she never even once lost consciousness putting her shoes on, when she asked me if I liked my baby nurse.

"What's a baby nurse? You mean the labor and delivery nurse?"

At this point, we were staring at each other, as if we were from separate planets.

"No," Jan answered, utterly puzzled. "The baby nurse. Didn't you use a baby nurse when you took the kids home from the hospital?"

It was then that I was hit with a brilliant concept for a new business! I decided I should probably include Jan in this start-up venture, since technically, it was her idea. I pulled her conspiratorially close, praying she hadn't blabbed about this to too many other people. "That's a great idea for a business! You get a nurse to come home from the hospital with you when you have the baby and have no idea what the hell you're doing. Because I was so tired I could barely string my thoughts together, much less take care of the baby. We should start this business!" Desperate to get off camera at this time, having been told for decades that television was a dying medium, and I was about to be a dinosaur (see, now this dinosaur is learning how to be an author!), I was always casting about for some business to launch. I think my lizard brain is comprised of mostly harebrained ideas and the occasional flickering of complete genius.

And even though it didn't technically come from my lizard brain, this idea was complete genius. It was way better than my roving celebrity cleaning business plan, which would have quasi-celebrities (i.e., me) cleaning the homes of actual celebrities because nobody can clean a house better in reality than I can in my mind. Way better than my mile-high exercise on the plane plan, which is basically a barre class at 30,000 feet but instead of a barre, one uses a tray "table" (tabled for now due to COVID-19). Even better than my public beach valet/caddy plan, which exists in fancy beach clubs, but imagine if everyone could enjoy the magic of having someone's teenage son carry their shit and set it up for them. Gold. (And I still think that one has legs.) But none of these plans are as genius as a nurse that comes home from the hospital with the new baby. Just as I was about to call my business manager, Rick Flynn, to let him know that I had found the zillion-dollar idea that would get me off television for good, Jan interrupted my ramble.

"Kel, you're kidding, right?"

Wordlessly, I set a gaze of pity upon my young protégée. Tilting my head to the right, while simultaneously down-turning my lips like a sad clown, I realized in that very Brady moment, I was suddenly the Marcia, and she was, well . . . Jan. See? This is the problem with Jan. She is so smart, hardworking, relentlessly professional, and a true innovator. But she lacks self-confidence, which I seem to have in spades. What I don't have is all the other shit that Jan possesses. Like the ability to shoulder great burdens in utter silence. My burdens are announced with a bullhorn. Together, we make one Jeff Bezos.

"No, I'm not kidding. This is the zillion-dollar plan. Think about it! We'd be giving a gift to new parents everywhere. Because, trust me, they don't know what they're doing, and that leaflet they give you in the hospital on the care and feeding of your newborn, is totally unhelpful."

Well, I'm sorry hospital leaflet makers, but it's true. Mark and I were utterly stupefied as we carried little Michael in his car seat right out of the front door of the hospital right after he was born, right past the security guard, like helloooooooo?! We simply couldn't believe they were actually going to LET US LEAVE THE HOSPITAL WITH THIS BABY! I think 99 percent of new parents feel this way upon exiting the hospital. The 1 percent who don't are just in denial. Or cult members. Or have a baby nurse.

You really had to see us back then. We certainly didn't look like capable adults. We looked like scared children, wandering around the hospital hallways, lost, clutching that leaflet, and carrying a newborn we found. Conversely, the month before Michael was born, we bought a wide-screen, picture-in-picture, TV. (Google it.) That television came with a 300-page instruction manual. While the eight-pound, ten-ounce person we were supposed to raise, and send to school, and teach to drive and turn into a productive, empathic member of society, came with a leaflet about how to take care of his penis after the circumcision and when we could expect the rest of his umbilical cord to fall off. Oh, and also a complimentary thin white, blue, and pink striped swaddling blanket with the hospital logo stamped on the bottom. Oh, and also a complimentary small bar of Dove white soap, a brand I still use to this day because the smell of it reminds me of my babies. The point is, a leaflet, soap, and a blanket do not a competent parent make. And that lady hadn't yet written *What to Expect When the Hospital Security Guard Lets You Leave with Your Child*, or whatever that book is called.

"Kel, I'm not sure if you're messing with me. I feel like you're pulling another Melanie Griffith. Is this another Melanie Griffith?" Jan implored.

Melanie Griffith, you ask? I'm sure you're curious what Melanie Griffith has to do with all of this. The short answer is nothing. But the long answer is legendary in the halls of *Live!*

About three weeks before Jan made the mistake of asking me about baby nurses, Melanie was a guest on *Live!* and Jan was her producer. Melanie is one of our favorite guests. She's a real movie star, but also a real human being. She is always lovely to everyone—both on camera and backstage. She's also, I believe, a bit of an earth mother and zeroed in on Jan's pregnancy. Instead of her spending her preinterview discussing the film or play or whatever project Melanie was there to promote, she spent most of her time giving Jan useful advice for how to make labor and delivery easier on her body. I'm certain Jan wished she didn't have to leave Melanie's dressing room to produce the segment. I'm sure she wished she could have stayed with Melanie until the second she went into labor because that's how soothing Melanie Griffith is. But Melanie wasn't finished. She saved one final tip for Jan, in what is still known to this day among the staff of *Live!* as "The Hallway Incident of 2003."

After the non-preinterview preinterview, Jan walked Regis Philbin to the studio to brief him on Melanie's segment. Melanie must have heard Jan's voice, and so peeked her head out of her dressing room door. In her famous baby doll purr, over Regis's head, she quietly yelled (in a way that only Melanie Griffith could) to Jan, "Don't forget to have your husband rub olive oil on your pussy so it doesn't tear when you push the baby out."

Boom. Just like that.

This happens to be great advice. I think. I don't know by experience as all three of my kids were C-sections.

But Jan was convinced I somehow willed Melanie Griffith to whisper-shout the word "pussy" in front of Regis to embarrass her. I did not. Trust me, if I did have that kind of power, I'd be dangerous. I mean, I would have paid real money to elicit that kind of level-four gobsmack from Regis on a regular basis.

"Kelly, you cannot be serious. Are you telling me you really didn't use a baby nurse? How did you manage? You had to have help? Who helped you?" Jan said in clear astonishment.

The elevated energy of the conversation drew the attention of our coworkers. A small but curious group began to form around us in the makeup and hair room where we had been talking. "She didn't use a baby nurse," Michelle Champagne, the *Live!* makeup artist told the others, not as a judgment, as much as a recap. This pronouncement seemed to cause mass doubt/confusion. Still, I decided to play along and not mention my idea for an at-home baby nurse service, just in case the others also wanted in.

"Nobody helped you? Nobody? That cannot be true . . . Wait, what about with Joaquin?" The questions were too rapid-fire to even attempt to answer for the group. I was just back from maternity leave from Joaquin myself, so I still had a bit of residual maternity brain.

"No, I had help. Of course, I had help. What do you think I am?" Frankly, I was starting to get defensive. I was also starting to feel embarrassed, like maybe I forgot to introduce something essential in my kids' lives, which was NOT the intention of the group, to be clear.

"Do you mean with Michael? What about Lola?" Suddenly, with every answer, I sounded like I was lying.

"I had my in-laws come help with Michael."

SILENCE.

Then, "YOU WHAT?"

In my memory the entire room yelled this in unison. The room, however, disputes this claim and wants this on record, so here it is. (But this is my book and I'm right.)

"My in-laws came and helped with Michael . . . and then my mother-in-law stayed for an additional three weeks," I said to the stunned faces standing before me.

That's right, I may not have had a baby nurse, but I had a mother-in-law. And not just any mother-in-law, mind you. I had an Italian mother-in-law. And Camilla Consuelos would certainly never allow a stranger to help take care of her baby's first baby, aka THE FIRST GRANDCHILD. (Insert inspirational *Lion King* opener here.) That was HER job.

I have since learned that baby nurses are real, and really amazing people who specialize in getting newborns on sleeping and feeding schedules, down to the minute. At the time, I had just never heard of them. I swear. The schedules baby nurses create are sacrosanct and unyielding and are not to be altered in any way. They also take over the night feedings, so that new parents can get some sleep, and perhaps not become basket cases. They are especially helpful to people who may not have extended maternity/paternity leaves. Or maybe people who host or produce morning shows. Or the rich. Or all dads.

My mother-in-law had a slightly different approach from a baby nurse. There would be no scheduling of any kind. Mom made sure to wake us every fifteen minutes to remind us to hold a mirror in front of the baby's face to see if he was still breathing. This technique almost always resulted in baby Michael waking himself, much to Mom's relief. Then she would offer to cook us breakfast at 2 a.m., and every half hour thereafter. At 5:00 a.m. sharp, Mom began planning that day's lunch and evening's dinner. During the baby's feedings, which happened on command and had to come directly from the breast, or the Sistine Chapel would collapse, Mom was careful to keep a watchful eye on the baby as he latched on, prudently sitting no farther than six millimeters away to assure the breast was producing enough milk using her X-ray vision. Which according to Mom, the left breast never was. "Mom, the pediatrician said he's enormous. One-hundredth percentile for weight. He's obviously getting enough milk." I didn't know how much Michael was actually eating, or how much my right versus my left breast was producing, but I knew without a shadow of a doubt that my baby was well fed. Mom, however, was unconvinced, explaining to me that even fat babies got hungry. Mark, for his part, slept through most of the feedings. Well, except his own.

My mother-in-law, in addition to being a milk production expert, is also an incredible cook, who never met a problem that couldn't be solved with carbs. She loves to feed her family, especially Mark, her youngest child. (Mark is my mother-in-law's favorite. It's so obvious. Ha-ha, I can't wait for Thanksgiving now!)

After Michael was born, we both had to stay in the hospital for five days. He was born via emergency C-section, and I suddenly developed a fever. I will not tell my labor and delivery story just in case someone is reading this while pregnant, but everything that could have gone wrong did, but that won't happen to you, so don't panic. Michael had to go into the neonatal ICU, NICU, as a precaution. The NICU nurses are an extraordinary group of people who I believe are angels living among us. The reassurance and empathy they give to their tiny patients, as well as the patients' terrified parents, is indescribable. You just have to see it to understand, but I hope you never do.

Michael, being born a solid eight pounds, ten ounces and twenty-two inches long, quickly garnered the nickname King Kong in the NICU. Most of his roommates were born premature, weighing only ounces. I felt an odd sense of shame combined with guilt when I came for his feedings, which was the only time I was allowed in the NICU. I avoided eye contact with the other parents when I was allowed to hold Michael and feed him without all the tubes and gloves that the other parents had to endure. And I knew we'd be leaving the hospital together in a matter of days. I also knew the other parents had months before they'd get to take

their babies home, and some of them never would. I knew the agonized look on their faces because I had the same look just a few days
before. I knew how that look felt.

I had a near nervous breakdown when Michael was taken into
the NICU after my C-section. I was carted into a recovery room
and left there with nothing but my worry. Whenever a nurse would
come in to check my vitals, I would ask to see Michael or Mark, and
the answer was always, "Let me find out." Then . . . nothing. After
about an hour another nurse would come in, check my vitals, and
answer the same question the same way. This went on for hours.
Eventually, a nurse came in and told me I wouldn't be allowed to
leave the recovery room until my heart rate, which was at 115 bpm,
returned to normal. After that declaration my heart rate jumped to
125, then 140, then 160. I stared at the rising number, willing it to
slow down, only to see it rise higher. Obviously, I was having a panic
attack while feeling my hormones drop. Naturally I began to wail.

"Maybe my heart is racing because I haven't seen my baby since
he was taken into the NICU, and nobody will tell me anything!
And don't tell me you'll go find out because you will just leave and
not come back! AND WHERE IS MY HUSBAND?" I didn't
recognize the sound of my own voice. My body seemed to be possessed. I was trembling uncontrollably and began tearing at my unbearably itchy skin, a side effect of my epidural wearing off. Just as
I was about to start screaming for help, my ob-gyn, Dr. Biggers,
came into the room. She was still in her surgical scrubs because she
had several patients go into labor at the same time that day. She
had been up all night, like the rest of us, but somehow still looked
like she had just finished a shoot for *Vogue*. She finally gave me the
long-awaited update.

Mark was with Michael in the neonatal ICU, which was mostly

precautionary due to my running a fever. The fever, she believed, was caused by having the epidural for so many hours during active labor. When the mother runs a fever, meningitis has to be ruled out in the baby, and so the baby goes to the NICU for a spinal tap. (YES, A SPINAL TAP!) I felt horrified that I potentially caused this situation by misreading when I needed an epidural. Reading the panic on my face, Dr. Biggers reassured me that she was certain that Michael was fine. She told me she had never seen a baby look so much like his father, and was positive Mark wanted to be a doctor because she had never seen anyone as happy to comply with medical protocol, as he was still wearing his scrubs in the NICU. I told her I desperately needed to see Michael and Mark. Dr. Biggers told me she would arrange to have me released from the recovery room (140), and that she would have someone give me a shot to control my itching and scratching (130), and get me back into the maternity ward where someone would arrange a wheelchair to take me to the NICU (120). And within a minute, my heart returned to normal.

Almost immediately upon my arrival to my room in the maternity ward, Mark entered in full medical regalia, looking like a doctor on a television show. His handsome smile quickly contorted into a stifled cry as he nearly collapsed onto me. Seeing Michael in the incubator with the endless alarms and various wires attached to his body, and the general chaos of the previous twenty-four hours had taken their toll on him. I rubbed his head to try to comfort him as best I could. Mark, in turn, reached into his pocket and pulled out a Polaroid of Michael that the nurses of the NICU had given him to show me. He looked so alone. My constant companion for all those months, the person I went everywhere with, was suddenly out in the world all by himself.

The aching in my heart was unbearable. I needed to get to him.

I pressed the button next to my bed to call the nurse. She arrived quickly, and upon my request, set out to locate a wheelchair. I wasn't yet able to walk, and the NICU was in another section of the enormous hospital. About a half an hour later another nurse walked in to check my vitals and give me pain medicine. I asked about my wheelchair, and she seemed confused and said she would go check. With every minute I could feel my anxiety level rising. Mark waited a while and then went down to the nurses' station to formally request a wheelchair himself. He came back into the room and said a nurse would be coming with one right away. Any relief I felt faded after an hour.

Mark, undaunted, went and asked again. I could feel the hope draining as hot tears started to well in my eyes. It was like reliving the recovery room all over. I pressed the button for the nurse once more. Again, another nurse entered and offered me pain relief, and I requested a wheelchair. I could see Mark struggle to keep his patience as he explained that we had requested wheelchairs for several hours to no avail, and that I hadn't seen our baby since the C-section. The nurse stuck to the script and said she'd go see about that wheelchair. It could have been a comedy skit, had it been funny.

When the door flew open, I expected to see someone else offering me Percocet instead of a wheelchair, but instead, I saw my angel. My best friend, Gretchen Randolph, came through the doorway bearing a huge smile, flowers, and a perfectly wrapped present. An avalanche of emotions came pouring out of me as we embraced. I sobbed on her shoulder, telling her about the recovery room, the NICU, and being trapped in the only hospital on earth without a wheelchair. Gretchen, mother of four and never one to be trifled with, immediately left the room. She came back approximately three seconds later, with a wheelchair. It might as well have been a Pegasus. "Let's go see my baby," Gretchen sang.

"Where did you get that?!" I needed to know how Gretchen managed to procure the chair that seemed so elusive to the entire hospital staff. "I went down the hall, saw it, and took it," Gretchen stated matter-of-factly.

"Did you tell them you were taking it?" Mark asked.

"No. I don't need to tell anybody. Now, do I have to drag you to see my baby?" There is nobody, and I mean nobody better in a crisis than Gretchen. She just handles life, and she doesn't tolerate the bullshit. She's also known to her family, friends, and multiple professional baseball teams as the Captain. My point is, the lady knows her way around a crisis. And in this case, a hospital. And so, she promptly, and without hesitation "borrowed" someone's wheelchair without a second thought.

It's true, you know, that old saying about how once you're holding your baby, you forget all the pain and suffering and everything else. Because I did. I forgot everything.

I forgot the twenty-four-hour labor. I forgot the fever and the emergency C-section that followed. I forgot hearing Michael's lusty cry that sounded like he was screaming, "WHY?" I forgot how Mark and I cried at the sound of his cry. I forgot him being taken away from us suddenly. I forgot the lonely recovery room and the anxiety of not knowing. I forgot that all of our friends came to the waiting room to celebrate the arrival of Michael only to find us missing. I forgot the look of a scared little boy on my husband's face. I forgot the relief I felt when Gretchen found the wheelchair. I forgot how hard it was for both Gretchen and Mark to lift me into it, and how agonizing it felt to sit up once that epidural had finally worn off. I forgot how far of a trek it was to get to the neonatal ICU, the temporary home of my son.

What I remember is the relief I felt when they handed me my boy, who recognized my voice when I called his name. How he locked eyes with me, just as he did upon his arrival the night before. He knew my voice. I felt the need to apologize. For the voice, but moreso for the rough entry into this world.

When we were finally home from the hospital, I sat uncomfortably on the sofa, my father-in-law's bed, watching the movie *Heartburn* and sobbing, with a flurry of activity around me. I promised Michael it would get better, as I gazed around our tiny apartment filled with people packed like sardines to meet Baby Kong. Mark disinfected each and every family member who walked through the door as the scent of actual sardines filled the air while my mother-in-law prepared an Italian feast for hundreds. I suppose a baby nurse would have told us to get all of these people out of the apartment, had she been able to fit into the room. I suppose a baby nurse might have diagnosed me with postpartum depression.

Even if I didn't know a thing about baby nurses then, or after my third baby, I always knew this. That women like Gretchen, my mom, my mother-in-law, and my incredible circle of female friends were the ones who saved me, got me my wheelchair, and pulled me out of the hormone shifting and into motherhood.

In the unsung hero department, a shoutout to my father-in-law who made sure I had my daily fiber, care of the massive diner bran muffin that I inhaled each morning. Second shoutout to the queens of the screen Nora Ephron; Meryl Streep, who created *Heartburn*; and Carly Simon, who wrote the score. That movie got me through that first day home from the hospital, not to mention those damn baby blues.

"Don't fuck with me, fellas! This ain't my first time at the rodeo."

—FAYE DUNAWAY IN *MOMMIE DEAREST*

CHAPTER SEVEN
IT'S PROBABLY JUST THE FLU

Mark was somewhere in Australia. He had booked a movie called *The Great Raid* for the Weinstein Company, which at the time was very prestigious and not yet pervy. I was finishing out my contract on the soap, while simultaneously working at *Live!*

With an almost five-year-old son, and an almost one-year old daughter, I found working two jobs enormously taxing, especially with my husband on the other side of the globe. The hours were especially long on the soap. So, when I was presented with a generous new offer to stay, I politely declined. It was not an easy choice, believe me.

I did find it ironic that in all the years I was only acting on *All My Children*, I had to fight like hell for the smallest pay raises during negotiations, but as soon as I got the other job, BINGO, money was available. It was as if after eleven years, the network found its wallet! Funny how that works, isn't it?

Show business makes absolutely no sense. Actually, this is true for most industries and most job offers for women. Let's get real.

The best part, however, was that even though the green new deal from the soap would have significantly increased my salary, it was also just a twelve-shows-a-year commitment. Twelve shows a year! My previous contract had me working twelve shows every three weeks. I'm not good enough at math to figure out how many shows I had been doing every year, but it was a lot. You have the app on your phone, so you figure it out. I do have to admit, the offer was tempting. But also, too little too late?

I weighed my options constantly in my head. I agonized over the details. It felt foreign to turn down a good deal. It actually felt foreign to be offered a good deal. If I turned it down, would I ever be offered anything again?

As an actor, it was hard to walk away from employment. Actors always believe that every job is their final job. At least the actors I know. Even successful, A-list, award-winning actors think that every movie is the last movie they'll ever be cast in. That every play is the last time they'll be asked to do a play. That every fragrance or auto commercial, no matter how bizarre or over the top, is the endgame.

And also, I'm sorry, but did I mention it was a good deal? Monetarily. I didn't like turning the money down because, well, money is money. I don't know about you, but I'm not a du Pont. And before you get on your soapbox about money not being able to buy happiness, you are probably right. But, money does buy food, and clothes, and pays for college, and does all sorts of things that might make one happy. And remember. I was now the proud parent of two little kids.

I knew, as an actor, I was never supposed to talk about doing the job for the money.

Actors are only supposed to talk about their passion for the craft. Their art. Their need to create beautiful stories by embodying other people. You know which actors say that? The rich ones. They can afford to make art because they made a boatload of money working on a successful trilogy or the Marvel franchise. Most actors are unemployed or underemployed, and simply must, at one time or another, do a job for the money. Okay, fine, are there actors who act for the love of acting? Probably, but I'm pretty sure we've never heard of them.

As far as the art I was making on the soap . . . Well, I had just strangled my mother on a yacht after someone roofied my punch because I witnessed her in bed with my husband, who had then thrown her body overboard because he had been roofied, too. (Who knew roofies made people so violent?) Then, I suffered a bad case of split personality, as one does, and wound up in another town, where I relapsed as an alcoholic, and then one of my personalities found out my mother was actually still alive, but not before I found myself in the clutches of some weirdo in a bar, and well, you get the idea.

And, with the money. It was a really tough call.

So, I had to view the offer from a time versus money matrix, which was and sort of still is omnipresent in my head, as well as in the head of every other working mother I have ever met. Even the working mothers who refuse to talk about it have the matrix written all over their forlorn expressions. Twenty-plus years ago, when my children were small, women really didn't mention their needs as working mothers. Probably because that would have been met with scorn and a possible demotion or pay decrease. Who knows, maybe it's still that way. So, women, myself included, shut our mouths and tried, and failed, to push down the guilt we felt about all the "missings." We missed the morning concerts and parent association meetings. We missed the coffee klatches and orientations. We missed the sign-up sheet for the class party, so we got cleanup duty ... EVERY. SINGLE. TIME! We were envious of our working mom friends who could set their own hours or were self-employed. We were always careful to play it off like we were managing it all. We pretended we knew exactly which teacher the other parents were complaining about, carefully nodding in the affirmative during the heated gossip sesh. We were ever mindful of the time versus money matrix ticking away, like a clock, in our brains, making sure we didn't have the stress of the matrix written across our faces as we picked up our kids from school, whenever we could. We made sure we were on time to take them to their best friend's house for the playdate, when we could. We tried, in vain, to remember the name of the sibling of our child's best friend, and sometimes the mother when she opened the door. We were dutifully present at all after-work school events, no matter how mundane, just so we weren't labeled absent mothers. We volunteered our time for every weekend activity, no matter how much we needed to do laundry, or get our roots touched up, or just have a mammogram. We were present at everything we could be present for, always trying to figure out which parent went with which kid. Always forgetting which classroom was the right one. Always feeling like there was some hidden directory that the other parents must've received at that damn orientation we missed. Always being nudged by that one mom, who was always there, who felt it was her God-given duty to exclaim, "It's been so long since we've seen you!" in a faux concerned smile. Always making sure that one mom, especially, doesn't know you keep that matrix in your head.

And always fully aware that there is no male version of this matrix. It simply does not exist.

So, I turned down the deal primarily because the time versus money matrix was finally swinging in my favor, and I did not want to upset that balance. And I knew, intrinsically, that those twelve shows, in the green new deal, would fall on a first day of school, or a school play day, or some important day that I should not miss. I had missed enough. I was done with the missings. Also, I just had a baby. Well, not exactly just, but she wasn't even a year old. It was time for a recalibration of the matrix.

Our daughter, Lola, was super quick. Not her delivery, mind you, that lasted an eternity. I mean she was quick in that I may look like a newborn, but trust me, I've been here before, way. She was a dream baby, and quick to reach and surpass all the normal milestones. (Whatever those are.) She seemed to understand everything that was going on around her right away. She also seemed to know about the matrix, and how short my maternity leave had been, and the decision I'd have to make about the green new deal, because money is green. Or at least it used to be, dear reader. Before crypto became a thing. Which I still don't understand, by the way. And being born a wise child, she let me sleep through the night rather soon. Women, sometimes, really get one another from the word "go," and Lola and I got each other. That is, until she turned eleven and became a total porcupine.

One day, shortly before Lola's first birthday, I received a phone call in my cramped nursery/office/dressing room. It was Bob Iger, the then president of the Walt Disney Company, reaching out to ask me to host an event in LA. (Yes, he called himself.)

We both had worked for Capital Cities/ABC before it was acquired by Disney. Although, he had been the head of the entertainment division, and I was an actor on a soap opera so basically equals. Bob was, and is still, one of the most easygoing, approachable, and likable executives in the entire upper echelon of executive land. He was at the time of this writing, my boss, so I have to say flattering things. He's also the most dynamic. His vision and leadership, combined with a savvy media expertise, helped him establish an ever-expanding global media/entertainment empire, with an equally expanding profitability. Did I mention that there is speculation he will also be president of the United States someday?

Okay, that's enough.

But back in 2001, he had yet to become the chairman of the Walt Disney Company and had apparently added event planning to his myriad responsibilities in his climb up the corporate ladder. Disney was launching a new animated film named *Lilo and Stitch*, and a premiere was planned at the El Capitan Theatre in Los Angeles. All I would have to do was walk the red carpet, introduce the film, and host the after party. Bob even invited the kids. I mean, it was a Disney film, after all! We'd be flown out on June 15 and spend the weekend in the Peninsula Hotel. There was just one problem. Actually, there were several problems. The first being that flying across the country with a toddler and a baby to see a movie seemed like a hare-brained idea at best. The second being, I really do not enjoy red carpets, movie premieres, and especially after parties. But the final, and most important reason, was that my daughter's first birthday was on June 16. So, I skipped the first few reasons, and simply explained that as much as I would "love" to attend, there was just no way.

READY FOR SOME DYNAMIC LEADERSHIP?

Bob quickly pivoted that the whole event would become a big party for Lola's birthday. A big Disney-sponsored first birthday party for my little girl! What could possibly be bad about this? That was, in no way, going to set her up for a lifetime of disappointment at all! I mean, what was I thinking, with my grand plans of a Fudgie the Whale ice cream cake and singing with the grandparents? Silly me.

Plus, and I should have led with this, because, in case you haven't figured it out by now, I tend to ramble, but I didn't feel well. I had a bug, a virus, the flu, what have you, and I just couldn't shake it. I had picked it up from four-year-old Michael. He just started an arts and crafts class, only he pronounced it "arts and craps," which I never corrected because that was a more accurate description of the class. Every week he seemed to bring home a new malady. Pink eye, strep throat, swimmer's ear. Swimmer's ear? How does one get swimmer's ear in arts and craps? Now it was this weird bug. I am very healthy.

I rarely get sick, and when I do, I can usually shake it in twenty-four hours. But this was lingering. It had been at least a week of feeling like . . . well, crap.

From working on live television, I had trained my body to never get sick during the week. Sickness was a luxury reserved only for weekends, vacation, or men. But this bug was sticking around week to week and really starting to piss me off.

Mark was on location, and completely out of pocket. The film was based on the true story of the Raid at Cabanatuan during World War II, and so there was a tremendous amount of pre-filming preparation. To make the movie as authentic as possible, the actors were sent to a two-week boot camp, where they were deposited into the southeast Queensland, Australian bush. All without their agents, managers, publicists, trainers, nutritionists, personal chefs, massage therapists, and cell phones. Not since the actual Bataan Death March had men known such suffering. I imagine morale must have been particularly low when they were assigned pup tents and roommates. That's two actors and two egos crammed into one tent. They were given rations, rifles, and regulation 1945 ranger gear. I know shooting a war film is why Mark became an actor, otherwise he would have stuck with ROTC in college. The Japanese actors had their own boot camp about a mile away. At night, both camps would engage in skirmishes orchestrated by the movie's technical advisers. This was like a grown-up version of capture the flag.

All the actors had to practice the unique speech patterns and lingo of that era. They smoked. A lot. They had to write letters home to their "doll faces" and "darlings." There was no internet or Wi-Fi in the jungles of the Philippines in 1945, or in the Australian bush in 2002, so with regard to technology, no acting was required.

Back in New York City, I made the decision to go to Los Angeles with the kids, mainly because the dynamic event planner (Bob Iger) would not take no for an answer, but also because my father-in-law said he would travel with me. That way he could be with us for Lola's birthday, and get to see his family, Aunt Cata and Uncle Louis. They lived in Oxnard but agreed to come to Los Angeles to see Dad, the kids, and me. And I suppose Lilo and Stitch.

We flew from JFK to LAX first class. (Not bad, Bob Iger, event planner, not bad at all.)

Here's a funny thing about getting on a plane and slithering into first class with two young kids—people are always so happy to see you, and unbelievably accommodating. Just kidding, people were immediately pissed and rolling their eyes. My response, in my head, was always, "Hey guys, maybe wait for them to freak out before you act inconvenienced, you dicks." But since we were in first class, I held that in, and ordered an orange juice for the kids and a tomato juice *pour moi* (that means "for me" in French), while my father-in-law ordered a mimosa. As luck would have it, the kids were angels on the flight, and robbed every one of those dicks the opportunity to be pissed off that day.

We checked into the very swanky Peninsula hotel in Beverly Hills, known worldwide for their personally monogrammed bedding, impeccably appointed suites, glamorous tea services, and elegant prostitutes. We were whisked away to one of the large and immaculate bungalows in the back of the hotel. This was no ordinary hotel room. This was like a chic and cozy cottage, complete with fireplace, full dining room, private hot tub, and gardens. (Not bad, event planner. Not bad at all.) I had a few minutes to unpack and get the kids and Dad settled with a room service lunch, before I had to get to rehearsal at the El Capitan Theatre.

My duties consisted of reading a few prewritten blurbs about the film and walking through a couple promotional spots. I didn't think this warranted a rehearsal, but the Disney side of operations was the exact opposite of what I had grown accustomed to at *Live!* We were a—ahem—live, freewheeling, and fly by the seat of our pants kinda program. The more imperfect the show, the bigger the ratings. Whereas any Disney production was flawless by comparison, probably due to the sheer number of people working to make it so. There were hours upon hours of rehearsal. Sound rehearsals, tech rehearsals, video rehearsals, and so many walk-throughs. And I still felt sick.

As soon as I arrived, I was met by an armada of production folks, a few executives from the animation department, the styling team, the director, and the always jittery PR team. (Why are they always jittery?) A production assistant, clad in her headset and clutching a schedule, asked me if I would like anything from crafty (craft service), and immediately handed me several menus from various fancy restaurants nearby, just in case I was dissatisfied with the selection, and wanted to order lobster from The Palm down the street. (Not bad at all, event planner, not bad at all.) I told her I was fine with whatever was at crafty and would go take a look myself. Coming from the soap and a live talk show had not prepared me for all this fuss. Disney clearly knew how to treat their folks. Having people catering to me was a novel experience. Actually, having lunch provided was a novel experience, but having someone bring it to me was equivalent to being in outer space. Maybe it was because *Lilo and Stitch* involved an alien?

I was feeling a bit peckish since it was technically dinnertime for me, still being on East Coast time. So, I sauntered over to the craft service table to peruse my options, which were utterly boundless. I couldn't believe the smorgasbord that was before me. How can there be so much food? Was this why the network continuously lost money? They certainly couldn't blame the shows on the East Coast. We had the same tray of stale bagels at *Live!* that we had at *All My Children*. For all I knew, it could have been the exact same tray. I made my move to the dessert table first. I casually placed a piece of ricotta cheesecake on a plate and ate it as I stared at the food in an attempt to decide what I wanted. I practically swallowed the cheesecake whole, it was that good. Although, when I swallowed, I thought maybe I noticed a soreness in my throat. I swallowed again, but I wasn't sure. Then I swallowed once more.

Ever notice that? If you suspect a sore throat, you simply must swallow two hundred times, or at least until an actual sore throat develops? I pocketed some of those fizzy vitamin C packets to take back to my dressing room, just in case I had caught a sore throat on the plane. Next, I pocketed some peanut M&M's for later, and a bag of regular M&M's to give to Michael when I got back to the hotel. I searched for a treat to bring home for Lola, hoping I might see something, besides cheesecake, to eat for lunch along the way. As a Libra, I have a hard time making decisions, especially when it comes to food, and especially-especially if there're too many choices. I settled on some hot water, lemon, and a Theraflu packet, the dinner of champions and hypochondriacs everywhere. Just in case I was starting to feel sick. Was I? I swallowed again.

The event was a supercharged, Hawaiian themed, magical Disney experience. The movie was adorable, and Michael had a blast. Lola seemed to enjoy the movie as well, then slept right through her megawatt, star-studded, red-carpeted, first birthday party. (Nice try, event planner.)

Back in the studio in New York on Monday morning, I realized I made a mistake. All that travel with two little kids, a packed work schedule, and a possible sore throat really took its toll. I could barely get out of bed to make call time and felt awful through the entire show. I felt even worse at the post-show production meeting, and horrible when I got to *All My Children* by noon. I called home to check on the kids. My babysitter answered and said my father-in-law was at the park with Michael, and that Lola was still asleep. I was relieved to hear that. When we got home Sunday night, Lola had been tough to get to sleep, and had woken up several times. She was fussy and wanted to nurse. That was something she did only occasionally at that point and only when she wasn't feeling well. I called the pediatrician to ask if there was a particular virus going around that I should be aware of. He laughed and said, "Always. There is always a virus going around."

The next day at work, I felt even worse. Michael Gelman, our show's EP and amateur internist, suggested I talk to my actual doctor, the one for grown-ups, about getting a prescription for this new drug called Tamiflu. He said it supposedly reduced symptoms from the flu or cut the duration of sickness. Not one to take medication except those readily available at craft services, I initially resisted, but ultimately realized I wasn't getting any better. I made an appointment for after work.

I sat in the office of my internist with Lola, sleeping in her stroller, next to me. I filled out the usual forms. Struggling against the pen chained to its clipboard, I swiftly drew a straight line down the NO column. Then, I got to the "how many drinks per week" page. Usually, this would call for a handicap, so as to not sound like an alcoholic. But, since I felt so awful, I wasn't drinking at all, so I didn't have to fudge my numbers. Zero drinks per week. It didn't look right when I checked that box. Even though it was true, it sure looked like a lie, so I crossed out zero, and checked one to three drinks per week. Yeah, that looked normal. The doctor entered the room just as I finished handicapping the drink section. He asked what brought me in. I explained about the bug from arts and craps, the flight, the work schedule, the possible sore throat, and my daughter nursing all night. I told him about my exhaustion, my nonspecific malaise, and how I never got sick. He felt my neck, carefully checking my glands, then did the old "say ahhh" with the tongue depressor, and the old "deep breath in" with the stethoscope. I asked him about that new drug called Tamiflu. He agreed that perhaps it might be something to cut the duration, if it is in fact influenza. He told me that a blood and urine sample would be required to make sure I wasn't pregnant. "When was the first day of your last period?" he asked. He might as well have asked me to draw Mesopotamia on a map. I stared at Lola, searching for the date. This was a question I could never answer. There was a time, before period tracker apps were available at the touch of a cell phone, when women were supposed to keep track of this data using nothing more than our memory and an abacus.

"I . . . Um, let's see. Well, it would have had to have been sometime in 2000, I guess. Right? Because she (Lola) was born in June of 2001, June sixteenth, so . . . doing the math . . ." At this point, I was hoping the person in the room who went to medical school might do the actual math, but he just stared at me.

"So, you haven't had a period yet? Are you still nursing? Exclusively, I mean." I was not nursing exclusively. I was hardly nursing at all. Once Lola experienced the flavors of actual food, she had very little interest in nursing. It had been at least two months since I nursed exclusively. "Could you be pregnant?" This was a question I could answer with certainty. "No. NO. NO WAAAAAAY. It's not possible." We both seemed surprised by my unusually definitive response. "My husband is in Australia, so there's no way."

Then the old "where there's a will there's a way" popped into my head for a second, and the doctor said, "Well look, because you are of childbearing age, I have to have a negative pregnancy test before I can prescribe Tamiflu, so why don't you just pop in there, and you remember how this works, right?" He handed me a urine cup and pointed me in the direction of the bathroom. I wheeled Lola in, did a semi-crouching tiger/hidden dragon move over the toilet to facilitate the stroller, because New York City is not for anyone with children, strollers, wheelchairs, or any sort of cast. Urine done. Toilet flushed. Hands washed. And hidden dragon risen, all without waking the sleeping tiger. Then, I pushed Lola back into the examination room and waited for my prescription.

A few minutes later the doctor came back with a PA. "Well, you're pregnant, so that explains you not having a period. Probably also explains why you're not feeling well."

"There has to be a mistake. There's no way! I just had a baby. She's right there," I said defiantly, as if pointing to a still sleeping Lola would somehow make them see the error of their ways. "Plus, Mark is in Australia, so there's actually no way. I mean there is no physical way. Because we never . . ." Or did we?

Did we? We took that two-day trip to Montreal. It was for our wedding anniversary. Mark's parents came and stayed with Michael and Lola. The trip was a surprise. I remember feeling conflicted about leaving the kids, not so much for myself, but for Mark, who would be headed to Australia for seven months. But Mark said that was exactly the reason he thought we should have some time alone, and that it was only for two days. He was persuasive. He has always been persuasive. It couldn't have been from that trip. It was just the one time. Okay, maybe it was two or three times. My point is, it was max five, but definitely not more than six times. But that was it. Plus, I was nursing. Kind of. "I TOOK THERAFLU IN CALIFORNIA!" I shouted, in tears, like I was confessing a crack addiction.

Suffice to say, I left the office without Tamiflu, but with a plot twist and a thrilling new character in the Book of Consuelos. And speaking of Consuelos...

I immediately went home and called his manager, explaining that I had to speak to Mark urgently. I was told, in no uncertain terms, that Mark was unreachable. Even if I needed him urgently, it would have to wait until the end of boot camp.

"What if there was a death in the family?" I asked.

"Oh no, Kelly, I'm so sorry, did you lose someone..." Great, now I was that asshole who invokes fake death for selfish means.

"No. Nobody died, I'm just saying that, if it was an extreme emergency, would I be able to reach him?" The answer was a definitive maybe. But I certainly did not have the balls to pull off a fake death, nor did I have the comfort level to tell Mark's manager that his client forgot to pull out. So, I waited. Two long, agonizingly thrilling weeks.

The phone rang at 6:00 a.m. on July 14. I knew who it was without even looking. I reached for the cordless phone on Mark's side of the bed, so as to not wake the kids. Usually at that hour they were already up, but a summer heatwave seemed to take the early morning rise out of them.

"Hello," I purred into the phone, trying to make the most of my predawn voice, the only time my voice sounded sexy.

"BABY! BAAAAABY! I'M BACK!" Mark shouted into the phone. He was obviously at a bar, and obviously drinky-drinky, happy-happy.

"I know, tell me everything," I whisper, in an attempt to

keep those kids, who both slept in bed with me on the weekends, asleep.

Mark proceeded to tell me everything. Over the course of forty minutes, I heard about the rations, the boot camp, the realistic-looking weapons, the tent, his tent mate James Carpinello, the drills, the SNAKES, the military raids on the faux Japanese camp. The night watch. The falling asleep. The stumbling upon an actual dairy farm, and almost being shot by a real farmer, with a real gun. He chain-smoked about a pack of cigarettes while he spoke, often with a mid-Atlantic circa 1940s accent. He spoke of his fellow Joes and their dames, and war being hell. I wondered if he was having a mental breakdown, and whether or not I should even tell him about the thrilling new chapter about to start in our lives.

But then he paused and asked, "How are you, love?"

How was I? It was the moment of truth. "I'm pregnant." I could hear him doing the math in his head, which very few actors can do, in their heads or otherwise.

"I love you, baby," he said rather calmly. "I had a feeling, didn'tcha?"

He had a feeling? No, I had had no such feeling. I thought I had the flu, or an autoimmune condition, or mono. "Do me a favor, don't say anything, because I haven't told work yet, and you know how it is there, so do me—"

But I don't get a chance to finish the sentence because mid-Atlantic 1940s Mark was back on the line, screaming into the bar, "HEY FELLAS, MY SWEETHEART'S HAVING MY KID!"

Yes, I had turned down the green new deal. And I recalibrated the matrix in my brain. But as it usually works out in the lives of mothers, the matrix expanded in spectacular fashion. And I wouldn't have it any other way.

"It's hard to be a woman. You have to think like a man, act like a lady, look like a young girl, and work like a horse."

—UNKNOWN GENIUS OF FEMALE ORIGIN

CHAPTER EIGHT

FOOL ME ONCE/FOOL ME TWICE

FOOL ME ONCE: PART ONE

I remember watching that painful moment on the television screen on September 17, 2002, as President George W. Bush stood at a podium in Nashville, before a group of schoolchildren, parents, and teachers. I also remember holding my breath as was often my habit whenever our forty-third president spoke. Not because of any political ideology, but more out of the sheer anxiety over what he might say or how he might say it. He was not, at that time, known as a great orator. But in the post-9/11 world, every word our president uttered, no matter how garbled or confusing, was breaking news.

"There's an old saying in Tennessee," he began, "I know it's in Texas, probably Tennessee, that says, 'Fool me once, shame on . . . shame on . . .'"

Oh NOOOOO, not that one. Not that stupid phrase. I always screw that one up. EVERYONE screws that one up. It's so screw up–able, that stupid "Fool me once shame on . . ." wait, how does it go again? But that day, the president of the United States endeavored on "shame on . . . shame on you. Fool me . . . you can't get fooled again!" Oh lord. Even I knew that was wrong.

In case you're curious and have the same mental/verbal affliction as former President Bush (forty-three) and I have, the actual rendering of that aphorism is "Fool me once, shame on you. Fool me twice, shame on me." Thanks, Google.

The reason I bring this phrase up is not just to demonstrate the inability I share with George W. Bush to properly quote pithy observations, but to illuminate the ease with which I am fooled. Or maybe not fooled, but the ease with which I believe.

Once upon a time, network television shows got big Nielsen ratings, and even bigger advertising dollars. Even in the middle of the afternoon. This was the time when the three major networks, then four with the addition of Fox, drew all the eyeballs. There were a few pay channels like HBO, and something called Prism, and of course Cinemax, which at the time showed mostly soft-core porn, and that was all.

No satellite TV. No World Wide Web. No internet. No social media. No e-books. No audiobooks or podcasts. There was only radio. Which meant, nothing to cannibalize the soap opera audience.

Daytime soaps reigned supreme. They spawned movies and hit records. There were racks of magazines at the grocery store checkout line dedicated to covering soap opera "news." The stars of soaps had mega fan followings, and sometimes those actors went on to become stars of the big screen.

A soap opera is an amazing training ground for newcomers trying to break into show business and earn the necessary and elusive SAG-AFTRA card to boot. They also serve as steady employment for seasoned actors who are tired of the merry-go-round of instability, and the grind of not knowing when and where the next gig will happen . . . or if.

But with the steady salary comes a grind of a different kind. As anyone who has worked on a soap can tell you, the gig can be like wearing "golden handcuffs." The oppressive shooting schedule means you can never get booked for other jobs. You're simply never available. My work days were routinely ten hours, sometimes longer. I didn't mind because I usually got to work with my husband, who sometimes played my husband on the show. This was very convenient. All of our friends were people on the show, too, so together, we were like a tribe.

When you work such long hours, it is crucial to work with people you love, and on sets . . . you never know. I was fortunate to work with a mostly wonderful cast. We were very close, like a large family. But as in all large families, there were one or two drunkles in the bunch.

Mark and I had a toddler and had just found out that we were pregnant with our second child. We had been trying to plan the next phase of our lives, and were both trying to move on to other, albeit different ventures.

I had a little over two years left on my contract at *All My Children*, and no interest in re-signing. Frankly, I just wanted to be a stay-at-home mom, at least for a while. I only had a nine day maternity leave with Michael, which, it goes without saying, was not long enough, and I couldn't imagine doing that again. At that time paid maternity leave for an actor was not a thing. Actually, neither was unpaid maternity leave. We were considered "independent contractors," so, if we didn't work, we didn't get paid. Full stop.

Plus, the amount of money I was spending on child care versus what I was earning (see chapter seven for the time/money matrix) stopped making sense to me. (And dollars.)

It was October 2000 when Angela Shapiro, the then president of ABC daytime, approached me over a lunch break during the Super Soap Weekend event at Disney Hollywood Studios in Florida.

Super Soap Weekend was a yearly soap opera fan event, like a Comic-Con for the most devoted watchers of the ABC daytime dramas. It drew huge crowds and ran from 1996 until 2008, says Google. I was only involved until the year 2000.

Like the soaps themselves, the event was a ton of work. Long hours and long lines of autograph seekers. We actors were constantly moved from one location to another every few hours, all around the park, with very little downtime. We didn't mind attending because the people were always fun. Soap opera fans are the best.

Plus, Mark and I got to bring Michael, and invite Mom and Dad Consuelos, who lived in Florida, to come and stay with us at the hotel and visit with their grandson at the happiest place on earth. So, all things being equal, this was not a work trip we minded taking.

Angela had, and still has, that rare combo of both high EQ and IQ. She was a company innovator with a keen business savvy and a keener knowledge of how to navigate the misogyny of running and programming a television network, without ever losing her sense of humor or her impeccably groomed executive patina. And even though she was frequently the only woman at the table, she still managed to have the biggest balls in the room.

Also, she makes me howl with laughter. She is one of the funniest people I've ever met, someone who can captivate a room with a single story.

At that point my morning sickness had segued into afternoon sickness as I failed in my attempt not to be nauseated by every single offering at the Disney lunch buffet when Angela walked over and casually asked, "Why haven't you hosted with Regis? I think you should. You'd be excellent. I actually think you are exactly what they are looking for. What if I can get you in the chair this week?"

I stared at Angela who, in the sweltering Florida heat and humidity, wore a gorgeous crease-free pantsuit with an immaculate frizz-free blowout. Not a bead of sweat was visible anywhere on her pore-free skin. There was absolutely no shine on her minimally applied makeup, which enhanced her delicate features. This was the kind of makeup that didn't exist on daytime dramas. I self-consciously blotted my face with my polyester napkin, which only repositioned the sweaty oil slick of television-grade foundation around my gigantic pores. I glanced down at the napkin and saw that it resembled the Shroud of Turin.

I would normally do anything for Angela, who was and still is a mentor to me. But this ask gave me an anxiety-induced cotton-mouth, followed immediately by lip-clenching nausea, even worse than I was already experiencing. I scanned the table looking for a glass of water or a saltine, but only found my reflection in the mirror behind the table. I immediately surmised the Florida humidity that eluded Angela's hair had found refuge in mine. I swallowed hard before I responded.

"Me?"

The ambivalence must have been written all over my face because Angela continued, "I know, I really should have had you host during Soap Star Week, but this is even better, so I'll give you some date options by the end of today."

I nodded, too afraid my lips would get stuck to my teeth if I spoke.

I didn't mention to Angela that I was pregnant. The only other person who knew was Mark—you know because he was there when it happened. I was early in my pregnancy and too paranoid that I might jinx things, so I kept my dry mouth shut.

What I wanted to say was, "Look Angela, I would do anything for you under normal circumstances, but I'm maybe eight weeks pregnant and I feel like a zombie. Staying awake is hard for me these days. I have a toddler and I work long hours, plus the smell of everything makes me sick. Especially early in the morning. So, I'm gonna have to pass."

Any actor auditioning for a role knows a couple of hard truths: (a) It is always better to be related to the producers or director of the project; (b) If not born gifted, the actor should try to read toward the end of the audition, but not too close to the end, and never before lunch break. The casting directors are hangry by then, and you do not want to audition over someone's pastrami on rye.

But again, it's much better to be related to someone involved with the project. Obviously show business is a meritocracy as well as a precise science.

Apparently the same principles used for actors are applied when talk shows are searching for a cohost. Unbeknown to me, by the time I showed up that first day in November 2000, everyone was sick and tired of looking for a cohost and apparently none of Regis's relatives were interested in the job. I would imminently learn that his curmudgeonly, irritated, slightly hostile uncle act was no act. Sure, it was his television persona, but it was also his genius. It's what made him Everyman and so relatable. And now Everyman was completely over the process of sorting through every woman to find a cohost.

He certainly didn't need one, and he especially didn't want one assigned to him from the network.

Who could blame him?

As it turns out, my "audition," as it's now called, was toward the end of this host search. I had not paid any attention to the search for Kathie Lee Gifford's replacement. I was usually working when *Live!* was on, and on the rare occasion I had the day off, my TV options were *Sesame Street* or nothing.

I had a preinterview the night before with associate producer, now friend, Elyssa Shapiro. Elyssa is a fabulous producer. She is very laid-back and not prone to panic, which I now understand is essential for the job. But back then, I wondered if perhaps she was on something. As Elyssa asked me questions about my life, my work on the soap, and Mark, I got distracted by the sound of gum popping in her mouth. To be clear, I too am a gum chewer/popper, but this was an entirely different level of mastication.

I don't know if you're anything like me, but I have always had a very hard time listening to other people chew. I could feel the sound somewhere in the back of my skull, which then shot all the way down my spine. Apparently this is a common condition known hilariously as "misophonia": *miso* (hatred) and *phonia* (sound). Not to be confused with hyperacusis—when sound is perceived as abnormally loud or physically painful—although now that I think about it, maybe I have that, too. Add that to my endless list of self-diagnosed disorders.

Anyway, Elyssa was preparing me for what to expect, and ran me through a list of dos and don'ts. Mostly don'ts. All the while, chomping on her Hubba Bubba.

"Don't look at Gelman (*pop pop*). Don't fade away in the interviews, but also don't lead (*crack, pop*). Regis will handle everything (*crackle*). Oh, and there will be a psychic." Long pause. "Are you okay if the psychic gives you a reading?"

Um. Was I?

"I mean you don't have to if you don't want to" (*crack, crackly crack*). In that split second a thought crossed my mind. What if this person is an actual psychic, won't they know I'm pregnant? (*POP! CRACK!*)

"No that's fine," I said, desperate to get off the phone because I was certain Elyssa had run out of gum and started chewing Bubble Wrap.

We said our goodbyes, then I pushed the antenna down on my first-generation Motorola flip phone (google it), and looked at Mark, who was driving me to the Chick-fil-A in New Jersey. That chicken sandwich with the bun and pickle was really the only thing I ever wanted to eat during my second pregnancy. Don't judge!

"What?" Mark asked. He could tell that I was conflicted. "What did she say?"

I chose my words carefully so as to not sound nuttier than normal. "That was Elyssa Shapiro. The producer. She said they are having a theme week with psychics. And she asked if I would be okay with the psychic giving me a reading. And I said yes. Do you think I should call her back and say no?" Mark turned his head toward me, and I was simultaneously floored by how handsome he was and also nauseated by him. I cracked the car window.

"Why would you say no?"

Men.

"Honey, I'm pregnant. We haven't told our parents. We haven't told work," I said flatly.

Mark laughed. "So? What, you're afraid the psychic is gonna figure out you're pregnant? Please."

That was precisely my fear.

"Mark! She's a psychic. That's what she does. Makes predictions and sees things and—"

I didn't get to finish because Mark started laughing out loud. "Oh okay, Kel, a psychic is going to make a prediction? Like the fortune-teller in Rome?"

You should know that we honeymooned in Rome, and Capri. It was EPIC!

Because we only spent $179 on our wedding, including airfare, dear reader, we really splurged on the honeymoon, staying in the super chic Hotel Eden, at the top of the Spanish Steps in Rome. Our room, a sumptuous and elegantly appointed suite, overlooked St. Peter's Dome. During our first night dining in the hotel's extraordinary rooftop restaurant, which is now called La Terraza, we enjoyed the breathtaking vistas of the ancient city. It was there, in the home of the Colosseum, one of the seven wonders of the world, that I Kelly Ripa, of Berlin, New Jersey, spied the eighth wonder and the true godmother of my brain . . . CHER!

I began to vibrate immediately, craning my neck to see if anyone else had seen her, but the rest of the diners seemed to be out to lunch. Was I hallucinating? Was I dreaming? Or could it be possible that ONLY I could see her? Did we have that kind of a connection? Or had I died and was I in heaven? Which would have made sense since heaven would be in Rome, and Cher would be in charge, because she is well, God?!

At some point, I became aware that Mark was having a lively conversation in Italian with our waiter, which would ordinarily make me very horny, but as we were in the same dining room as Cher, it just sounded like irritating gibberish.

"Kel, Kelly?" Mark said, and I realized that even though I'd only been in Italy for less than twelve hours, I was starting to understand the language.

"Si," I fired back coyly, careful not to lose sight of Cher.

"Babe, be cool," Mark said, in what was starting to sound a lot like English. Be cool? Who could be cool at a time like this? "You ready to order? Do you want me to order for you?" Mark asked. I decided that the only chance I had at capturing Cher's attention would be to order loudly, for myself, in Italian.

Why I thought that was a great plan is the ninth wonder of the world.

I inhaled deeply and stated with as much fanfare as I could muster, "QUESTA MACCHINA, NON E GIAPPONESE. QUESTA MACCHINA E ITALIANA!" In case you're curious, and don't speak Italian, that meal I ordered from the stunned waiter translates thusly, "This car is not Japanese. This car is Italian." Proving that the Berlitz Learn Italian cassette I had crammed on the flight over was worth every lire.

That night after dinner, we strolled hand in hand, walking off the incredible meal, taking in the breathtaking sights of the ancient city, and window shopping, when we were approached by a fortune-teller. Mark had warned me that pickpockets lurked in every corner of every piazza.

Mark and the fortune-teller had an animated conversation in Italian. I smiled in spite of my edginess because unless Cher was in the room, listening to Mark speak Italian was one of my favorite things to do back then, and still is. One of these days I'm going to learn to speak Italian myself. (Says every year.)

Mark, I assumed, would translate what the fortune-teller was sharing, so I kept hypervigilant—with one eye on the traveler, who was now holding my hand in his hand, and one eye on the lookout for potential gypsies, tramps, or thieves. Still one of my favorite Cher songs.

Mark was emphatic in his responses. His Italian is always emphatic. He laughed, he gesticulated, he made affirmative sounds. If I had closed my eyes, I would have thought he was on the phone with his parents. But I didn't dare close my eyes at a time like this. We could get robbed.

"What? What's he saying?" I asked.

Mark was guffawing so hard he could barely get it out, "He's telling me that I should stay away from you. And that by no means should we get engaged."

BASTARDO!

Meanwhile, back in the New Jersey Chick-fil-A drive-through . . .

"Yes, I remember. So, you really don't think I should worry?" I was still uneasy.

"I'm positive, baby. You've got nothing to worry about." He leaned over and gave me a kiss, which immediately made me nauseous.

I couldn't sleep a wink that night, unable to shake the feeling that the psychic would know I was pregnant. I rolled over to look at Mark who was, as always, sleeping like a man, which is the same as sleeping like a baby, only completely through the night. I tried to will him awake so he could say something to make me feel better. Then I tried flipping around in bed. Nothing. Then I tried making passive-aggressive huffing sounds. He was like a dead body, but one that was breathing. Then I gently kicked him as hard as I could. Et voilà. (I picked up the Romance Language fun pack from Berlitz.) "What's going on?" he muttered, slightly irritated.

"I can't sleep." We stared at each other waiting for the problem to solve itself.

"You nervous, babe?" He pulled me close and started to kiss my neck and rub up against me.

(Now why can't a woman receive some level of comfort, support, or a foot rub without it leading to a sexual encounter?)

What was he going to do? Sex my anxiety away? Apparently that's exactly what he was going to do. Not that I was complaining because let's face it, I was wide awake anyway.

However, four and a half minutes later, I was right back to square one and he was sound asleep again. I kept going over every possible scenario in my brain, when suddenly my long-deceased grandmother popped into my mind vividly. I hadn't thought about her in quite some time, but I suppose I had been triggered by the idea of a psychic into remembering my own psychic episode years before. In 1974 my parents took us on a family vacation to Walt Disney World. My grandmother, with whom we lived, was supposed to come with us, but decided she wasn't up for the long drive to Orlando, Florida. As we were leaving, she gave my sister and me gifts to keep us amused in the car. Linda was gifted a Mr. Potato Head, which back then was a bag of metallic eyes, ears, and lips that were placed into an actual Idaho russet. Initially, I felt envious of her fabulous gift. But then my grandma handed me a tiny purple purse with a Kewpie doll on the front, staring out from a magical little window. As I looked at the doll, I felt a sudden overwhelming rush. I still don't know how to describe the feeling, but it compelled me to throw my arms around my gram and say, "Please don't die, Gramma."

As I felt the air leave the room, I knew immediately that I had said something unspeakable and taboo. I don't remember much more, except what has been repeated to me by my parents for decades.

I spent the entire drive to Orlando begging my parents to turn the car around. I was insistent that we had to get home because Grandma was going to die. My mom made frequent phone calls home so that I could speak to Gram, reassuring both of us I'm sure. But no amount of hearing her voice assuaged the feeling of dread. My relentless begging cut our time at Disney short. My parents were at a loss as to how to calm me down. The hysteria only subsided once we were in the car headed home, but I remained vigilant. I kept asking if we would make it in time, telling my dad we had to go faster or we wouldn't be able to give Gramma the souvenirs we bought for her.

I stayed on the armrest of the car the entire ride home, and when we turned onto our street, I could see my grandfather standing on the porch of our house. He was waving his arms the way people do to warn of trouble, and I knew we had missed her. And, we had.

So, while I didn't believe in fortune-tellers, I was still a little wary of psychics.

That morning, in the makeup chair at *All My Children*, I was seriously starting to have second thoughts about the guest-host gig. There was a general excitement and buzzing about all around me that felt very odd. Doreen Gillis was everyone's favorite makeup artist in the building because she was especially good at hiding exhaustion. I liked her because she got the job done fast. That morning she was moving at double speed. Richard Esposito, my hairstylist, was swiftly blowing my hair into a sleek straight do.* Everything felt like too much, too fast.

When the restoration process was complete, which in those days took less than forty-five minutes, we all loaded into an SUV and headed to the *Live!* studio over at 7 Lincoln Square. It seemed silly to take a car service when we were less than six blocks away, a maximum ten-minute walk.

After my sitcom Hope and Faith *was canceled, because apparently, once I joined the talk show, the creatives at ABC decided I was an actor, Richard Esposito wound up becoming Alec Baldwin's hair stylist on* 30 Rock, *whereupon his biting sense of humor behind the scenes was noticed and he was written into the show playing "Richard Esposito, hairstylist."*

What I didn't know at the time was that talk show hosts DON'T WALK!

We arrived four minutes later, and pulled directly into the garage, which looked exactly as it had when Mark and I had smoked cigarettes and ignored each other back in 1996.

I got out of the car along with Richard and Doreen, as well as the *All My Children* publicist who had insisted on coming for some reason, though I imagine any excuse to get out of our dank studio for a field trip was worthwhile, if simply to an even danker studio. We were greeted and taken to a small empty dressing room. Too small for the four of us, so I asked the publicist to grab Richard a coffee he didn't ask for. I needed to breathe.

There was a knock on the side of the open door, and Elyssa Shapiro walked into the room to introduce herself. She was adorable, and younger than I expected. My age.

Actually, she is six weeks older, which is something I continuously remind her of and hold over her head to this day. That's right, Elyssa Shapiro is six weeks older than me. (Now it's in a book!)

She dove right in to brief me just as the PR person came back with Richard's unwanted coffee. Richard saw my eyes counting the number of people in the room and asked Doreen and the PR rep to accompany him to the green room to look for bagels. Once we were alone, Elyssa's gum made its entrance. The snapping, crackling, and popping started immediately, as if all three Rice Krispies elves were having an orgy in Elyssa's mouth.

I tried to stay focused on the task at hand, which was not throwing up.

"Okay, so really just basically everything we went over yesterday. No big changes" (*POP CRACK!*). "Just remember, don't look at

Gelman. And don't forget to participate in the interviews. I mean, don't just fade away after host chat. But let Regis handle everything. Really only speak if he's not already speaking. And don't speak when he doesn't want you to. Just go with the flow. And don't forget the psychic is here, and she's going to give you a reading if you're still okay with that" (*POP POP!*).

I was just about to weasel my way out of the psychic reading portion of the show, when suddenly, in the doorway appeared the *Live!* executive producer, Michael Gelman.

Did Elyssa mean I couldn't look at him in the dressing room? She really didn't specify. I stole a brief glance. He didn't strike me as a diva, but you never know how people are off camera. I averted my eyes just in case.

"Hello, I'm Michael Gelman, the executive producer, how are you . . ." said Gelman, who seemed perfectly friendly for someone who didn't want any eye contact.

I glanced up sheepishly a second time. He was holding out his hand to shake mine, which I delicately obliged with a small curtsy. Just in case.

He then assumed a deep squat position right there in front of the door and twisted the top half of his body against the bottom half until we all heard a loud crack. I paused waiting for a scream, but instead, he let out a euphoric sigh.

I was suddenly spellbound and realized not looking at Gelman might be more challenging than it sounded.

It was only after he rose into a tree pose that I noticed he was clutching a bunch of newspaper articles in his left hand, which he began to read to me. These were supposed to be my talking points in case I forgot how to think for myself. He read aloud the parts he found most pertinent or humorous or were already highlighted. I wondered if I should mention to him that I actually knew how to read all by myself, or if this was just part of his process and maybe he read to all the cohosts.

I was trying to stay engaged but being read to has always put me to sleep. While I attempted to suppress a yawn, Gelman segued into the rundown of the show. He repeated everything Elyssa had just told me, almost verbatim. He then told me that they were not looking to hire a permanent cohost, and I should just go out there and have fun. (FUN?) Just be me. (Right.) Try not to fade away after the host chat. (CHECK.) Try to participate in the interviews, but not too much. (GOT IT.) Try to predict when Regis is finished asking the questions. (UM, OKAY?) Oh, and under no circumstance should I ever look at Gelman. (HUH?) There it was again. (SO CONFUSING.)

I feared that the very act of being forbidden to look at this man might lead to me having an eclipse situation on my hands, or rather my eyes. (You know you've been tempted to look.)

And with that, Gelman vanished with less than five minutes to air. I couldn't believe how low-key everything was. People were meandering backstage like nothing was going on.

My natural instincts were to run down the hallway screaming, "FIVE MINUTES TO AIR! FIVE MINUTES TO AIR! WHAT'S WRONG WITH ALL OF YOU? DON'T YOU SEE THE CLOCK?"

But I resisted that urge when I noticed another clock that said it was seven minutes to air, and yet another that said it was 2:20. Every single clock had a slightly different time.

Thankfully the sound guy knocked on the open door to mic me, so my panic time was cut short.

I turned to him and asked the obvious, "Um, so do you know what time it is? I mean, will someone come and get me or . . . should I be somewhere?"

The sound guy looked at me like it was his first day as well. "I think he'll get you," said the sound guy. I smiled and nodded in the affirmative, wondering who HE was. He didn't mean Gelman, did he? I couldn't handle trying to find my way to the set with my eyes closed. Plus, he was just here, why didn't he just bring me with him? Wait a minute . . .

He didn't mean THE HE, did he?

Doreen and Richard entered and sat me down to give me one last touch-up, and then I heard a familiar voice. "Regis is here to get his cohost, thank you!" said Regis Philbin.

I made a mental note that everyone in the building seemed to refer to themselves in the third person. I then attempted to present a demeanor of calm by flashing a winning smile, only to have my upper lip stick to my TEETH. Using nothing more than my sandpaper tongue, I pried my upper lip loose, with a sound akin to the tearing of masking tape. I reached for a final glug of water, but the terror-induced cottonmouth was unimpressed with my adorable attempt to quench it.

"Kelly is ready," I said in a high-pitched squeak, invoking the third person rule for myself. Regis then scanned the room, unsure which one of us was me. I made another mental note that the third person rule was for employees only.

Regis was warm and friendly, and even though I'd met him many times, and had also been a guest on the show many times, he seemed to have no memory of ever seeing me before in his life. Which now, in hindsight, I understand perfectly.

"Well . . . look at you," he said, as we began our walk to what I assumed might be the studio since the show was about to begin in fifteen seconds, yet still people were milling about rather casually.

"Just relax and let Regis handle everything. Okay? This will be the fastest hour of your life," he offered.

"Don't even look at her . . . sons of bitches!" he yelled to absolutely no one while laughing to himself. He then took a sip out of his coffee cup, which appeared to have orange juice in it, yet I couldn't help but wonder if maybe his OJ was fortified with something stronger. I eventually learned that this strange turn of phrase had nothing to do with me, but was one of the Reege's many preshow rituals, which, in the future, I would pick up and make my own.

"I'll pull out the chair for you, okay, sweetheart?" he offered in a very paternal way. I found his kindness reassuring.

"Sure, um, okay, I—"

But I was interrupted with, "Save it for the air. Save it for the air," he said, twice. And then every single day that we worked together going forward.

I heard the audience roaring, then the show's theme music.

There was a small monitor backstage, and I could see the show had begun. I felt the sudden urge to run back down the hallway screaming, "SOMEBODY HELP ME! Angela, I changed my mind!"

I shivered at the thought and played it off like I was cold, which I was, come to think about it.

We were standing in the wings waiting for the stage manager to give us the cue to move, when I heard the voice of Tony Pigg, the show's iconic announcer. "And NOW, here are Regis Philbin aaaaannnddd Kelly Ripa!" And just like being shot out of a cannon into a fevered dream, I found myself in the chair.

The audience, made up of mostly older women, was clearly in

love with Reege. He had been having his coffee in their kitchens for a long time, and they adored him. He had become an even bigger star recently with the success of his prime-time game show *Who Wants to Be a Millionaire*, so he was probably spending time in their living rooms as well.

We kibitzed over the preselected items from the newspaper that were both light on news as well as substance, a hallmark of the show I would come to learn. I answered the questions posed to me by Regis, noting that he was in no way, shape, or form looking at me, as much as he was looking past me. Or behind me? The entire time we spoke, there was no eye contact. I wondered if I was not supposed to look at Regis either. These rules were so confounding.

Finally, curiosity got the better of me and I turned to look in the direction of Regis's gaze. And there, perched on a stool, was that rarefied raptor Gelman, clutching his cue cards.

SHIT! I had done it! I looked at Gelman! What would happen now?

I swear, I only glanced for a second—second and a half max. But it was too late. I felt a tapping on my shoulder. As I turned back around to snapping fingers, "'Scuse me, got a sec?" a visibly exasperated Regis demanded, to the howls and guffaws of the women in the crowd. I took a stab at laughing as well, but I failed to find the funny when my lip got stuck to my teeth once again.

After twenty minutes, we took our first commercial break.

Without a word, Regis got up and sauntered over to the thrilled and cheering audience. He signed copies of his books and CDs and chatted with audience members. He told jokes, answered questions, and tried to give as many people his undivided attention as he could. He knew they traveled a long way and stood in a long line to meet him, so he tried to make those few moments worth their while.

I then spied Gelman moving with deliberation toward the phone on the studio floor. I assumed he was calling security to have me removed immediately for wanton and reckless eye contact.

Elyssa walked over to either hit me in the face with pepper spray or take a large hook and drag me off the set, but instead she reassured me that "host chat" had gone even better than she had dreamed.

She seemed genuinely thrilled with the way it was going. I wondered if we were experiencing the same show.

I was convinced that the mere act of looking at Gelman, accidentally or otherwise, would probably result in the show's immediate cancellation.

"OMG, that was so funny, I was cracking up. When you looked at Gelman" (*POP CRACK!*).

Suddenly, the stage manager was counting us down again. Regis made his way back to the chair with no sense of urgency, and uttered to the room, "Killing myself for a mere five hundred thousand a day. For what?" The audience boomed with laughter. Then he turned to me, "Think that's funny, do ya?"

No, but I certainly wasn't about to tell him that, especially since I already had two priors. One for illegal use of the third person and the other for felony eye contact.

Before I knew what hit me, the psychic segment had arrived. I tried to black out any thoughts in my mind, which was usually a piece of cake for me. Blackness. Think of nothing. Don't think about your grandmother. While thoughts of Gramma suddenly swirled in my head, Regis read the introduction for psychic medium Char Margolis!

Char was adorable, petite, friendly, and laser focused on me.

CHAR: Okay, I was picking up someone deceased with an "E" initial . . .

ME: Yes . . .

CHAR: And in her name, is there an "l" or a "d" in it if you spell it out? Or is there an "m" or "n" in it?

ME: Ummm . . .

CHAR: But it starts with "E," right?

ME: Yes!

CHAR: It's not an Eve, or Eva, or . . .

ME: No.

CHAR: Esther or something?

ME: Yes!

CHAR: Is it Esther?

ME: Yes, yes!

CHAR: I knew it was an "E" female. Is this your grandma?

ME: Yes, yes! (HOW DID SHE KNOW THAT?)

CHAR: Okay, her spirit is with you, and she wants you to know that she watches over you, she watches over. I heard you say earlier that you're married, and you have a husband and a son, so she watches over your son and she's also showing me another baby!

ME: *BLACKS OUT*

CHAR: And she's saying that she's going to watch over you when this new baby comes, and it's soon! It's not far away. You're not pregnant yet, are you?

REGIS: Excuse me, are you expecting?

ME: *Still processing*

CHAR: Uh-oh!

ME: I haven't told my boss yet . . .

REGIS: Are you kidding me?

CHAR: Oh my god, oh my god! Oh my god I am so happy for you!

ME: My sister-in-law doesn't know yet . . .

And there it was. You could have heard a pin drop at once, and then uproarious joy the next second. I stood there in shock.

REGIS: Kelly Ripa is PREGNANT! News on the show!

CHAR: You heard it here first!

And then it was over. Regis was right, it was the fastest hour of my life. Elyssa walked me backstage, saying things to me that I did not hear. I saw people lining the hallway backstage who seemed to be smiling at me and offering congratulations, but I felt like I was underwater. So, I defaulted to smiling and nodding in the affirmative. Once back in the dressing room with Richard and Doreen, I felt like I had resurfaced. They were applauding and hugging me. Which made me nauseous.

I tried to sneak through the doors at 320 West 66th Street hoping nobody had seen *Live!* The front desk security guard greeted me with a warm "Congratulations" and a "Good job!" Uh-oh, things weren't looking promising. I headed to the elevators and up to the dressing room. When I got out, the second security guard wished me congratulations, to which I offered a conspiratorial "Shhh" in response.

But honestly, who was I kidding?

I walked into our makeup and hair room, in search of Mark, or a saltine.

"CONGRATULATIONS!" Everyone yelled as I walked in. It

was as if they had never seen me on television before. Hair, makeup, wardrobe, actors, all ran over to offer me hugs and pats on the backs and "Good Job!" and "You were hilarious." I could feel myself about to vomit. I headed to my dressing room to look for Mark, or a saltine once more.

The door of my dressing room was adorned with a slew of yellow Post-its, each bearing the name and number of an agent from all the top talent agencies. CAA, Endeavor, William Morris, ICM, United. "Kid, I'm gonna make you a star!" I said to myself, imagining what I would hear if I returned those calls. Apparently, top talent agents only watch talk shows and not soap operas. Instead, I removed each of the sticky yellow squares from the door and pushed my way inside, hoping to find a box of saltines magically unwrapping itself.

Just then, Mark entered the room and pulled me into a warm hug and long kiss. I felt around in his jacket pockets for crackers to no avail.

"First of all, you were hilarious. You're so smart and quickwitted. You looked gorgeous. Glowing! You were glowing. We were screaming in the makeup room when the psychic came out."

My stomach lurched at all of Mark's flattery, so I held up my hand. "You can't just kiss me without offering crackers. You know that. As a prophylactic."

"Prophylactic crackers got it. Are you feeling sick?"

He seemed to have forgotten my sleepless night and my worry about that segment with the psychic. Because I WAS A PSYCHIC TOO! I just knew she would know.

"Yeah but our folks . . ." I said, but Mark was way ahead of me.

"That's who I've been on the phone with. Babe, everyone is thrilled. Nobody is upset that they heard about it on the air." I was dubious, but I focused on the task at hand, which was finding the damn box of saltines and then our executive producer.

"Well, I guess we better let Jean know."

No sooner had the words come out of my mouth than an announcement came over the PA system. "Kelly Ripa, please report to Jean Dadario Burke's office." (Yes, working on a soap is a little like high school, and I had just been called to the principal's office.)

Every aspect of our show was tightly controlled. The executives had creative authority over the colors and lengths of the actors' hair, so I was pretty sure I should have informed them that I was expecting before a psychic told them on national television.

I stepped into the hallway and headed down to the basement where the producers' offices were located. No, you read that correctly. The producers' offices were in the basement.

This ain't Hollywood.

I dragged Mark with me, even though Jean hadn't called for him. He was, however, half of the reason I was pregnant, so I thought he might like to share in half of the responsibility. Plus, everyone found him charming, especially Jean, who I thought also might like a reminder that it does, in fact, take two to tango.

We got out of the elevator on the bottom floor and hung a right into the *All My Children* executive offices . . . in the basement. An intern was stationed at the phones and looked up at us like she knew we were about to get after-school detention.

She called into Jean's office, "Kelly and Mark are here." Then, with a curt nod, "You can go in now." The door opened to an impossibly petite Jean Burke. She was the only person I knew who was as tiny as Susan Lucci.

She shook her head, "What am I going to do with you?"

I suppose that was her unique way of saying congratulations.

"Have a seat." We both sat down like children in time-out.

"So, when were you planning on telling us?" she asked me specifically.

I leaned forward and explained to her that WE weren't planning on telling anyone for at least another few weeks or so. And that I didn't expect a psychic to share my happy news with the world, much less my employer.

Then, I mentioned my hope that the pregnancy would be written into the show this time around.

The first time around, my character Hayley wasn't pregnant. This meant that I, Kelly the actor, was also not supposed to be. At first "the belly" as it was known, was ignored. But like Glenn Close's character in *Fatal Attraction*, "the belly" WOULD NOT BE IGNORED, DAN!

Anyway, "the belly" was at first hidden behind purses, luggage, doors, and lots and lots of tables. But alas, no amount of ignoring "the belly" made it less real. "The belly" craved the spotlight like an aging Hollywood starlet and refused to comply with production orders. Eventually the rest of me joined "the belly" in protest, and the writers were left no choice but to bury my character alive in a cave, from the eyes down. I was told the only part of me that didn't look pregnant was my forehead.

Jean informed me that the writers had no intention of writing my pregnancy into the storyline because another character was going to be pregnant, and the show couldn't possibly have dual pregnancy plots.

I looked toward Mark hoping he might charm Jean into advocacy, but he sat there silently nodding in agreement.

"Does a pregnancy have to be a storyline? Can't Hayley just be pregnant and get on with it like people do in real life? Can't she run the private eye firm, the nightclub, the AA meetings, and the beauty arm of Chandler Industries while being pregnant?" I implored.

Jean said it sounded like Hayley had enough on her plate to balance, so adding motherhood might be too ambitious.

I suggested Hayley drop the PI firm because that was ambitious, not to mention ridiculous.

Jean promised me she would talk to the writers and make some suggestions.

Before you google it, in 1997, "The belly, chapter one" was thwarted from making a star turn due to an Erica Kane pregnancy. And no, it wasn't a geriatric pregnancy storyline. Before you burn this book, all pregnancies are considered geriatric when the mother is over the ripe ol' age of thirty-five. These are the medical rules, dear reader, not mine. So calm down! For the record, Erica Kane is still thirty-five.

Spoiler alert: The writers did wind up giving my character a pregnancy storyline, immediately after I came back from my four-week maternity leave when my daughter Lola was born. So as luck would have it, I got to be "pregnant" forever. I think it was a total of eighteen months with the real and reel pregnancies. You know, just like an elephant.

So, I believed that the folks at *All My Children* wouldn't ask me to hide my belly a second time around. I also believed that doing that favor for Angela was a one and done. Turns out, I was wrong on both counts.

FOOL ME TWICE: PART TWO

Call it instinct. Women's intuition if you will. But every internal warning mechanism I possessed shouted, "WALK AWAY FROM

THIS JOB OFFER! YOU DON'T NEED THIS KIND OF HASSLE. YOUR LIFE IS GREAT JUST HOW IT IS." It was, in fact, the strangest vibe I've ever gotten after receiving an offer for a job. Over at *Live!* they had been searching for the right person to cohost for quite some time, and, supposedly, I was it.

But it didn't feel like the folks at *Live!* were happy with the decision. From my perspective, it felt like a force majeure.

I was standing in my kitchen with a bucket of extra crispy KFC because with this pregnancy, I really craved fried chicken. (With Michael, I craved whole lemons, rind and all. Joaquin, I just couldn't eat a thing.)

I was writing down the details of the offer on a nearby KFC napkin with my brand-spanking new agent on the line. It wasn't the money that stood out, but the phrase that accompanied it gave me major pause.

"They want to make sure you know who your boss is," he said rather dubiously.

"What does that even mean?" I asked in earnest.

"I-I . . . wish I could tell you" was his exasperated response.

A lot had transpired in the two months since I had first been asked to guest cohost on *Live!* With the exception of the napkin, I was not journaling during this period, so I'll do my best to recall the conversations.

Almost immediately following that first appearance in November, I got another call from Angela asking me to cohost again. And it was an easy gig, psychic pregnancy reveal notwithstanding, so I did it.

Soon after that, there was a request for a third day.

However, before that third appearance, I was given a list of reminders.

Mostly the executives at *Live!* wanted to remind me that they were not looking to hire me permanently, which I found amusing since THEY kept calling ME. Never before had so many men lined up to tell me how uninterested they were in me. At least not since high school.

I was invited to lunches and meetings with these same men whose jobs I didn't understand and whose titles were extraordinarily synonymous:

Senior VP of blah blah.

Executive VP of blah blah.

Executive of blah.

Senior executive in charge of blah blah blah.

They showed me comprehensive Neilsen ratings books, thousands of pages of ratings for the show broken down by year, month, week, day, hour, and minute. Sexy stuff, right? I feigned knowing what it all meant, while pretending it was fascinating. (It wasn't.)

Maybe they were trying to bore me to death.

Maybe they thought my indifference was an act, but I was too busy working on the soap while raising my family to care about a job that didn't exist. Because when I was told that the executives weren't looking to hire me as cohost, I believed them.

Fool me twice . . .

As soon as I arrived that third morning, I noticed a vibe shift, or a cooling off.

My agent said they didn't want me bringing an entourage to the studio. He said there had been complaints. This confused me as I had only been bringing Richard and Doreen, my hair and makeup team.

I had never heard of a three-person entourage, but keep in mind, I had left my day job to run down the street and host the morning show, which meant I would then go back to work and resume the role of my character. In the spirit of efficiency, I thought it would be better to have my makeup done just once at my day job, and then simply touched up at *Live!*

Regis greeted me forty-five seconds before the show started with, "Uh-oh Gelman, it's got an entourage."

IT?

I felt my face get hot, and my heart start racing.

I flashed a strained smile and said, "By 'it,' did you mean me?"

Then came the familiar reply, "Save it for the air."

Did he really want me to save THAT for the air?

Maybe it was all in my head, but I was certain the vibe shift from backstage continued on the air that day.

I left the *Live!* studio in a state of confusion. I certainly would never be invited back to cohost again. I wondered what I had done to bring about this drastic change because as all women do, I blamed myself. Luckily, though, I was too busy to dwell on it. And, I still had a toddler and was very pregnant, so there was that to contend with.

I went back to my dressing room at *All My Children* and was met again by a yellow square on my door. This time the note came from Angela Shapiro, who I assumed wanted to tell me that I wouldn't have to worry about hosting *Live!* ever again.

But instead she informed me that they wanted to make me an official offer to become the new cohost. The permanent one.

Who did? I asked.

The network.

Okay look, it's very complicated, but *Live!* is run differently than most programs of its kind. I'll give you the Cliffs Notes version.

The show started out local on the affiliate station WABC in New York. Then, the ABC/Disney syndication division, Buena

Vista, decided to test it nationally. Still with me? It sold to myriad affiliate stations across various networks and became a hit, and the two factions, ABC and WABC, have been at war as to who is in charge ever since.

This meant that the network wanting me as the cohost all but guaranteed that I would be the antichoice inside *Live!* Especially by the inner sanctum and the executives from the local affiliate who kept telling me they weren't interested in hiring me for the job. In a shocking turn of events, they had been telling the truth. I wish I had understood the dynamic between the two divisions back then. I would have run. But I didn't. So I didn't.

"Um, Angela, I have to tell you, I really don't think they like me over there. I don't think it's a good idea. I have no idea what happened, but something clearly did. I think you better find someone else. Someone he likes."

"It's not his decision to make, Kelly. It's not you, so don't take it personally. You are the breath of fresh air the show needs. I will protect you. Just think about it. Discuss it with Mark, and let's circle back at the end of the day."

Meanwhile, back in the kitchen, I was still trying to figure out who my boss was. Michael waited as patiently as a three-year-old who hadn't eaten dinner yet could. He was bouncing up and down with the anticipation of what could possibly be in the red-and-white paper bucket. I nestled the phone in the crook of my neck and moved around the kitchen table, laying down placemats, plates, glasses, as well as knives and forks, as if I was presenting a home-cooked meal to my family. I bumped into every chair, including the high chair, due to my now obviously pregnant frame. My belly was much bigger the second time around, and when I turned suddenly, I bumped into Michael, knocking him to the ground.

I tried to write down the different points of the offer.

Mark walked into the kitchen, and spying the forlorn expression on my face, threw up his "what gives" hands. I pushed the oil-stained napkin across the table toward him. THEY WANT TO MAKE SURE YOU KNOW WHO YOUR BOSS IS . . . and I pointed toward myself. Mark still looked confused, so I blurted, "They want to make sure I know who my boss is." Then, my agent seemed confused, so I told him I needed to bring Mark up to speed.

Mark had the same reaction as me. "What does that even mean?"

"No idea. No, I take that back. You know what it means, guys? It means I shouldn't take this job. It feels really wrong. What kind of an offer starts with, you better know who your boss is? It's just so weird!" I said while biting into a delicious buttermilk biscuit.

Then, my husband piped in with, "Kel, you might have to decide if you can tolerate weird in exchange for better hours and more money."

As I sat down to cut up Michael's chicken into toddler-safe bites, I passed the phone to Mark, who put the call on speaker so we could both listen while the lengthy list of "deal breakers" was being presented.

The list would have been comical to anyone in the entertainment industry had they been listening. I thought they were petty, for lack of a more accurate descriptive. Usually, the breaking point of any negotiation comes down to money, which this did as well, but the executives at *Live!* were also willing to blow up the deal over much smaller issues. I'm talking the most basic of basics.

I wasn't permitted to use my own hair and makeup people.

I can't state enough how standard it is to have a dedicated makeup and hair team on any show, much less one bearing the "talent's" name. But this was the number one deal breaker and the most consequential flash point of my entire contract. Not only were Richard and Doreen not permitted to do my hair and makeup in the *Live!* studio, but they couldn't do it before the show either over at *All My Children*. Even if I paid them myself! I was commanded, yes commanded, to use Regis's hair and makeup team. I pushed back that it made no sense for me to have to go to the second studio, wash my face and hair, and have it all redone for the soap. They insisted it was a deal breaker as *Live!* had a very specific look. We laughed at the absurdity of the thought of what that look might be. Having said that, I was relieved when makeup artist Michelle Champagne and hair stylist Diane D'Agostino were not only talented, but kind and welcoming as well.

But at this point, we were at a standstill over item one. Which again, is never a good sign.

But wait, there was more.

There would be no wardrobe services or budget. None. Zero.

I know I sound like a broken record, but THIS NEVER HAPPENS. ON ANY SHOW!

There would be no paid maternity leave.

On brand. And obviously, very helpful considering I was quite pregnant at the time.

I was not permitted to have an office. Not that I asked for one, but once I knew that having one was forbidden, I simply had to have my own cubicle. It was like being commanded not to look at Gelman all over again.

My name had to be smaller than Regis's name on the *Live!* title card and branding. A game of inches, which speaks for itself. But on that we agreed.

Seniority, after all.

That word. Seniority was used quite a bit during that negotiation and my early years on *Live!* However, it seemed that seniority would be elusive to me, something I could never achieve, even when I was the person on the job with the seniority. As it turns out, "seniority" is a masculine word.

Look, the reason I'm walking you through all of these details, all of this minutiae of my work history and obviously poor negotiation skills is not to trash anyone or garner any sympathy. There is real shit going on in the world. I understand that people in the real world have real problems. I, too, am a real person, so I know my complaining about being offered a job making more money for theoretically working less hours is not going to win any tiny violin contests. I'm just trying to contextualize things.

And I feel that I owe it to myself to correct the record out there. I now know that by taking the "high road," which is woman code for shutting the fuck up, I allowed false narratives to be attached to me.

Bethenny Frankel summed it up beautifully when I was a guest on her podcast. In describing her relationship with the media, and not commenting on inaccuracies to try to minimize the news cycle, she put it this way: "[My divorce] was completely analyzed and dissected by the media. It is their job. It is their right. I couldn't get off the ride. I wanted everyone to stop talking about it. But because it didn't end, it would keep resurfacing. And it was just pretty much a nightmare. I mean, everything about it, the actuality of it was a nightmare. But then living it in the media was a nightmare. And in many ways, I brought this on myself."

Even though I had a live daily talk show I chose not to dignify fabricated stories and correct the record no matter how tempted I was. Why sell their rags for them?

But by my allowing false information to live on, unchecked, it became true as far as those in the media and the viewing public was/ were concerned.

Even certain broadcasters I liked and respected were unwilling to be curious about well-established, well-documented events at *Live!* People who knew better.

The biggest misconception about my place on the show was that Regis had hand-selected me, guided me, and was my best friend, and then left, after which I never spoke to him again. I think that is a basic misconception about on-air personalities in general. The audience assumes that they are watching two best friends. I get it. I used to think that Regis and Kathie Lee were married. That's the assignment of a morning show host. Rarely is that the case. Working on morning television is like any job. Except that America gets to do your performance review every single day.

Podcasts like this one helped fuel this narrative:

INTERVIEWER: What about Kelly? How often do you see or speak to her?

REGIS: I haven't seen her, I don't see her. She lived downtown, and now I hear she's on the East Side.

INTERVIEWER: Have you seen her since the show ended in November 2011?

(If the show ended in 2011, where have I been going every day?)

REGIS: No, I haven't.

INTERVIEWER: Wow. Is that weird?

REGIS: No, it doesn't bother me. I was over there yesterday (at ABC) as a matter of fact to do something for them. No, I don't see her.

(We saw each other in the elevator.)

INTERVIEWER: Because you had a good run with Kelly.

REGIS: Yeah, sure.

INTERVIEWER: Who did you feel like you had the most of a click with? I know you've had a lot of cohosts in your time.

REGIS: Hmm, well, you know, I didn't have that many hosts. No, I did have a lot—in California as well. Mary Hart, that's how she got her start in the business.

INTERVIEWER: Yeah, by the way, think of all these women who worked with you who became hugely successful . . . Mary Hart, Kathie Lee Gifford, Kelly Ripa. You made these women.

REGIS: Made them what they are!

(For the record, we all had jobs when we were hired.)

That unfortunate podcast was pounced on by the press and elevated that false narrative.

Nobody blamed Regis when he left the show the way he did, because to be clear, he announced he was leaving on live TV. And nobody blamed him for not reaching out to me. Including me. But I don't think that I should be blamed either.

Would I have preferred a heads-up? Of course, but his exit wasn't about me. He had his reasons for leaving the show. Nobody gets that more than I do.

I just wish I hadn't become the target, of the media or otherwise. Especially since I was the one person kept out of the room, when that huge show-changing decision was being made.

Later that year, when walking a press line for *The Hollywood Reporter*'s annual power issue, in which I was featured, I was asked if Regis had congratulated me, or if I had heard from him since he left the show.

I considered embellishing for a split second, saying that we had traded phone calls, but it felt too dishonest. So, I told the truth.

"No."

And yet, here again, I was dragged through the mud.

The reality is that I would have traded places with him in a second. I was scared to death, and suddenly responsible for keeping our very popular show on the air, all by myself.

In the years following his departure, Regis was invited back on the show many times, but always declined. So it was a genuine thrill and surprise when he finally relented and agreed to be on our annual Halloween show, with Kathie Lee to boot!

Everyone backstage and on set was very excited to see Regis because frankly, nobody was funnier or more robust in their hatred for our Halloween show than Regis. Plus, after years of declining the invitations, the fact that he chose this show as the one seemed downright miraculous.

I heard him before I saw him. It was like no time had passed. He was yelling at Gelman about the "horror of Halloween!" And "what the hell am I supposed to be again?"

Then I heard, "Regis is supposed to be Regis, only from twenty years ago! Like a flashback! Get it?" Gelman barked.

"Why can't Regis just be Regis?" was the counterbark. It brought back all the old memories of the parts of the job I rather enjoyed. Especially the chronic explaining mixed with the endless exacerbation plus the confusing referring to oneself in the third person. And so, I decided I would make my way into the makeup and hair room and take my chances with an off-camera conversation.

He gave me a big smile and a hug and exclaimed, "Hello there, miss . . . star."

Then, Gelman swept in with, "You remember Kelly Ripa." I

didn't take it personally. Because, as America knows, we had a long-standing joke that he could never remember my name.

So, imagine my confusion when just a year after that Halloween show, Regis appeared with Larry King—whose infamous interview style of no preparation, no preinterview, no research—led to this puzzling exchange:

LARRY KING: Do you keep in touch with Kelly Ripa?

REGIS PHILBIN: Not really, no.

LARRY KING: Not really no, do they ask you to go back even for a day?

REGIS PHILBIN: Never once did they ask me to go back.

LARRY KING: You're kidding.

REGIS PHILBIN: She got very offended when I left. She thought I was leaving because of her. I was leaving because I was getting older, and it wasn't right for me anymore.

LARRY KING: So, you mean she took it personal?

REGIS PHILBIN: Yeah, I think so. That was eleven years ago and I—

LARRY KING: Haven't heard?

REGIS PHILBIN: Never have.

I will never fully understand that interview. Or why my name was dragged into these interviews in the first place. I was certainly never asked for a comment or clarification, or my perspective. Not that I would have given it—I just wanted the story to go away.

In the Larry retelling, Regis claimed he retired because he was getting older and no longer wanted to work. As a response, I became angry with him, stopped speaking to him, and hadn't seen him since he left the show.

The main problem with his story—it just wasn't true!

And yet, the media seized. I had gotten mad at Regis for retiring. I had dropped him. I was the bad guy.

Sure, there was video footage of that Halloween show readily available. And me inviting him over for dinner to see my kids. None of it mattered. I could have pressed the issue. I could have kept the news cycle going.

So, fool me once, fool me twice, fool me a thousand times, for not setting the record straight in real time.

It wasn't easy, and it wasn't fair. Maybe me being in that chair in the first place wasn't fair to Regis, and me staying and enduring the fallout certainly wasn't fair to me.

Right before his departure from the show, we were on a break from filming our final TD Bank commercial when he began telling me about the last time he walked away from a job.

Usually during breaks he held court with the crew, screaming in quasi-mock fury that it was taking far too long to shoot a thirty-second ad. This time, though, he seemed to need to get something off his chest. He was telling me about his soon to be published book and recalling the sections about his time working on *The Joey Bishop Show*. Regis said Joey hated having him as a sidekick and was awful to him.

So awful in fact, he quit twice, both times storming off the set in the middle of the broadcast.

He became hyperanimated, his skills for storytelling firing on all cylinders, and I felt like I was there, watching his old humiliations unfold. His humorous delivery belied the fact that his feelings were still hurt, so many decades later.

I understand the feeling perfectly.

He asked me if I would mind him giving me some practical advice, which I am grateful for and will keep between us.

It's easy in a job like ours to lose sight of the things that are important. And sometimes I do. But the reality is I had a lot of fun over the years at my day job. I got to sit next to one of the greatest storytellers of all time. The few occasions I socialized with Regis outside the office, over the decade we worked together, I truly enjoyed. He was an even better storyteller in person. I think he would have said the same.

I learned a lot over the years, mainly that context is almost always overlooked, that something repeated often enough becomes the truth. And the good outweighs the bad . . . mostly.

I was able to raise my kids with a certain continuity almost never available to children who are raised in "show biz" households. Same school. Same city. Same home. Same friends. I have been able to live a relatively normal life, which if you've ever seen my show you would understand is all that really matters to me.

I earn a great living and have enough resources to allow for more philanthropic endeavors. My parents raised me to know what matters. I could have pursued many opportunities to branch out, both on the broadcast and acting side, had I so desired.

But what sometimes gets twisted, is that all of those opportunities exist BECAUSE of *Live!* And whoever has the great good fortune to ascend to that rare seat behind the host chat desk channels a universe of infinite possibilities, harnessing entirely that spontaneous, electrifying, and explosive energy. All while precariously perched atop a *Live!* wire.

"Beauty
fades.
Dumb lasts
forever."

—JUDGE JUDY

CHAPTER NINE
AGING GRACEFULLY: THE BIG LIE

They say that one should grow old gracefully. I don't know who "they" are exactly, but they are wrong, and they most certainly never had a job working in front of a camera. Of course, given pandemic work from home conditions for the past few years, most of us work on camera now. So, I hope they feel like an asshole, because they truly are.

The current on-camera reality has seen a boom in cosmetic procedures. I would imagine that some of the most thriving businesses these days besides TikTok and Amazon are the ones owned by plastic surgeons and cosmetic dermatologists. This is not something I know for certain, but there has to be some correlation between the size of my plastic surgeon's house and the amount of time we are now required to be on screen. It just stands to reason, and they deserve it. They do God's work, after all, or at least the work God should have done. It's as if the entire world has woken up to what I have known for nearly all of my thirty-plus years in show business—aging is not for pussies and should be avoided at all costs by everyone with the exception of a chosen handful of people. Men, of course, get to age, but only the men who look good doing it.

Social media trolls get to age, but only the ones with dogs as avatars and private accounts. These people always fit the same profile. They are very triggered by anyone in a bathing suit or on their way to exercise class. The bio that appears underneath the avatar almost always says something along the lines of: "proud gramma, love my guns, my Bible, and my country."

Radio hosts get to age, but only if they remain on the radio and don't dare venture into television. Unfortunately, the pull to the camera seems too strong for many a radio star to ignore. The more of a face for radio a deejay has, the greater their need to be on camera. Lucky us.

Writers also get to age. Especially the ones who go by their initials.

TV, film, and theater critics and tabloid journalists all get to age and simultaneously point out how aged everyone else looks while using a headshot from 1979 next to their byline (the one taken right after their first face-lift).

Of course, I say all of this with a wink and a nod because I know someday I'll be faced with my face, and I hope I have the courage to go through with the Botox on my face should I ever need it. HA! Keep reading. The reality is people's opinions toward cosmetic work changes over time, along with their needs. And when I say cosmetic work, I'm talking everything from teeth whitening, the gateway cosmetic procedure, to a full neck lift, which I haven't had yet but will soon, perhaps by the end of this book. Frankly if I didn't work on camera, I'm not sure I would even own a hairbrush much less get Botox, but my foray into injectables began innocently enough. Truly, I am a soap and water kind of person. I only recently started a beauty "regimen" every night before bed because I had Fraxel, a deep laser procedure to get rid of my melasma, which is the discoloring of the skin caused by, among other things, pregnancy. I hate to wear makeup and only do so when I'm on camera or at an event where makeup is required like the myriad clown conventions I've attended, not to mention the Academy Awards. So, I'm pretty much forced to wear it every day. But there's makeup and then there's high-definition TV makeup, which is industrial-strength spackle meant to plug all holes. The melasma had forced me into wearing makeup even when I wasn't on camera. So, the Fraxel was a double blessing. Not only did it get rid of all the discoloration on my face and make me look shiny and new and made it so makeup was just a work thing, but my dermatologist taught me how to take care of my skin beyond soap, water, and makeup-removing wipes.

I first had Botox the old-fashioned way—in my armpits because I was told it would help with my chronic sweating. Yes, I did sweat a lot, but once I started working on *Live!* the sweat poured off me, or at least that one hour I was on the air. Years later I would come to realize that I was suffering from chronic anxiety and not just hyperhidrosis, which is really just an SAT word for "sweats through her clothes." Anyway, this was my initiation into cosmetic procedures. Now, this is in no way a suggestion that you should stop sweating because sweating is good for you and important. It is vital to regulating your core temperature and ridding the body of toxins. I think. Look, if you're a med student reading this book, take what I'm saying with a grain of salt. But if you're a person who works in front of large groups of people, sweating more than normal, and antiperspirants aren't doing the trick, even the prescription kind, perhaps Botox is for you. Apparently, this was a common procedure that women and men had been doing for a long time. Most of my friends and coworkers had Botox. Just in their faces. Not their armpits.

When I had my pit-tox, I was a target for the tabloids. This was pre-reality television, so I guess they needed something to focus on, and I was an easy target. The *National Enquirer* in particular was obsessed with me. The CEO of American Media, the parent company of that tabloid and many others, was David Pecker, an aptly named prick. He had to step down from his position in recent years when he became the subject of an investigation into illegal use of campaign money to pay off a series of strippers and porn stars for his good friend and eventual president Donald Trump. The point is, this is a man with a lot of integrity, so you know you can trust what he puts out there. Week after week, the *National Enquirer* published one work of fiction after another. Frankly, I was shocked by the amount of attention they focused on me. What their articles lacked in journalistic integrity and, well, facts, they more than made up for with creativity. Although after a while, even I became bored by how similar they all were in tone and content. The articles seemed to target people who would believe anything, like all of my relatives in South Jersey. The "writers" liked to keep their "readers" focused on a series of ideas: Me being afraid of losing my husband. Me being threatened by my husband's success. Me being jealous of literally everyone else on television. And most importantly, my appearance and all of my "procedures." I read that I had a full face-lift. Chin implant. Cheek implants. Nose jobs, yes plural. Full veneers on my teeth. A brow lift. Skin resurfacing. And my personal favorite, the headline blared, was "KELLY'S SECRET BOOB JOB. WHAT WENT WRONG?" The tabloid used a picture of me standing in a formal dress, flat chested, as proof that I had a boob job, and something must have gone horribly awry. I was shocked when board-certified "doctors" would weigh in on the procedures I allegedly had. I found it laughable that nobody bothered to account for when I could have possibly had these surgeries since I was on live television every single day, but should a tiny detail like that get in the way of a good story?

Eventually, the stories ended. Just like that. One day the tabloid journos stopped writing about the Botox shots in my forehead and Restylane in my lips and silicone implants in my face. And that's when it dawned on me . . . I must look like shit. And I knew that it was time to actually get some procedures, for real.

I walked into Dr. Brandt's office almost a year to the day after I had first seen him for my sweaty armpits. He came dancing into the room, as was his custom, singing his hello. Dressed in head-to-toe Prada, he looked like he just stepped off the runway in Paris and not out of the lab where he spent 99 percent of his time.

"Dr. Brandt, I was thinking maybe this time I could try a little Bo (what he called Botox) maybe in my face? I don't know, I just feel like I always look like I'm frowning or thinking deeply, and I'm not. I mean I'm not a deep thinker." I rambled ceaselessly.

Dr. B threw his arms up toward the heavens, like he was testifying before God, and cried, "I thought this day would never come!" I wondered if Dr. B was relieved.

I pressed forward, "I have just been worried that maybe I am not ready for such intervention since I'm only thirty-eight."

Dr. B stared in disbelief. "Oh honey, you are ready. You've been ready since you came in for the armpits." What? How could that be?

"Why didn't you tell me then?" I was incredulous.

"Because I'm here to enhance, not to push." This is why Dr. B was the best. He didn't push, he just gave you what you wanted, when you wanted it, and would suggest the best way to solve your concerns.

There is a reason every on-camera person I knew went to Dr. Brandt. Even the ones who pretended they didn't. No wonder I was so confused about my own aging. I hadn't seen it done. I mean, I had seen my face age, but I seemed to be alone, since everyone around me was unwilling to talk about what they were having done, I just assumed it was my work schedule plus having three young children that was making me age in dog years compared to my peers. And

Mark, who for the record refuses to age. But that's just genetics, damn him.

Oh no. What I realized was, they were all having Botox and fillers, and more in Dr. Brandt's office. It was just that nobody was talking about it. It wasn't until Dr. Brandt's untimely passing in 2015 that I realized how far and wide his reach truly was. His memorial service looked like the Oscars meets the Tonys meets the Emmys meets Fashion Week.

It's been said there is nothing like that rush you feel after your first hit of heroin. Well, I don't know about that, but it is certainly true when it comes to Botox. I actually saw the difference in Dr. Brandt's office as the years of sleepless nights from nursing babies and waking up early for work melted away. I held the mirror in front of my face and watched, as Dr. B swung the needle around, millimeters from my eye, modifying the lyrics to show tunes to match his every move. "One singular sensation every little Bo on her face . . ." And like magic the elevens in between my eyebrows vanished before my very eyes. So did my crow's feet. These were the things that really bothered me about my appearance. I smile and laugh a lot, which is good emotionally but terrible when it comes to creating laugh lines. I find it ironic that the happier a person feels, the older it can make them look. Would I notice these things if I didn't work on camera every day? Of course not. I am not as narcissistic as this chapter would indicate.

I left the doctor's office with a spring in my step and a newfound appreciation for Jennifer Bassey, the uber talented and glamorous actress who played Marian Colby on *All My Children*. Our dressing rooms were across the hallway from one another and back then, I couldn't understand her fixation on aging. Imagine that, a twenty-something actress who couldn't understand the plight of her fifty-something counterpart. Jennifer had a super-magnifying mirror in her dressing room that I was convinced was the source of her agony. Jennifer would tell me constantly that I needed to "hop on the Botox train sooner rather than later." Cryptically, she would add, "It is almost too late." I would always dismiss her, telling her I didn't understand how or why anyone would deliberately inject botulinum toxin into their face. Then I would arrogantly and ignorantly tell her that there was something to be said for growing old gracefully.

Jennifer, ever ready with a clever retort, would respond. "Darling, imbeciles grow old gracefully. You're not an imbecile, are you?" *Not anymore*, I thought to myself as I walked home from Dr. Brandt's with my complementary frozen peas in a latex glove for swelling. You'd be amazed at how good frozen peas in a glove feels on the skin. Now that I think about it, I must have looked like an absolute lunatic walking down the street with those purple latex gloves, which looked like they had hands in them because the peas added a certain human characteristic to the gloves. Of course, I live in New York City, so nobody even batted an eyelash. PS: Ask me what I have in my dressing room, today? Yep, the Bassey mirror, as I call it.

The next morning, I sprung out of bed and ran to the bathroom mirror to see if Claudia Schiffer was staring back at me, and she was not, but a very rested looking Kelly Ripa was. That's all I've ever wanted. I know what I look like and I'm not searching for miracles, I just don't think anyone should ever have to look as exhausted as they feel, and when I'm your president, Botox will be on the ballot!

I sashayed into work that morning like I was in a Calvin Klein commercial waiting for my producers and coworkers to fall on the floor from the youthful beauty before them; however, there was basically no acknowledgment whatsoever of my youthful transformation. Except from the only person who really mattered, Michelle Champagne, the show's long-suffering makeup artist. I sat down in the makeup chair for what I liked to call special effects, and immediately Michelle trilled, "Someone looks amazing." In my mind, I gave Michelle an enormous bonus. We were both astonished at how the process of putting on makeup seemed to take half the time and half the product.

"Why doesn't everybody do this?" I asked. Michelle explained that everyone did do it and that I was just late to the game.

My audience has long been my confessional and this day was no different. When Regis asked me what I had done the night before, it was always more of an opening way for him to tell me what he had done, but not on this day. I regaled the audience with tales of my Botox. I walked them through the entire process. The cleaning of the face, my bravely refusing the numbing cream, watching the elevens disappear, the complementary latex gloves with frozen peas. The audience, comprised of mostly women, leaned in, smiled, applauded, and then looked at me as if to say, what took you so long, honey?

I stood back and waited for the inevitable tabloid backlash, but there was none. Of course. They couldn't make up a story, so they had no story. I suppose I had put them in a bind. What would the headline read? "KELLY RIPA FINALLY GETS THE BOTOX WE'VE BEEN TELLING YOU ABOUT FOR SEVEN YEARS!"

I was officially a convert. But I used and still use Botox sparingly. I believe when it comes to the face, less is more. Same with filler. It's to fill in the gaps, not to create a separate face on top of your actual face. When I was a toddler, I fell on the sidewalk, creating a scar on the right side of my face by my temple that everyone always thought was a dimple. I suppose that was because it was only visible when I smiled. So, when I went back to Dr. B for my second Botox treatment ten months later, he asked me if I would like him to fill in my scar with Juvéderm. "You mean my dimple?" I asked.

"No, I mean your scar. That's a scar isn't it?" I guess I had grown so used to everyone calling it a dimple that I forgot it was actually a scar. Just a dash of the Juv was all it took, and a scar that had been on my face for almost thirty-nine years was gone. But alas, fillers felt too seductive a mistress, with such immediate gratification. I knew I was going to have to put a strict limit on myself. Only for the scar. No crazy lips, no bagel head. (Google it, but be warned it's gross and creepy.)

I kept myself honest, until one day in the beginning of 2014. I was reading the Sunday *New York Times*. Our kids were bigger then and tended to sleep in on the weekends. So, for us to stay in bed on a Sunday and read the paper felt like a crime of luxury. I stumbled on an article in the Style section about, what else, pioneering techniques in plastic surgery. The article was about a surgeon right in New York City performing something called fat transferring. Not even knowing what it was, I knew I wanted it. But as I read on, I became obsessed. With fat transference, a doctor sucks the fat out of the fat parts of one's body and places it in the breasts. THAT . . . IS . . . GENIUS! I mean, it's all of the fun of a boob job but none of the pick a material, pick a shape, over/under muscle decisions. And, with a side of fat deposit displacement. Yes, please.

I read the article to Mark out loud, who said all the things husbands say to survive in their marriages. "No, you're perfect, I'm a legs guy. You don't need that. Don't do it for me." I'm not sure why men still labor under the misconception that women do things for them. It is a patriarchal thought process that this book isn't going to solve. This book is the Jacuzzi. Next book is the pool.

"Listen to this," I harangued, "fat transfer breast augmentation uses liposuction from other parts of your body and then injects said fat into the breasts. This is a breast augmentation option for women who are looking for a relatively small increase in breast size and would prefer natural results." I never had bigger than an A cup. And now, after nursing three babies, I had what I described as an AA cup long. I believed that this procedure would increase the volume, not size, and solve my conundrum of *dem damn titties*.

I stared at Mark expectantly, and right away I saw he was scared to death because he didn't quite know how to respond. "Don't you think that sounds amazing?" I asked. I could tell that he thought I was setting a trap.

Finally, he spoke. "Immunity?" What the fuck did that mean?

"The fuck does that mean?" I demanded.

"I need to have immunity if I'm going to answer this question." He wanted immunity. *He must have joined some male empowerment group that I was going to have to infiltrate and dismantle in my spare time*, I thought.

But what I said was, "Yea, sure sweetie, immunity."

He began with extreme caution. "Well, I feel like this could be a slippery slope. And it's one thing for you to do topical stuff, I mean you're in and out of the office in ten minutes, but this sounds like a major procedure that would require recovery time, and I think you're perfect the way you are." He added that last bit of bullshit in for good measure. I saw where he was headed. He was worried about recovery time . . . meaning he was worried that he would have to take a hand in running the household. He likes to think of himself as more of a general, lobbing orders from command central, and if I had this surgery, Mark would have needed to get in the foxhole with the terrorists (i.e., our children).

"So, you're worried that my recovery time will be more work for YOU," I said, my body perfectly still, my pupils shrunken and focused on their target. Mark, now feeling the threat of being backed into a corner, rose out of the bed, I assume to make himself look as large as possible. But I also watch Nat Geo, so I rose, too. Together we started making the bed, never taking our eyes off each other. Measuring our words like we were sworn under oath at a Senate Judiciary Committee hearing.

"I am only worried about your health, and I think you're—"

I cut him off, "Perfect the way I am. Yes, I know you've said that already."

I want you to understand that as I am reading this back to myself, I am cognizant that this all sounds insane. I would like to take this opportunity to apologize to Mark. I would like to, but I can't, as I'm on a deadline, and like I said before, I'm a creative and therefore not good with schedules. Also, he doesn't deserve it unless he apologizes first.

Mark told me that if I felt like this was something I really wanted to do, he supported my decision to have a consultation. And then he retreated, waving his white flag, into the shower. As he rinsed off his loss from the battlefield, I decided to postpone my plan to infiltrate his male empowerment group and join him because, well, it was Sunday.

I booked my appointment for March 7, 2014.

I immediately felt welcome in the small but cozy office. The doctor was warm and engaging and was rocking a pair of knee-high stiletto boots under her lab coat, which told me she was a freak off the clock. Just as my mind was starting to wonder about the S&M habits of the doctor, she told me about her other job in which she removed the excess skin from people who were suffering from obesity and had lost a tremendous amount of weight, all pro bono. This showed me she was an empath and made me feel deeply ashamed of my perverted sexualization of this obvious saint. I explained to her that I liked my body in general, I'm very athletic and fitness is important to me. It was just *dem titties doh* . . . and she nodded as if she'd heard it all before.

She then excused herself so I could get undressed. I stared at myself in the full-length mirror in my paper robe and saw Gollum staring back at me in the surgical overhead lighting and thought about how they should invent a procedure that allows doctors to just pull everything up from the top of one's head, sort of like a ponytail of skin, or a bed that forces people to sleep upside down, like bats. The doctor came back in and looked me over. She spun me in a circle, making a general hmm sound. She then told me that I was not a good candidate for fat transference because I didn't have enough quality body fat to perform the liposuction.

"What about here?" I asked, while swinging my backside toward the doctor's face and squeezing my saddlebag area.

"No, see, that's just loose skin, no fat, just skin. But hang on, wait a minute, you have a little here. Your flanks have some fat." Wait, what? I was too embarrassed to ask what flanks were, and I was on emotional overload. First, I found out that the part of my body that I always assumed was fat was really just loose, which we can all agree is worse. And then I found out that a part of my body I never even knew I had was the only part of me that was carrying fat. "But not enough. Not for this procedure. And I don't recommend gaining weight just to suck it out because there's no guarantee that your body will gain the weight where you need it." I thanked her for her candor and put my clothes back on.

I walked home somehow even more deflated than how I walked

in. I reminded myself that I had three healthy children and a husband who loves my deflated ass and not enough flank fat. I stopped into a pharmacy on my way home and bought a pack of Reese's Peanut Butter Cups and a Snickers.* I guess having a doctor telling me I didn't have enough fat for a faux boob job accelerated my appetite. I sunk my teeth into the first peanut butter cup, a candy I hadn't eaten since Halloween in the eighties. It was delicious. I tried to eat it slowly. Around the edges at first, then I let the peanut butter part melt in my mouth. I licked my fingers, remember this was 2014, there were no masks and people licked their fingers. I could see people staring at me enviously. With great dignity I put the second peanut butter cup away to save for dessert and opened the Snickers. I had no idea they still made Snickers. Doctor's orders I told myself, even though I'm fairly certain this is exactly what she said not to do. I marched over to Park Avenue because they always have the cleanest streets and the doormen tip their caps and say hello even if you don't live in the building, which I love and makes me feel fancy. That day was no exception, save for the fact that every doorman remarked that I had an awfully big candy bar for such a little lady. I wanted to tell them about the flank fat but chose to spare them since they probably had enough bullshit to deal with.

I made it home with two half-eaten candy bars (though if you're persnickety, one is a bar, and one is a cup, but you get what I mean) all hopped up on sugar and disappointment and reminded myself, before I walked through the door, that those I live with were not where I was, emotionally.

I saw Mark sitting at the kitchen table on the phone. He smiled and waved for me to be quiet and give him a second, but I remind

---

All candy bars should be multiplied by two.

myself that he had not recently consumed eighty grams of sugar and should therefore be taken with a grain of salt. HA!

I sat down next to him and pulled out some work to show that he was not the only one doing things and also so I could eavesdrop. Unfortunately, he was not talking to anyone important or eavesdrop worthy—something about life insurance and a living will and executors, blah blah blah. I just wanted him to hang up and ask me how my appointment went.

Eventually he did hang up and asked how my day was. "Fine," I told him.

"Why are you so late?" Finally.

"I went to see the doctor." Blank stare. "About the procedure." Blank stare. "The one I read to you about in the newspaper."

Ah. The lightbulb went off in his head. "Yea, so tell me. What'd the doctor say?" I told him the doctor said I wasn't a good candidate. "Why, because you're too young?" Mark asked. Too young? Why would I be too young? There's no age requirement, I explained.

And then Mark dropped words on me I will never forget. "Well, honey, if you go to a doctor for a face-lift and they tell you you're not a good candidate, that's probably why." I let that sentence hang there in the suddenly stifling atmosphere. Face-lift? FACE-LIFT? What the FUCK?

"I DIDN'T GO TO SEE ABOUT A FUCKING FACE-LIFT. I WENT TO SEE ABOUT THE FAT TRANSFERRING!" I'm pretty sure the neighbors heard me, and potentially my family in New Jersey. South Jersey. Mark looked confused, as if he had no idea what in the hell I was talking about. My theory was finally proven correct. This man does not listen to a single thing I say.

So, to recap, on March 7, 2014, I found out that I don't have fat in my butt, I have loose skin. The fat I do have resides in my flank section. Still not sure where that is. I'm not a good candidate for the "au natural" boob job, and my husband thinks I need a face-lift.

There's nothing graceful about growing old. What's even less graceful is allowing the opinions of others to infiltrate how we view our own aging process. I often think the most vital cosmetic procedure is one that doesn't exist yet—removing the thumbs of internet trolls. Just because you have a thought doesn't mean you should express it anonymously in a public forum. The opinions of internet trolls may have weighed heavier on Dr. Brandt than anyone could have imagined. Those who live in the public eye are targets, and some folks can handle it, while others fall prey. As someone who has lived through the tabloid years at their peak and now enjoys being the target of regular internet trolling, you can say all you want about celebrities signing up for that when they become famous, but no one signs up to be judged and harassed for doing their jobs. If only Dr. Brandt could have stuck around long enough to learn that the comments folks make online are just reflections of how they feel about themselves, their lives, their own aging process. That's just the truth. Fortunately for the trolls, they get to remain anonymous, their looks hidden. Free to move with impunity through cyberspace, onto the next target.

So, if you're going to ping me on Instagram about how terrible Botox is for me, or that my neck looks terribly old, or that I'm setting an awful example for my daughter and women everywhere, fine. I can take it. Troll me. Sure, I'd be pissed, but my face would never betray my feelings. That's the beauty of Botox. But remember, not everyone can handle it. So maybe, think twice.

"If you feel like an outsider, you tend to observe things a lot more."

—ANDERSON COOPER

CHAPTER TEN

THE WHITE HOUSE CORRESPONDENTS' DINNER

Congratulations! If you're still reading, you've made it more than halfway through. I appreciate your dedication. I'm not sure I would do it for you. We'll see.

Every once in a while, opportunity knocks, and when it does, make sure you hit the floor like you're hiding from the Jehovah's Witnesses. Otherwise, you might receive an invitation to the White House Correspondents' Dinner. We didn't hide, thus proving my theory that if you hang around long enough you will get the ubiquitous invitation to the famous nonpartisan dinner. The "Nerd Prom," as it's known in the press. Whether you're a correspondent or not, this is one of those events that everyone on the planet is invited to eventually. If you haven't been invited yet, fret not, I'm certain your invite is in the mail. Anyway, it was an invitation I had been dreading. Don't get me wrong, I had been invited in the past, but always had a very good excuse as to why I couldn't attend. Like being nine months pregnant or washing my hair.

If I'm being perfectly honest, I have a severe case of social anxiety disorder, and I tend to say awkward or inappropriate things when under duress, so the last thing I needed was to spend time with political journalists or actual politicians. People think that because I'm an extrovert on television I am one in real life. Surprise. That's why they call it acting. In real life, I am much more comfortable hiding under my bed during any party, even those not occurring in my home. But, I had promised Mark that this was the year I would try harder to get out more and meet new people. Mark is what is clinically known as a social butterfly. Or excessively friendly. Basically, the man has never met a party he hasn't loved or felt perfectly comfortable attending. I guess you could say he is the yin to my introvert.

Anyway, back to the dinner. We were invited to sit at the USA Today table, which I was told was a prime location. Front and center. But honestly, I was a little disappointed that we were front and center. We were surrounded by the illuminati, Academy Award winners, authors, and generally controversial figures that I love to look at from afar, up close.

So, I guess how the dinner works is like the basic principle of the Met Gala, but for people who read. Various news organizations like ABC, NBC, CBS, CNN, FOX, CNBC, Huffington Post, Washington Post, New York Times buy a bunch of tables that support the White House Correspondents' Association (whatever that is). As an invited guest, you are expected to be famous, famous adjacent, or infamous. I like to consider myself the latter two. It is also your duty to look nice. Check. Make sparkling conversation. Check. And not shit yourself. More on that later.

Our reasons for attendance at the event that particular year were threefold. We were going out of genuine curiosity, but it was also our wedding anniversary, and nothing says I love you like hanging around Washington political operatives and the press. But most importantly, we were going to support our friend Jimmy Kimmel who was slated to emcee. Jimmy's big Italian family flew in from California by way of Brooklyn and collectively we were all nervous as hell. This is pre–Jimmy hosting the Oscars or the Emmys or such big television history-making moments, so we weren't sure if he could handle the pressure, meaning we weren't sure if we could. On a separate note, Jimmy's dad looks exactly like Wolf Blitzer. Not really going anywhere with that, just thought you'd like the visual fun fact.

We took the Acela train from New York's Penn Station to DC. The train was super exciting. Rachel Maddow swanned right past us and Mark was poking at me to tell her that my father-in-law watches her every night and that our kids refer to her as his girlfriend. In a surprise move, I decided to restrain myself and keep quiet. But there were famous celebrities, recording artists, journalists, and news anchors as far as the eye could see. It was a packed train, but fortunately for us we arrive everywhere at least an hour early or Mark will think we're late, so we were the first ones to board. The hard part was waiting for our seat mates to arrive and hoping against hope that there would be two cool people sitting across from us and not people from Fox News. As luck would have it, we hit the seat mate jackpot when Holly Robinson Peete sat down across from us. She is fabulous. She's a working mom just like me, but unlike me she somehow looks put together and perpetually twenty years old. Holly is a woman's woman, and I could instantly tell it was going to be an easy ride.

Mark, Holly, and I plotted and put our luggage on the empty seat to rearrange our belongings, so it appeared that the seat was occupied. If Sharon Stone walked on, we planned to move the bag and try to entice her into our corner. But if it was Bill O'Reilly? Sorry Bill, this seat is taken. We kept our heads together in loud animated conversation, lest anyone think we welcomed them into our circle. Funny how it never occurred to us that we got on an empty train and watched it fill up around us. Perhaps nobody wanted to sit next to our lame asses?

When the train left the station, our conversation turned to the most important issue of the weekend, hair and makeup. Or lack thereof. Apparently, the Nerd Prom was a way bigger deal than we had realized, and all the good hair and makeup people on both coasts were booked a year in advance, so we were all using the same four, exhausted, local hair and makeup people usually reserved for the Washington, DC, news broadcasters. Not that there's anything wrong with that, but it is a definite look. "How do you want to look tonight?" "Oh, I don't know, maybe give me the full Lou Dobbs," said no woman ever. Also, this year's Nerd Prom was just two days ahead of the Met Gala, and so it seemed that there was a shortage of all creative craft types across the board. And I, as usual, had my period. There is a persistent theme in my life. For all major events, I have my period. Any party, award show, gala, school fundraiser, or even my honeymoon, I have my period. Oh, and all vacations. Especially vacations. It's my body's fun game with me. Relaxing? How do you feel about bleeding out? Look if you're squeamish, maybe they'll give you a refund on this book. I don't know. I've never returned a book. Not even the dreaded *Fifty Shades of Grey*. That's not authentic rough play. Trust me! Having said that, I'd like to sell even a quarter as many books as that woman did.

In what felt like eight minutes, we pulled into DC's Union Station. Naturally, because Mark had arrived first and chosen our seats as close to the door as possible, to ensure we were first off the train and first into our taxi. I bid a hasty adieu, which means goodbye in either German, French, or English, I think, to Holly and we vowed to stay in touch. This is a vow all people in show business make, but seldom mean. With the exception of Holly, who actually means it. I often wonder if doctors in medical seminars embrace one another and vow to stay in touch only to never speak again. Probably, minus the part about embracing and vowing to stay in touch.

Mark was now at least thirty paces ahead of me because I made the fatal error of saying polite goodbyes and wearing an attractive but ultimately impractical Manolo Blahnik pump. I like the way my heels sound in the cavernous Union Station. Echoey and slightly menacing. *Click, click, click . . . pant, pant, pant. Click, pant, click, pant.* I work out, so I can never understand why I am so out of breath fast-walking through Union Station. Mark got so far ahead of me he was already out of Union Station and into a cab before I got through the lobby. I wanted to linger to see if anyone fabulous got off the train from the other cars, but Mark was like a military operative, and telling me by text that we were currently only six minutes early and therefore late.

I love Washington, DC. I really do. It's my kind of place. I like the monuments. I like the gentle climate, the good food. I love the politics that infuse everything. And I simply can't get enough of the hotels. They are old-school and sophisticated, and the rooms are spacious and elegantly appointed. They always have chic bars and interesting books in the rooms. And sometimes you have a view of the White House. We usually stay at The Hay-Adams: "Stewed in rich history and surrounded by the most iconic monuments of our nation, The Hay-Adams, recently named the #1 Hotel in Washington, DC, is the hotel of choice for discerning guests. Enveloped by views of the White House, St. John's Church, and the scenic Lafayette Park." Or at least that's what the website says (it lives up to the hype). We've stayed there numerous Easter weekends with our kids and can honestly say we've never been treated better. It's elegant, but somehow warm and familial at the same time. This trip, however, was different because we'd be staying at The Jefferson. Again, it was Correspondents' weekend, so everything was super booked. I must admit, I was not looking forward to staying at The Jefferson because I felt like I was cheating on my wife. Mark explained to me that that's not how infidelity worked and that as our preferred hotel was booked, it wouldn't feel "cheated" on. The Jefferson is a "Washington, DC, hotel that is at once classic and contemporary . . . [and brings] delight to the details," according to their website. As far as the battle of the websites go, The Hay-Adams one, The Jefferson zero.

As our cab pulled up to The Jefferson, I must admit I was impressed by the chic boutique Beverly Hills–ness of it all. In my head, I begged the forgiveness of The Hay-Adams. The Jefferson's facade is positively elegant and the crowd out front was bustling. I immediately started speaking with a foreign accent, which I do when nervous or in situations I deem fawncy. "Thank youuuuuu sew maaaahch Beckford," I said to the man who opened our cab door, sounding like any actress from the 1940s, mildly British by way of South Carolina.

"My name is Chris," said Beckford. In your book you can call him Chris, okay? Mark rolled his eyes and explained to Beckford that I was recently hit in the head and developed a disorder that makes me sound like an asshole. I sauntered away from the cab and left the luggage for Mark and Beckford to deal with.

We entered the opulent lobby of The Jefferson, and I was mentally transported to Versailles or Kris Jenner's house. Coffered ceilings and antique tapestries and artists of note hung on every wall. Which artists? I don't know, I'm not a docent. And with its prewar Park Avenue black-and-white floors gleaming, my Manolos made that Union Station sound again. I felt as if I was floating like a swan on a halcyon lake. Once again, I began speaking like a member of the royal family. Mark strode ahead of me to the concierge, but some very efficient staff member headed him off and greeted us both. "Mr. and Mrs. Consuelos, welcome to the Jefferson."

"Hoooow doooo youuuu doooo," I responded with a down-turned palm, arm extended like Audrey Hepburn in *My Fair Lady*. I could see reflected on the front desk man's tie clip that Mark was rolling his eyes again.

"Exciting weekend," said the front desk man.

"Oh, 'tis," I replied, and Mark jumped in front of me.

"Pardon me, but would someone at the concierge know how to tie a bow tie?" Now I rolled my eyes. How was Mark making the Nerd Prom all about him? He's not a nerd. Even in high school he wasn't. Mark was popular. He was in the homecoming court. He was in a three-way for Pete's sake. (According to his yearbook—in Florida, but still.) But apparently my popular, prom king husband, who has been to a thousand award shows, has never learned how to tie a bow tie. The man can take off my bra with one hand. Theoretically. If I were to ever need a bra. But I digress.

"I'm certain that will not be a problem, Mr. Consuelos, and will Mrs. Consuelos be requiring anything?" Mark turned to look at me, and I realized I was staring at myself in the front desk man's tie clip. "And might I add that it's great to see you again, Mrs. Consuelos, I'm so glad you returned." This snapped me out of my tie clip reverie, and I actually looked at the front desk man, whose name I didn't know, in the eye, then scanned his chest. Name tag, name tag, where was his name tag? This would not be happening at The Hay-Adams. I usually do this thing where I pretend to know someone even if I don't, just to save myself the embarrassment of introducing myself to my uncle or cousin. But this guy, I was certain I'd never met before. He didn't even look a little familiar. Mark was now looking at me quizzically.

"I'm sorry, have we met? Perhaps at The Hay-Adams? That's where we usually stay," I said wistfully.

He laughed. "No ma'am, right here at The Jefferson."

"No, you must have me confused with someone else, this is our first time staying here, and please, no need to call me ma'am, I'm only forty-two."

Now the front desk man chuckled, then leaned in and in a conspiratorial voice said, "Oh, okay, your secret's safe with me." And winked.

"No. No secret!" I was now speaking in an elevated volume so that Mark and anyone else who passed by knew with absolute certainty that I (a) was from New Jersey and (b) had never been to this hotel before and therefore this guy obviously had me confused with Charlize Theron or Michelle Pfeiffer. "I have never been here before. Ever," I stated, emphatically.

"Perhaps it was at the Ritz-Carlton. I used to work there," he answered, sheepishly.

Okay, that's it. "Yes, I did stay at the Ritz-Carlton, for Laura's wedding," I said, more to Mark than to the front desk man.

"Ah, that's it," said Mark, who then dragged me to the elevator so we could review our master plan.

Mark and I had worked out this plan many years ago after one too many experiences with one too many makeup artists looking to re-create the wheel. And trust me when I say this, I really am just a wheel folks. I was worried about working with unfamiliar hair and makeup people. I had been burned in the past. No, literally burned, with curling irons, flat irons, and eyelash glue. Don't ask. Our devious agreement was that any makeup and hair procedure taking longer than forty-five minutes would compel him to enter the room and state that we needed to wrap things up. That way, I would have enough time to undo whatever had been done to me. Apparently only three people, Kristofer Buckle, Michelle Champagne, and I seem to be able to plaster this fresco.

After an endless walk down the elegant corridor, we arrived at our room. The deluxe suite. We had been offered the option of selecting the color palette for our suite between gold and platinum. Naturally, we selected platinum because we didn't want our desperation to show. The front desk man was blathering on about Wi-Fi and in-room dining and gym hours and then finally asked, again, "And will Mrs. Consuelos require any assistance?"

Um, hello? "Yes, please, I'm expecting hair and makeup to arrive in the next twenty minutes, if you could please send them up when they get here."

Mark ran into the bedroom, I assumed, to get some cash to tip the front desk man who stood in the doorway awkwardly waiting.

"So," I began, "how long were you at the Ritz-Carlton?" I can never allow silence.

"Oh, I was only there for the summer of my senior year in college, three years ago." I looked at him sideways, still searching for a name tag.

"Oh, well I was there in 1995, so you couldn't have seen me then."

And he looked at me like he'd dug up the crypt keeper. "No ma'am, I was only in grade school back then." Then he leaned in and with a whisper said again, "Don't worry, your secret's safe with me."

This again! Now I was annoyed. "No secret! I HAVE NEVER BEEN HERE BEFORE." He was grinning from ear to ear like he had something on me, and I felt like I was in the *Twilight Zone.* "Look, you obviously have me confused with someone else." Grin. "Seriously." Wider grin. "Why would I pretend I've never been here before?"

The smile vanished and he leaned in for the kill. "So, HE doesn't find out . . ." gesturing toward the bedroom and his tip. That was it. I was done. I was about to pack up and head to The Hay-Adams and beg for a broom closet. Anything but this.

"Find out WHAT?" At that point, I was genuinely curious about whatever my sexually adventurous look-alike had done. Judging by front desk's face, my twin definitely was living a way more exciting life than me. "He can hear because it wasn't me," I said, gesturing toward wherever Mark was. After what felt like three years, Mark sauntered back into the foyer wearing the hotel robe (because he needed to change into a robe that minute?) clutching a twenty-dollar bill, which he deposited into front desk's hand.

"Are you two still discussing you not remembering being here?" Seriously? Mark is the WORST wing man.

"Yes, sir."

And with that he swept out the door as Mark swanned toward the bedroom.

A minute later, Mark yelled, "You know they say everybody has a twin."

"Yea, well mine raised hell here with what's his name and he's never forgotten it, and by the way, thanks a lot for the backup and for leaving me alone with that weirdo."

"Just wanted to see if you still had feelings for your imaginary boyfriend. Now get on this king-size deluxe platinum bed." He smiled the megawatt smile that usually renders me helpless, but I rejected the idea outright. My makeup and hair team were due posthaste and I needed to shower and wash my hair. I never understand why we can't ever arrive the night before an event and relax into being somewhere. So, no relaxation for me, no booty for Mark.

Just then, the doorbell rang, and I welcomed the lovely hair and makeup team who seem extremely competent. I asked them to set up in the deluxe platinum living room. (Can you tell we don't get out much?) The shower was sublime, with a television in the mirror. It was built in, so when it's a mirror it's a mirror, but then you hit a button that says TV and suddenly you can watch television on the mirror! Amazing! (WE DO NOT GET OUT MUCH.) All I wanted to do was luxuriate in this marble palazzo of a bathroom and enjoy the complimentary Wanderlust Red Flower soaps and shampoos. I mean, what does Wanderlust smell like? Mystery and heaven and not wanting to get out of the shower. (WE DON'T GET OUT MUCH, BELIEVE ME.) I could feel the foreign accent welling up within me, but I stuffed it back down. I washed my hair and body in record speed, especially for that beautiful bathroom, I'm certain. I wrapped myself in the thickest, thirstiest terry cloth towel, and wrapped a second one around my hair, like a debutante.

Then, I passed the magnifying mirror. A MAGNIFYING MIRROR! I was proud when I resisted the powerful pull. I knew too well the havoc it could wreak.

"So, how do you want to look tonight?" I'm always amazed when makeup and hair ask this question. Does anyone ever say, "You know, I really want to look like shit tonight"? I just figured that given my bone structure, and with enough time, the experts would be able to make me look like Faye Dunaway in *Chinatown*. Am I asking too much? Hello? I'm asking you—the person reading this book. Oh, forget it, just keep reading.

Because I had no plan, I just I stammered, "Um, maybe like not too done?"

The hairstylist chimed in, "And for hair?"

Oh boy. "Um, I was thinking like, um, sexy, wavy? Like not too done? Like wavy but not curly?" And then, I did it. I googled an image of Sarah Jessica Parker. It always comes down to googling an image of SJP as Carrie Bradshaw, doesn't it? Hello? I'm talking to you. And there I stood, holding the photo this woman has obviously been shown two hundred times before because she nodded enthusiastically.

"Yes, that's a fabulous look for you." And then she added that on *Live!* she thought I always looked so pageant-y. And my hair generally looked very matronly.

Okay . . . It's one thing for me to complain about my hair and makeup on *Live!*, but I don't recall asking for your opinion, lady.

I have learned over the past few decades on camera that if you have five minutes to get ready, makeup and hair will get you ready in five minutes. But if you have three hours, the team will need four. The latter was happening, as I saw a very thin barreled curling iron toiling away at my hair. I attempted to self-advocate, as my therapist had taught me. "Hey, do you think that barrel is a little thin? Because my hair really gets very curly, very easily."

Clearly she was used to hearing this from Lou Dobbs because she had an answer at the ready. "No, because I like to put the curl in so I can take it down later because this is all going to fall in loose waves around your face. Sexy and undone."* With that, I thought I heard the makeup artist suppress a chuckle.

Meanwhile, over in special effects, the makeup artist was still applying eye makeup thirty minutes in. She explained her plan was "a big dramatic eye and then clean underneath with foundation and blush." Two words really stood out to me in this description. BIG and DRAMATIC. These are two words that I distinctly remember not using when I described what I was going for. I cannot fathom how BIG and DRAMATIC fit with "natural and not too done." I suppose now I can see how I had been vague.

And as usual Mark was nowhere to be found. Remember when he was supposed to come save me if things were taking too long? That only works if your husband doesn't have narcolepsy. I, of course, could not see myself while I was sitting in the chair because the mirror was too high. So, I was going by feel, intuition, and length of time being spent on my makeup and length of my actual hair, which seemed to be more Shirly Temple and less Sarah Jessica Parker by the minute. I repeatedly texted Mark as the ordeal drifted into the two and a half hour zone. I know what I look like. I'm not the prettiest, I'm not the sexiest, I'm not the most glamorous, but I'm also not the most hideous. For heaven's sake, it usually takes me a half hour to get myself ready, and an hour if I'm being done by professionals. How does Lou Dobbs actually sit still this long? At his age, he must need several pee breaks.

Finally, I was enveloped in a cloud of hairspray and face-setting powder so large that I am convinced that we had created a new hole in the ozone.

Then, thank merciful God, there came a knock at the door. I heard the bedroom door open, and Mark staggered out, clearly having just woken up. "Coming!" he yelled. He opened the door to find the woman from the concierge desk, sent to help him with his bow tie. "Hey, I'm sorry, I just woke up from a nap. Can you come back in five minutes so I can shower and get dressed?" Mark turned on his heels and was about to saunter into the bathroom when I yelled to him, hoping that he would remember our deal and help me out of my nightmare.

"Hon! Don't you need to um . . ." Mark turned to me, and I saw him wince. He actually winced. I saw fear in his eyes.

"Wow," Mark said. "You look so glamorous, you're so tan. Incredibly tan." What?

The makeup artist then weighed in with her thought process. "I just didn't want her to look washed out next to you. You've got that incredible Latino skin, so I added a liquid bronzer to the foundation to give her that glow. Sexy right?" God lady, what's he gonna say?

"And your hair is so flouncy!" Mark choked out next. What the fuck did he just say? Flouncy?!

"Yea, I like to put the curl in so I can take it down later and all this is going to fall in loose waves around her face. Very sexy and undone." I was actually mouthing the words along with her.

Suddenly, there was another knock at the door and this time, I stood to open it. The concierge was back, and she, too, winced upon seeing me. "I know," I said. "You're here for Mark's tie?"

"Yes, ma'am." Another ma'am, a personal record.

"Ladies, thank you so much, I'm so sorry but I have to get dressed. You'll be okay seeing yourselves out?" I said while moving toward the bedroom and my salvation.

"But I still have to glue on your lashes," said makeup.

"Yea, and I really need to give you one last spray, so it stays flouncy," said hair. But I was done.

I ran into the bathroom, looked in the mirror, and was greeted by a dirt-colored face wearing jet-black liquid Kabuki eye makeup. My hair was in tight Shirley Temple ringlets. Like I was in a pageant, which was painfully ironic. I didn't know where to begin, so I turned on the shower. Mark entered the bathroom and was breath-taking in his Ralph Lauren tuxedo, his bow tie still untied.

"Are you gonna be ready to leave in five minutes?" he asked, as if he hadn't seen me.

"Um no, I'm not because I sat in the makeup and hair chair for almost three hours because someone never came to help me." (Tears welling.) "So now I have to start over."

"Are you crying over hair and makeup? You have three healthy kids and a husband who thinks you're beautiful, and you're crying?" This again. *Why do these always have to be my options?* I wondered. Like, isn't it possible to have three healthy children AND good makeup for the one night a year we go out? Is that asking too much? I realize that Mark is right, by the way. But I would like to acknowledge that having a hair and makeup disaster on the one night you decide to leave the house does not encourage you to leave the house more often. And it did little to help with my social anxiety situation.

"No, I'm not crying," I whimpered. I turned off the shower and stood in the steam while trying to brush the wiggy-ness out of my hair. The problem is, like I told the lady, once it's curled, it's curled. While battling with my hair, I took a makeup wipe and smeared off 90 percent of the "bronzed" foundation. Then I took another, then another. I couldn't believe how brown the makeup wipes were. Terra-cotta actually. I got out of the steam bath and saw that my hair now resembled an old, forgotten Barbie's. My face was even more startling with just the heavy eye makeup on a naked face. I dried off as best I could because I was now sweating from rage and social anxiety and just the sheer speed at which I was moving to make it into the car in five minutes. Boom foundation. Boom blush. Boom gently taken down freakishly heavy eye makeup. Boom done in four minutes. The hair was what it was. I stepped into my gorgeous Brian Atwood heels and regretted not buying them a size larger, then slithered into my dress, which I loved. Erdem, borrowed of course. It was a dark elegant floral pattern, form-fitted with an elbow-length sleeve and jewel-encrusted belt. I felt pretty, as long as I didn't look at myself from the neck up. I asked Mark, who is absolutely the most elegant man I've ever seen, to zip up the back of my dress. Mark did the deed, and leaned over and whispered, "You look beautiful. I don't know how you fixed it so fast, but you did. By the way, can you tie a bow tie?"

Somehow in all the drama, his bow tie never got tied. The concierge couldn't do it, the man from the front desk who thought he knew me couldn't do it, and apparently the hotel asked a sales associate from a retail store nearby to come do it, and HE couldn't tie it either. So now it was my turn. Apparently it's harder than it looks on the YouTube video we googled. I made a first attempt. No dice. I tried again and I could feel heat coming off Mark's body. I did worse the second time and my hands started to shake. Mark walked away toward the mirror and gave it a go himself, doing a terrible job. Now, his hands were shaking, too.

"Okay, here, give me one more chance," I said, as I watched the video again, step by step and yelling for Mark to pause it every three seconds as I followed Chris from YouTube to the letter. Mark wriggled and coughed like he was being tortured, and I remembered that he had been napping during my torture, which made me want to choke him with this bow tie. "STOP!" I was now in a full sweat and semi-hypnotized by Chris's droning voice. Eventually, we got it. It wasn't perfect. It was a little crooked if I'm honest, but at least it was done. I saw Mark studying it in the mirror with a disappointed grimace and decided that I didn't care. I ran to put on extra deodorant, because the flop sweat was real, and grabbed my purse.

Evening bags for these events are always a joke, but this one was tiny even by evening bag standards. My stylist from *Live!* had put my outfit together for me because, well, that's her job. And she must have known I would need to put things in my purse, right? Like a lipstick. A phone. A compact. Gum. A protein bar. Nope, there was simply no room. I was faced with the ultimate Sophie's choice. The purse was so small I could either take a lipstick OR a tampon. Not both. I tried every which way to compel both lipstick and tampon into the purse. I tried stacking both vertically and horizontally. I tried crisscrossing. I tried to fold the tampon. The bag was so slender it barely even held the tampon because it was a Kotex security and don't you dare judge me. I needed lipstick, but I needed the tampon more. I slid it in and forced the Judith Lieber kiss lock shut. It popped open. I tried again, it popped open again. I tried a third time and it finally held, and we were off, with Mark graciously agreeing to hold my lipstick.

We walked at a clipped pace toward the elevator. While we waited, Mark looked at himself in the reflective surface and tried to adjust the tie. When the elevator door opened, we both got in and looked at ourselves with complete contempt. Mark turned to me and said, "My bow tie is crooked."

Because I couldn't resist, and because I'm an asshole, I said, "Well at least you have three healthy kids," as we reached the lobby level. We moved quickly toward the front of the hotel where the car service (Mark sprung for a car service) was waiting.

As we passed the concierge and front desk, my friend shouted, "Enjoy your night Mr. and Mrs. Consuelos." I turned to say thank you and saw him holding his quiet finger up to his lips. He was the asshole, I decided.

We got into our car, which was the very last in a long line of cars, limos, and SUVs stretching around the corner. "Hello there, my name is Matthew, I'll be your driver for this evening," and I don't know how, but I was immediately aware that Matthew had no idea what he was doing.

Matthew turned around and looked at us expectantly. "Where to?" Oh boy.

"Um, the White House Correspondents' Dinner? Um, do you have the address? We were told you have the address and parking pass and everything." Matthew then opened the glove box and started digging around in a pile of old napkins while making Donald Duck sounds with his mouth, and it dawned on me that this was why I never left my house.

I am nothing if not aggressively passive-aggressive and I let out a long, irritated breath. "Pfffffffffwwwwwwwwhhhhhh." This way, Mark would know that this was somehow his fault. Mark took out his phone and pulled up the itinerary that my assistant Lauren had diligently put together for us, a minute by minute breakdown of how the night was supposed to go.

"Okay, so we have the pre-dinner cocktail party that starts at six, so we need to get to the Washington Hilton, okay? And we need to be dropped off at the T Street entrance? Okay?"

Matthew looked at us blankly and said, I kid you not, "Ohhhh keyyyy. Do you know where that is?"

"No, we don't because we're not from here, so . . ." We were still not moving, and it was 5:50. In Mark's special ops brain, we should have been there twenty minutes ago because we had to walk the red carpet in order to get to the cocktail reception in order to pick up our credentials and be photographed for our press passes. Don't forget we were going to be in the same room as the president of the United States. You think they let just anyone saunter in? Well, obviously they do, but you need a pass. The Nerd Prom is a bit of a security and logistical jigsaw puzzle, and with a driver who apparently had never been to Washington, DC, before, well it was apparently our lucky night. I worried that Mark was going to take the wheel himself, but instead he Google Mapped it and started giving Matthew detailed instructions.

Fortunately, we were not far, but Matthew was convinced he knew a better drop-off spot. As Mark instructed him to go right and around to the back of the hotel, Matthew countered, "No, I'm going to drop you off this way because there's less traffic." I suppose he sensed Mark's unease with being on time instead of early.

We knew right away that we were in the wrong spot. There were security barriers and people crowded behind them trying to get a look at the who's who. Security guards and German Shepherds lined the entrance. As we approached, we were immediately waved away. My Brian Atwood shoes screamed, "I told you so." We tried to explain that we belonged in a way that didn't make us sound insane, but to no avail. I was getting more and more uncomfortable as we walked to yet another entrance. Finally, someone inside who looked like an authority saw us, and thank God, recognized us. Sort of.

"Hayley and Mateo!" she screamed, using our soap opera character names from a decade ago. "Now why are you two at the wrong entrance?"

"This is where we got dropped off," Mark explained, giving this lady the full Mateo Santos charm. Mark has an extremely seductive quality when he wants it. He can summon sex appeal out of thin

air and lay it on whoever needs it in real time. By the time Mark/
Mateo was done with this lady, we were snuck in through a VVVIP
entrance, past the red-carpet press line, directly to where our credentials were waiting for us, and whisked to the cocktail reception
hosted by USA Today in the Independence Room.

We entered and were redirected to a small room off the main
cocktail reception area to be photographed. I thought to myself,
Well, at least we can prove we were here. As soon as we walked in, we
bumped into Johnny Galecki and his girlfriend at the time, Kelli
Garner. Johnny played my brother on the sitcom *Hope and Faith*,
and Mark and I adore him and Kelli, even though she misspells her
name.

I think Johnny and I felt equally uncomfortable in social
settings, especially large overwhelming events such as this, and
took comfort in the fact that we'd both be at the same table until
we'd find out we wouldn't. USA Today had several tables and we,
the table entertainment, would be divided among them. At this
point, I was just hoping I'd be seated somewhere near Mark, who
I'm sure was off somewhere adjusting his tie. We were then introduced to editors, editors at large, sports columnists, entertainment reporters, and people from digital, back before digital was
really a thing. I was trying my very best to not be self-conscious
about my hair and makeup because I do have three healthy children, but I kept raking my hand through the mess on my head,
which seemed to be getting curlier by the second. I already knew
how my makeup looked because everyone kept asking where I had
been on vacation. I was in the Independence Room and ironically
felt utterly trapped. I knew Mark was getting nervous because we
hadn't begun to make our way to the ballroom. There was only a

half hour before the doors opened and it's a ten-minute walk to the metal detectors, so that meant we'd only be twenty minutes early, and therefore late.

As I looked toward Mark who was sipping a tequila* and repeatedly checking his watch, my eyes fell on his tie, which was now perpendicular. He saw me looking. He instantly became the *Mona Lisa*, his eyes everywhere. "What? Is it crooked?"

"Just a little," I answered, and I grabbed that tie and psychically threatened it to stay parallel. "You're so handsome," I said as I twisted that tie 180 degrees in the opposite direction with all my might.

"You ready?" Mark asked expectantly, so I know my answer had to be yes no matter how not ready I was to walk into an enormous ballroom filled with celebrities and politicians armed only with a single glass of wine* and my lucky tampon. As we began our walk down the various corridors we became a herd of elegant sheep all queuing up to pass through security. I heard a familiar voice behind me and turned to see the stunning Alicia Keys and her husband, Swizz Beatz. They are kind and warm and normal, but for the fact that they are a thousand percent cooler than everyone else. I wondered if they ever felt socially awkward or nervous like I did right then, and always. I felt it coming, and so did Mark because he rubbed my arm. "Please don't." He really knows me. He knows that anytime I see or hear Alicia Keys, I feel the need to sing "Fallin'," her hit song from her debut album, *Songs in A Minor*. Fortunately for Mark and I suppose Alicia, they moved toward the metal detector on the left and Mark made sure I stayed put in the right lane.

I could hear the security guards telling everyone to have their purses open and to place anything metallic in the plastic bins, just like at an airport. Mark begrudgingly placed his wallet, cell phone, and sunglasses that my purse couldn't hold for him in the bin and walked through. *Beeeeeep.* "Sir, go back. Do you have any metal on your belt?" the security guard asked while he saved time and pulled out the wand to wave over Mark's crotch. "Lucky wand," I heard some guy say from the cheap seats. The beep came again, right on his crotch. "Sir, did you empty your pockets?" the guard asked.

"Yea, I thought so," Mark said while reaching into his pocket and pulling out my lipstick, which apparently had a metallic tube. Side-eye all around.

"Ma'am," my fifth ma'am for those of you keeping score at home! "Please have your bag open," security yelled. I wanted to explain that if I opened this bag it would never shut again, but there was no time. There was a long line and everyone from Hollywood was setting off every conceivable alarm in the universe. It is as if they dressed not only to impress but also apparently wearing plutonium. I immediately opened my bag because I am a rule follower and in some form of spring action hydraulic fuckery my gigantic tampon launched out of my bag and into the air, spinning like a member of the Olympic diving team, in slow motion of course. "Projectile?!" questioned one of the guards, loudly. "No. It's a tampon!" I had screamed. Silence.

Complete and total silence.

You have three healthy children, I thought to myself as I bent down to pick up my tampon, which seemed to be somehow more offensive to everyone than an actual projectile. It also had transformed into the size of a roll of Bounty paper towels with a small rope at the end. I could feel the heat of humiliation rising from my feet and drenching my body in a flop sweat.

"Sorry, it's a small purse," I explained to the guard with the dog hoping he would hit me with pepper spray, that way I would get to go home early. I stood up and was waved through as the man behind me passed through the metal detector in one second flat.

"Kelly, I work for the *Washington Post*." Oh, thank god a journalist. "My wife loves your show . . . now she loves you even more," he said. I looked and he was pointing to his elegant and sophisticated wife. I can't imagine a tampon had ever fallen out of her purse.

"I'm sorry you had to witness that," I said.

"That's why you're the most relatable woman on TV," she answered. Once again, it was the sisterhood to the rescue.

Mark turned to me and pulled me in to whisper in my ear. I leaned in close because I was mortified and needed a reassuring word.

"Don't they make smaller tampons?" Oh, Mateo Santos. You know how to sweet-talk a girl.

For the record, they do make smaller tampons—they are great if you get a nosebleed. And if we ever leave the house again, it will be after menopause.

A few notes:
* *As for Lou Dobbs's hair and makeup team, I now realize that "undone" has regional definitions.*
* *All alcoholic beverages should be multiplied by three.*

"A good marriage is one where each partner suspects they got the better deal."

—UNKNOWN

CHAPTER ELEVEN

THE REVERSAL OF PSYCHOLOGY

Mark and I are in couples therapy. And by "in" couples therapy, I mean we are currently binge-watching the Showtime docuseries *Couples Therapy*.

We are watching separately, of course, as Mark is currently living in Vancouver for his job.

For many years, I have felt like Mark and I could benefit from real couples therapy. To Mark's credit, he has agreed to attend sessions twice. Both times, he refused to return after the initial session because he became convinced that I had somehow manipulated the therapists (Yes, there were two. One he selected, one I selected.) to advocate for me. He just knew that I had "gotten" to them somehow and prejudiced their opinions. I'm not sure how I would have found the time, but that didn't seem to matter to Mark. Plus, I'm fairly certain any good couples therapist would not fall prey to manipulation by one half of any couple he or she was treating, as being a neutral third party is sort of the role of a couples therapist, even if I was clearly right. But what do I know?

Mark and I both grew up in households where therapy of any kind was NOT a thing. As a kid, I was actually threatened with therapy. I was routinely told, in no uncertain terms, that if I didn't stop (insert normal childhood development here), then

I would be sent to a shrink, and my entire school as well as the whole neighborhood would know I was crazy. (I love seventies parenting.)

Mark was reared with a similar opinion of therapy. Perhaps this is due to his having spent his formative years in another country. Apparently, therapy in Europe in the seventies was also not a thing. Maybe it was a financial consideration. Maybe it was because we have parents of a certain age, a generation of adults who did not dwell on thoughts or feelings or happiness or trauma. Maybe our parents just couldn't help simultaneously ignoring their own, and their children's, emotional needs. Maybe that's just the way things were when we were kids.

Maybe that's why Mark and I are riveted by this docuseries and can't stop watching these brave couples in marital crisis. We marvel at their openness, their raw emotions, and wonder how long it would take our parents to die from embarrassment if we appeared on this show. These couples are analyzed with devastating efficacy and empathy by Dr. Orna Guralnik. (I highly recommend giving this show a watch and then decide for yourself which member of the couple you are. It is a fun game.)

The big takeaway from this series, Mark and I noticed, is how impactful what happens to us as children can be, and how that plays out in our relationships in our adult lives, over and over until we break the cycle. This is, of course, an oversimplification of the show and therapy in general. But I don't mind telling you that as we watched, we both wondered aloud what we have done to our own children and how we may have ruined their future happiness. Mark wondered less than I did but acknowledged that a lot of his own obsessive-compulsive behavior was passed on to him from a certain family member . . . who shall remain nameless, but I will put it in code later. I would say at least two to three of our own children have inherited that very same quality. I will not say which ones . . . but they are boys.

I question whether or not any of my high-functioning social anxiety disorder, my low-functioning borderline personality disorder, my wanton reckless agoraphobia, my unchecked egomaniacal grandiosity, my narcissism that has not progressed to malignancy, or my probable undiagnosed ADHD* has affected my kids, but they seem to be doing great. Don't you think so? What was I saying? Where were we? Sorry, I got distracted by my own reflection in a spoon.

I would go so far as to say that our children are, for the most part, abundantly normal, boring even. They haven't been paying attention, clearly.

I will get Mark into couples therapy, the actual clinical process, and not the Showtime series. But it will take some maneuvering on my part, some good old-fashioned reverse psychology. Luckily, I have practice, as this is my go-to method for getting Mark to agree to almost anything. I'm not sure if reverse psychology is based in actual psychology, or taught in psychology classes, but it works like a charm. The only thing is, this technique is exhausting, and when I employ said methodology, it usually signifies that I'm at the end of my rope. Why I have to signal the end of my rope to get my husband to agree to anything is clearly one of the many reasons we need to talk to a professional. Between us, dear reader, Mark is usually right, but he cannot know that, ever.

---

*All psychological disorders above are self-diagnosed.

And my assertion to always being right must be maintained if we have a chance of making this marriage work and getting from twenty-five to fifty years.

I have utilized reverse psychology in our marriage for anything from real estate acquisitions to choosing the right nursery school for our kids. Mark always has strong opinions about all things, and there is always much discussion. So much talking. So, after many years, I have learned that I must always lean hard into the opposite of what I want to get the desired outcome because simpler methods will not prevail.

I'm not that demanding, really. I mean, I don't think I am. Maybe Mark has a different opinion, and maybe when he decides to write his own book, he can dispute this claim.

I would rather choose my battles. Meaning, I would choose not to have any battles at all, if I could. But Mark's insufferable OCD sometimes prevents him from giving an inch. A therapist might say this is because he was born into a military family, and he has a strong need for order and control. A therapist might also say that because there was less order in my childhood, that it could be described as not as structured, I craved having someone with a schedule. Someone who took charge. Although, who knows? I'm not a therapist.

However, I will say this: In the often-exciting haze of our twenty-five-plus-year marriage, we mostly agree. And I mostly don't have to resort to reverse psychology. We are basically on the same page and happily so. Two things now sit at the very top of our "marital resistance list." These are two things we just have a hard time with, both personally and as a couple.

One I feel is justified, and the other . . . well, keep reading.

The first is the vow renewal. This is a tippy-top, no fly list, under any circumstance, NEVER thing. From our standpoint, a vow renewal always feels like a jinx. Or at least a precursor for divorce. The last-ditch, pre-divorce celebration, if you will. We have all read about various high-profile couples renewing their wedding vows over the years. Usually we don't personally know them, but as with all well-known people, we feel like we do, and we feel like we have a vested interest in their marriage or relationship. Even though it's clearly none of our business, we want good things for these strangers we think we know. But, whenever Mark and I read about a vow renewal, we always have a sinking feeling, a sense of impending doom. Probably because we always know where it's headed, which is to a lengthy and messy divorce. It's just happened too many times. We've even gone to the ceremonies and then had to take sides in the divorces and THEN gone to the subsequent remarriage weddings. But I will admit, the gift is never quite as good the second time around. So, just don't do it.

BUT, if you're planning a vow renewal while reading this, I'm sure you'll be fine. I'm talking about what we've seen, our personal feelings about it, and why we've never done it. So, don't cancel the deejay just because I weighed in. I'm clearly jaded and judgmental and have no idea what I'm talking about. This is NOT, I repeat, NOT a self-help book! (Even though I'm right on this one.)

The second thing we resisted is actual couples therapy. And by we, I mean Mark initially, and then me ultimately. For at least twenty years I thought our marriage would benefit from learning how to communicate the "right" way. You know, with "I feel" statements, and all that. We were young when we got married.

We would fight about the most inane, ludicrous things. I always chalked it up to immaturity on both of our parts, but Mark seemed to think that if I felt like we needed therapy, then I should absolutely go and see someone about that.

So, I did. Every Wednesday at 4:00 p.m.

I know what you're thinking, and you're right. An hour midway through the week is not nearly enough time for one to assess how screwed up things are and will get. I mean, usually I need at least two insufferable dinners with people I do not like, which I anticipated with such dread, that I would unknowingly fight with Mark instead of deferring the invitation, followed by a weekend of Soul Cycle classes surrounded by people who never learned the phrases "Please," "Thank you," or "Excuse me" to really have an accurate picture of how unstable I feel. Midweek is too soon. Not enough has happened in the week to remind me of why I need therapy. Monday would have been the perfect day for the appointment. It would have been like watching *Last Week Tonight with John Oliver*. We would have been able to take all my feelings from the week before, big picture, and zoom out, analyzing them from every side.

But, my therapist, the one I asked/told my mom about, was so in demand that I took what I could get. Which happened to be hump days at 4:00 p.m. Half of what was going to happen to me, around me, or because of me, wouldn't have happened yet, from a therapeutic standpoint. So, I spent a great deal of time in my sessions anticipating what might happen with the rest of my week. That is, until my therapist taught me how to troubleshoot the tough moments and manage my anxieties about what I can't control.

At times, in my sessions, I would get extremely emotional.

Other times, I'd be like a stone. Sometimes, I would come in toss-ing twelve pieces of nineteen different thoughts, and she would catch every single fragmented idea, midair, and put the word puzzle together to help me understand what it all meant. I bet she could solve a Rubik's Cube in under a minute, and then help the Hungarian sculptor, Erno Rubik, figure out why he was so fixated on puzzle games and colorful shapes. Probably had something to do with his mother.

After a few months of sessions, one Wednesday I strode into the comfortable homelike office on the Upper West Side and an-nounced with complete confidence that I was suffering from de-pression. My therapist stared at me for a beat, then asked me to continue. I told her on our Sunday drive home from Long Island I was reading a *New York Times Magazine* article on depression, and realized I had every single symptom. I read the entire article out loud to Mark, mostly to keep him from falling asleep at the wheel. But also, to aggressively passive-aggressively let him know that my depression was somehow his fault. And I wasn't talking just about regular depression mind you, the kind that makes you feel sort of bummed out. No, I was talking the clinical kind. I knew I had it.

I leaned toward her conspiratorially. "I read that article, and man it was like reading about myself. I probably need Lexapro. Or Wellbutrin. Or Prozac. Or Paxil. Or Zoloft. Or Cymbalta. Or Luvox. Or Celexa. Or Latuda. Or—"

My therapist stopped me. She asked me to tell her exactly why, besides the article, I believed I was suffering from depres-sion. I knew this question was coming because, like I said, I read the article, and this was one of the questions a therapist should ask.

"I have a hard time getting out of bed in the morning. I almost always wake up crying at the thought of having to go to work. I feel like I'm in physical pain. My hair hurts. I have no energy at all. I'm very easily distracted. When I'm playing with my kids, I feel like I've forgotten to do something at work, and when I'm at work, I feel like I've forgotten to do something for my kids. I cry in the shower. I cry myself to sleep. I cry backstage. I sometimes want to cry in the middle of the show. Sometimes I feel like I can't breathe. Sometimes I realize I'm not . . ."

There was a long pause, and she acknowledged that my descriptions of my day-to-day experiences indeed sounded depressing. She then asked me how I felt during the weekends and on vacation. "That's the thing, I feel great heading into the weekend, but I'm always aware of Sunday. Because by the time Sunday rolls around, I feel like a kid trying to figure out how to get out of school."

She took another long pause, and then continued. "And what about when you take a vacation?"

I stopped to think about my last vacation. "I start counting the days until I have to go back to work from the time I'm fastening the kids' seat belts on the plane. You know. It exhausts Mark to listen to it. Only six more days until I have to go back . . . now my kids have started to pick up on it. They'll say, 'Don't worry about it, Mommy, we still have so many days.' And that's just what I say out loud. Plus, the tabloids always use a two-week hiatus as an opportunity to write a really shitty cover story about me while I'm away. Sometimes they even figure out where we are and send a photographer to ruin the trip. It's always something. It's just . . . you know, it sucks." I reached for a tissue because I am excellent at feeling sorry for myself. Why focus on the fact that we were able to take nice trips, when I could focus on the tabloids' fiction writers?

"But what about your other symptoms? Are you able to get out of bed? And are you in physical pain on vacation?" she asked. Because she knew, as you now have likely figured out, my mind had started spinning.

"Oh. Um, no. No pain. I'm able to get up and really enjoy my time away. It's just the clock in the back of my head that's always ticking."

We sat across the room from each other, in comfortable club chairs. I looked toward the sofa and wondered if anyone was ever in bad enough shape emotionally that they laid down during their sessions. "Well, I don't think you're suffering from depression. Typically, depression doesn't go away on the weekends or during vacation. That's not usually how it works. What I think you suffer from is workplace apathy. I think your job makes you miserable."

I wondered what pills cured that.

She wasn't wrong. At that time, a different time, a pre–#metoo #timesup time, a pre–women belong in the room where decisions are being made time, I. Was. Miserable (see chapter eight, "Fool Me Once/Fool Me Twice"). Suffice to say, I left the office that day without a prescription but with some breathing techniques for when the shit really hit the fan.

See that? Again, I just drifted into the darkness, and this chapter is on couples therapy.

Anyway, by the time Mark proudly exclaimed one day a few years ago that he had found a therapist for us to see together, I was ten years into therapy on my own. I had spent ten years focusing on my marriage, work life, childhood, and all the things that I wanted to fix about myself. Ten years is a long time, and I had declared myself cured, ostensibly, so I politely declined Mark's offer. Now, I won't say that Mark is not used to hearing no, but I will say that it is not a word he is very familiar with. He is, frankly, the most persuasive person I've ever met. He could talk the underpants off a nun. (Just kidding, nuns.) What Mark did not realize, however, was that in my near ten years of therapy, I had been working on one phrase, well two, but one of the phrases is a single word. Write this down if you're audio booking, or highlight it, because it is so simple, and yet the most effective way to negotiate anything to your advantage. Ready?

"No. That doesn't work for me."

That's it. That's the entire argument. Now, the words are simple, but the move is harder to execute than it looks. You, dear reader, are going to want to throw an apology in there. Trust me, it is human nature to want to apologize for all sorts of things that have nothing to do with you. How many times have you apologized to a person who bumped into you on the street because they were looking down at their phone?

The trick is to never say, "No, I don't think so. I'm so sorry, that really doesn't work for me right now." Do you hear the difference? That leaves the ball in the other person's court. Whereas "No, that doesn't work for me" takes the ball out of the court altogether and runs it over with a bus.

I had come to this phrase in my work with my therapist because after ten years, something emerged. And that is my tendency to accommodate others around me to my own detriment, pushing aside my own needs for the comfort and happiness of others for the sake of harmony. I'm sure this comes from my desire to create calm in an unpredictable and chaotic career, but the fact is by doing this, I made myself miserable. I yes'd myself into workplace apathy, anxiety, and self-diagnosed clinical depression. The really bad kind. And so, I needed a way to communicate my own desire, or lack of desire, effectively. With my therapist's help, I had rigged the system in a way that felt as if I could stand up for myself without being an asshole. I no longer needed couples therapy for that.

When Mark invited me to therapy, I decided I would really go buck wild, and leave it at no. Just, "No." I didn't even add the "Doesn't work for me." A baller move, I know. Mark looked as if a foreign object had flown out of my mouth.

A deafening silence followed, then, "No? Just no? That's it?"

"Yep, that's it. Just no," I said, and sauntered out of our bedroom with Mark close behind.

"Why?" Mark asked with great incredulity, because, like I said, he is not used to dissent.

Then I pulled out the big gun. "It doesn't work for me," I said, cool as a cucumber, like I had just thought of this powerful sentence and hadn't been rehearsing it for years.

Mark looked baffled, "What doesn't work for you?"

I must admit that having Mark in a position of vulnerability, watching him struggle to navigate not getting his way, was oddly thrilling. It was akin to catching a great white in a tiny guppy net. Like I had harpooned Moby Dick with a pea shooter. Like I had captured Neptune's trident with my bare hands and now owned the sea. (Can you tell it's Shark Week?) Mark was shocked. He was trapped. I had dragged him to the depths of my obstinance. It was there, at the bottom, where he would sink or swim.

You know, going back and proofreading all of this makes me realize how off the rails I sound. Or at least off the deep end. (Shark Week actually lasts a month.)

Maybe I'm not cured after all. Maybe I'm an asshole who can only receive pleasure from creating pain. And NOT the fun kind. Perhaps I'm hooked on the high of the makeup after the breakup. Remember, that's how I caught the shark to begin with. I'll have to talk to my therapist about all of this.

But, in any event, I held firm, telling Mark that in no way, shape, or form would I go to couples therapy with him. Ever. (See how exhausting this reverse psychology is? I mean I just got lost in the ocean.)

Mark, to his credit, made an appointment for us to meet with a therapist anyway. When I refused to go, because I am obstinate to the point of self-sabotage, or because I forgot how reverse psychology worked, he endeavored ahead without me. I must admit I was impressed. But then he came home irritatingly euphoric from his first couples therapy session. There he was all pumped up on the natural endorphins that occur when you pay clinical experts to unpack your emotional baggage, talking a mile a minute and regaling me with stories of his obsessive, unyielding demeanor and self-centeredness, as if I'd never met him before. Then he told me that I should definitely come to the next session because the therapist was really surprised I didn't show, and that I would really like him because he wrote a book on marriage.

Okay, two things about that: Number one, why on earth would the therapist be surprised I wasn't there when I specifically refused to go? And number two, and I can officially say this now, who HASN'T written a book?

But I had a sinking feeling that they were both right. Maybe I was pushing this reverse psychology just a little too far.

Spoiler alert! I'm totally going to go to couples therapy with Mark, probably right after this book comes out.

But Mark doesn't need to know that yet.

"When all else
fails, there's always
delusion."

—CONAN O'BRIEN

CHAPTER TWELVE

THE GOOD NEWS: YOU CAN'T DIE
FROM EMBARRASSMENT

You cannot die from embarrassment, believe me, I've tried and it's physically impossible. Of course, you may want to die, nobody's trying to take that away from you, but physically you just won't. You don't get to this level of mediocrity after thirty-plus years in show business without knowing how to embarrass yourself, and still somehow live.

Of course, there are always people who don't embarrass. They are called shameless or sociopaths, and they usually live forever.

Which brings me to Richard Gere. No, he's not a shameless sociopath. But Richard Gere and I once starred in a performance art piece, which was equal parts thriller, comedy, tragedy, and, um, I suppose horror. Surely you must have heard this story somewhere before . . . it is legendary . . . one for the record books . . . ringing any bells? NO? Well, buckle up because even if you're not a fan of his films or his stance on Tibet, I guarantee you will love this performance.

Andy Cohen, Mark, and I were at the beautiful waterfront home of Jane and Jimmy Buffett to celebrate Anjelica Huston's birthday. Before you start complaining about how out of touch and elitist I am, let me state emphatically that (a) yes, I am, and (b) seriously, this is really the only chapter where I get even close to a glamorous and fancy schmancy name-droppy life. Unless you count the chapter on the White House Correspondents' Dinner, which I certainly do not.

Back to the officer (me) and the gentleman (Richard Gere). Let's, for the sake of expediency, from now on refer to Richard Gere simply as Richard Gere. We were having a lovely dinner, and when I mean lovely, I mean nobody hosts a dinner party better than Jane Buffett. She just does it right. From the perfectly sublime menu (I'm talking fried chicken with buttermilk biscuits and lavender honey, hunny), to the always exciting guest list (think very A-list, with Mark and me thrown in to keep it real), to the casual elegance of her luxurious southern charm (she has outdoor furnishings that I'm certain are for only indoor use, under a giant magnolia tree with electric blue laser lights that beam down upon a fifty-person picnic table).

Back to *American* (Richard Gere) *Gigolo* (me).

Dinner was served buffet (pronounced: "Buffett," like Jimmy) style. I should explain that Mark hates to navigate a buffet. He gets overwhelmed, or he gets confused, or maybe he just likes when I serve him. Who knows? But when there is a buffet, I usually navigate it twice if the plates are big and the selection is amazing, or only once with two plates balanced on one hand if it's just so-so. Since we were at Jane's, I already knew it was going to be a two-trip-down-the-buffet-line kinda night. The first plate for Mark was a no-holds-barred experience. It was the kind of plate I would make for myself if I had a metabolism. Thinly sliced juicy medium rare skirt steak, a buttermilk fried chicken breast and also a fried drumstick, a piece of grilled Long Island corn, some avocado and tomato salad, sautéed broccoli, collard greens, and a heavenly ramekin filled with creamy three-cheese mac and cheese. Also, two biscuits. The plate was embarrassingly large, and every guest stared and said the same thing: "Kelly Ripa, you do not eat all that food!"

"No, you're correct. I don't eat any of this food. As a matter of fact, I'm just dropping this off to the father of my children."

Well, you would have thought I shit in the pool with the scornful look that instantly appeared on everyone's face. "You're getting your husband's plate?" "Is something wrong with him?" "Why can't he get his own food?" said the women. Then, "Jeez that would be nice." "I wish someone would get me my plate." "Hon, how come you never get food for me?" said the men.

"Because you don't look like him and you need the exercise," is what I would have said, but Jane beat me to it. Again, Jane is perfect.

As I dropped off Mark's plate, I saw that he was wedged between Andy Cohen and Marci Klein, daughter of Calvin and producer of *SNL* and *30 Rock*. (I promise this name-dropper chapter is almost over.) I gave Mark a kiss for good measure since everyone was still clutching their pearls at my having stormed the buffet table for my man. I then returned to the table for my sad plate, a sensible salad and a French serving of mahi-mahi. A French serving means basically the size of a credit card. No wonder French women don't get fat, they're starving. (There's a whole book about it. Don't come for me.) Every seat was taken except for a spot at the very end. Directly across from . . . you guessed it, Richard Gere. Be cool, I thought to myself as I slid over to the Richard Gere part of town.

As I attempted to sit down elegantly, my foot got caught in the hem of my dress because the more you pay for a dress the more likely it is to have a faulty hemline and cause you nothing but embarrassment as you try to look chic and effortless. Naturally, it is impossible to sit down with one's shoe caught in one's hem without exposing one's bosom. Although, in my case I suppose they're more like pecs than breasts. Either way, I'd only had a single glass of rosé* so I was not nearly ready to show Richard Gere my 32 AA longs.

Alas, with tangled foot and tearing hemline, I sort of crashed down at the table with my sensible salad sadly scattering over various plates. "Stuck the landing," I said to no one in particular since nobody bothered to look up. Silent eaters. Oh no, the worst. Eating with them is akin to eating in a monastery or a library or that cult where you can't make noise. I have to say at this point our end of the table looked like a big dud fest. Meanwhile, all I could hear were fits of uproarious laughter coming from the center of the table, aka Mark/Marci/Andyland. Heads all around were craning to hear what all the fun was about. Back in Silent Town, I decided to try my hand once again at breaking the ice. For heaven's sake, the man had been on my talk show a dozen times and couldn't be lovelier. Why am I such a socially awkward asshole? *Kelly*, I thought to myself, *just be normal. Say hi. Nice and easy. Nothing too weird. Just breathe and be yourself, but normal.*

"RICHARD YOUR SON HOMER IS SO HANDSOME AND SUCH A LOVELY YOUNG MAN . . . I MET HIM AT MARCI'S BEACH BONFIRE LAST WEEK AND WHAT A GREAT KID YOU'VE GOT THERE—CHARMING, PO-LITE, PERSONABLE, JUST A GREAT KID. SMART, TOO, A CHIP OFF THE OL' BLOCK, I SUPPOSE."

Now all eyes were trained at our end of the table since apparently my normal, not too weird intro into an off-camera conversation with Richard Gere was a fawning, screaming run-on sentence about his teenage son. Heat came from the bottom of my feet and rose up to

---

All alcoholic beverages should be multiplied by three.

the top of my skull. Through my skull actually. And without fail my hyperhidrosis kicked into high gear. It's a clinical problem, look it up. I can't do everything, I'm busy writing this book.

Richard Gere looked up from his plate of vegetarian fair and smiled that megawatt movie star smile, and I could actually hear Joe Cocker and Jennifer Warnes sing "Love lift us up where we belong, where the eagles cry, on the mountain high." If you haven't seen *An Officer and a Gentleman*, please put this book down and go to your viewing device and download it now. This book will keep. I promise. Best sellers are timeless.

"Thanks, he's a great kid, isn't he?" Richard Gere said in such a way that revealed he is used to women screaming awkwardly in his face.

"Who knows what tomorrow brings," I sang softly, but caught myself and covered by having a fake coughing fit. I asked him what his son was into academically, athletically, and Richard Gere answered in a very engaged, down to earth way. I'd love to tell you what he said, but I left my body at that point and was where the eagles cry on the mountain high. I do remember at one point wondering if Richard Gere could pick me up as easily as he did Debra Winger, but knew that I should hold that question deep, deep down in my soul and never let it out of my mouth.

At a certain point, dessert was served. It was a glorious smorgasbord of mini strawberry shortcakes, chocolate brownies, apple pie, peach crumble, homemade ice cream, and a giant bowl of fresh berries. I'm talking strawberries, raspberries, and blueberries with fresh whipped cream and mint on the side. I didn't want to lose my spot next to Richard Gere, but I also didn't want to lose out on the strawberry shortcake (Mark's favorite), or the fresh whipped cream with berries (mine). Yes, I eat dessert. You think I can survive on a piece of fish that can fit into a wallet? In the name of expediency, I decided to only take one spin around the dessert table. This meant I was going to stack my desserts very strategically. Two shortcakes, one apple pie with a peach crumble stacked on top. It was like dessert Jenga. I skipped over the various ice creams because that required a bowl that I did not have a hand to carry and headed right to the chocolate brownies. I was immediately deflated by what I saw. All of the delicious, gooey-center brownies were gone and all that was left were the overcooked, over-hardened end bits that nobody wanted.

Damn it, I thought to myself. Should have headed directly to the brownies first. Rookie mistake. This was not my first go-round of the dessert table for heaven's sake, but Richard Gere had obviously gotten into my head, and I was making sloppy dessert errors. "To hell with the brownies," I said out loud and moved on to the berries and whipped cream. Actually, I'm lying. I just hit the whipped cream. I piled that deliciousness onto the pies and crumbles in one mountainous dollop. Think Richard Dreyfuss in *Close Encounters of the Third Kind*. You've never heard of that movie, either? I'm starting to think you picked up the wrong book.

I headed over to Mark in the hope that he wouldn't be too broken up about the missed brownie opportunity only to find the cool kids at the center of the table had their very own dessert cornucopia that had been hand delivered by a waiter who was very obviously flirting with Andy. Naturally, all of their brownies had been eaten in a flash and they were looking for some fruit to offset the gooey goodness of all those center brownies that they had eaten like pigs and to hell with anybody else who may have wanted one. *Well, you know what? I'm seated next to Richard Gere, so I don't need your damn brownies or your funny conversations or any of the cool shit that's going on over here because Richard Gere and I are probably going to talk about the Dalai Lama, so fuck you.* Which I did not say but thought very loudly as I dropped the plate of cake/pie stew a la whipped cream next to the empty brownie trough and stormed off. Ingrates.

I made my way back to the mature, heady end of the table and paused briefly to google the Dalai Lama, just to have relevant talking points. Hey, a talk show host always prepares to be glib when totally not well versed on a subject. Truthfully, if being glib was an Olympic event, I would be Michael Phelps minus the fast metabolism and extremely long arms.

As I returned to my seat, I saw that Richard Gere appeared to be eating a piece of key lime pie. Excuse me? I had not seen key lime pie anywhere. Was there a secret off-menu offering for Golden Globe winners?

I tried once again to take a seat, elegantly, and damn if my foot didn't get caught in my hem again. I crash landed, just as I had before dinner. "Picnic tables are hard for you to navigate, huh?" said Richard Gere. At this, I threw my head back to laugh a howling cackle and wondered if Richard Gere thought I was reminiscent of Julia Roberts in *Pretty Woman*. Now I know you've seen that one so shut it.

Apparently, my cackle caught the attention of most of the table as I realized everyone was now staring at me and talking in hushed murmurs. I heard words like "drunk" and "out of it" and "on something" being batted about. I felt a wave of embarrassment as I thought how my attempt at impressing Richard Gere had made the rest of the dinner party think I was on something more than just those one to three glasses of rosé.*

All alcoholic beverages should be multiplied by three.

Suddenly there was an audible and collective gasp and the sound of a loud smack. I turned toward the noise and saw what everyone had actually been talking about—a woman who was passed out facedown on a stone pathway leading to the house. I wasn't sure how or why she had fallen, but I did know she was down. And not moving. Everyone at the party, in one quick motion, bolted—either for their car, or the house, or anyplace that wasn't that path. The only people left behind with this woman were Richard Gere, and me. Oh yeah, and Mark. I guess he remembered I had the car keys.

"Call the paramedics," Richard Gere stated with as much command as Zack Mayo reincarnated. I knelt down beside Zack—er, Richard Gere—and attempted to administer first aid.

Mark rolled his eyes and flatly stated, "I'm not calling the paramedics. She's had too much to drink. Or something."

"Just call the paramedics!" I shouted perhaps with too much zeal. Take that, Debra Winger.

Richard Gere spoke gently to the woman on the pavement while cradling her head. Immediately, I regretted not falling on my face and only tripping over the hem of my stupid dress. "Hon, can you tell me your name? How old are you? Are you in any pain? Did you take any medication, because it's very important we know . . ."

Richard Gere is an angel and deserves the Presidential Medal of Freedom, I thought to myself. I was awakened from my reverie by the voice of Mark, who once again seemed to have lost his friend group and was now trying to glom on to mine. "Let's go, she's fine," he said.

"You are a monster," I hissed, "clearly she is not fine." Actually, she was laying/lying (never sure which one is which) in the arms of

Richard Gere, so she was probably faring better than 99 percent of the human population. I worked my way to the other side of the woman, whose name we still didn't know. I wanted Richard Gere to see me and to know that we were in this thing together and that I would never abandon him like that hooker Julia Roberts did in *Pretty Woman*. Or the way that two-timing Diane Lane did in *Unfaithful*. Or the way that underserved political wife Lauren Hutton did in *American Gigolo*. Or the way that model Cindy Crawford did in real life. No sir, I was in it for the long haul. If only Richard Gere would have opened his eyes, he would have known.

"I think I'm dying from embarrassment," the woman on the pavement said, as she slowly came to while trying to cover her face with her napkin.

Doing my usual awkward chatter, I chimed in with, "You can't die from embarrassment. Trust me, I'm living proof!" Richard Gere laughed. A genuine laugh. His laughter was like the purest form of crack cocaine and immediately I wanted more. I knew I would have to wait because the woman on the pavement took precedent.

"Are you in any pain? And have you taken any medication?" Richard Gere asked again. The man had the patience of Job. Mark suddenly appeared with a phone in his hand and started asking the woman on the pavement the exact same questions that Richard Gere, the saint, has already asked.

"Why are you bothering her?" I said, somewhat annoyed.

"Because you told me to call the paramedics and they are asking!" Mark barked like a caveman. Then he asked the woman on the pavement, "How old are you?" The nerve.

"You do not have to answer that," I responded.

Mark cut me off, "Yes she does, 911 is asking."

"Hon, how old are you?" Richard Gere cooed.

"Forty," I purred in reply. Now Mark, Richard Gere, and perhaps even the woman on the pavement were staring at me like I had a screw loose. Although who was the woman on the pavement to judge anyone at this point?

Mark made a break for the front of the house (thank god), and I was finally alone with Richard Gere. Well, except for the woman on the pavement, who was still between us.

Damn her. Richard Gere seemed to be preoccupied with her well-being, despite my best efforts at ignoring her occasional moans of discomfort, so once again I decided to try my hand at small talk. I learned from watching the TV show *Survivor* that people who go through traumatic experiences together are sometimes bound to one another for life, and this was certainly traumatic.

"At least we'll have a story to tell our grandkids!" is what fell out of my mouth. (Where the eagles cry, on the mountain high.)

Richard Gere didn't get a chance to respond to how happy he was about our being bonded for life because suddenly, headed in the direction of our special private moment, was Mark Consuelos, accompanied by a Long Island EMT carrying a jump bag.

"Hey Richid, hey Kelly. Yous doin' a movie out here?" he deadpanned. You gotta love Long Island. From the regional accent to the familiar greeting, this guy had seen it all and was not impressed by any of it. Certainly not as impressed as I was. He took out a flashlight and shined it on the woman on the pavement. "Do you know how old she is?" "Do you know if she's taken anything or had too much to drink?" he asked Richard Gere as if he was placing an order at Burger King.

"No, she said she didn't have anything to drink. She just sort of fell facedown on the pavement," Richard Gere said with authority—which of course made sense since he has played a doctor in the movies.

"So embarrassed . . ." murmured the woman on the pavement once again. Obviously, she hated to have to share the spotlight with Richard Gere. "All I had was a pot brownie." Yes. The woman on the pavement who had assured us that she hadn't had anything to drink, and no medication, declared that she had eaten a pot brownie. No wonder I couldn't get my hands on any of the brownies.

Suddenly the EMT was shining his flashlight in Richard Gere's handsome face and mine. I wondered if he thought we took pot brownies. "Don't look at us, I had berries and cream and he had the off-menu key lime pie!" I declared. And with that, Mark stated that we should go home and get out of the way of the EMT so he could do his job. It was a cock block if ever there was one.

"We didn't want to move her in case there was a neck injury, and really just wanted to wait until you got here," Mark told the EMT, as if he gave one rat's ass about that woman. Then the EMT took out his cell phone and asked Mark if he could get a shot of the two of them together because his wife and mother were Mark's biggest fans. He handed me his phone, and I took a secret selfie with Richard Gere and handed it back to him. Take that, Mr. EMT.

And then, I double kissed Richard Gere good night as one does, and yelled down to the stoner on the pavement, "I hope you feel better soon."

For the next two months I told the story of Richard Gere and me saving the life of a stoner on Long Island. I told all my friends. I told Mark, who reminded me every time that he was there, and that I was making a way bigger deal out of the event than it was, because he is a hater. I told the people at the King Kullen. I told everyone at

Soul Cycle. I told my shrink. I told my mom. I told my audience. I told myself that one day when Richard Gere needed a young starlet to play a caring surgical resident, I would be the first and only person he thought of.

An addendum: After an entire summer of telling my Richard Gere story, I wound up at the home of our dear friend Sandy Gallin, may he rest in peace. Sandy, much like Jane Buffett, was a consummate host. At Sandy's you always enjoyed the best food, guests, and stories—it was always a two-trips-around-the-buffet-line party. As I queued up for Mark's plate, who did I see standing right before me in line? Bathed in a halo of glorious light? That's right. You can hear the song, can't you? ("Who knows what tomorrow brings? In a world, few hearts survive.")

Richard Gere was standing right in front of me, luminous with his tan skin and flesh-colored loincloth. Or maybe it was a white linen shirt and beige trousers. It's hard to remember every detail. Either way, I began to tremble at the thought of our previous encounter, just two months ago. Should I put my head on his shoulder? Embrace him from behind? I didn't have much time to fantasize about our greeting because right away, Mark barreled over, hand extended, megawatt smile blazing. "Richard! Mark Consuelos, great to see you." I like that Mark always introduces himself to everyone, whether he's met them once or six thousand times. I find it positively charming, although at that moment, I was beyond irritated that he was interrupting my alone time with Richard Gere once again. Especially since I was already getting his plate, so there was no reason for him to be here.

"Hey Mark, how are you?" said Richard Gere, his own megawatt smile on display. This was like *GQ*'s version of an MMA fight.

Boys don't fight over me, it's embarrassing, I thought to myself. They began a game of conversational badminton. "How's your summer been?" "Too short." "Same." Blah, blah, blah. Back and forth.

To the untrained ear it probably sounded like regular small talk, but I knew better. I decided to put an end to all this cocksmanship and blurted, "Do you remember when we saved that woman's life at Jane Buffett's house during Anjelica's birthday party?" There was a pause, perhaps too long a pause, then a flash of recognition on Richard Gere's face. Thank god.

He looked into my eyes, smiled, and then asked quizzically, "You were there?"

Mark fell over laughing. Like a cackling hyena. Richard joined in the laughter, although why, I'm not sure. "Yes, I was there. Right there," (by your side) I stammered. "How can you not remember? We were on the ground with that woman until the paramedics came." I tried not to look or sound as crushed as I was. Good bye Golden Globes. Good bye *Vanity Fair* Oscar party. Good bye Dalai Lama.

"Yea, I guess there was so much going on I wasn't really paying attention," Richard Gere said with a chuckle. Not paying attention to the greatest costar you have ever had? Will ever have? Suddenly I felt like Paula back in the factory. Or Vivian back to hooking on Hollywood Boulevard. Or oddly, Leon the pimp from *American Gigolo.* (Just google the reference, I can't do all the heavy lifting here.)

Needless to say, Mark was merciless. To this day he has never let me live down my conviction that I should have become a celebrated trauma specialist, but also that I would make the greatest costar/love interest Richard Gere has ever had.

A second addendum: Several years later, I was asked to give one of the eulogies for my dear friend and cosmetic dermatologist Fred Brandt. As I mentioned previously, Fred was the greatest doctor, but also one of the greatest characters I've ever met. He was incredibly funny and never took himself or the beauty business too seriously. He was the doctor to the stars, socialites, other doctors, and regular people. His heart was the only thing bigger than his talent. His memorial service was jam-packed with the glitterati of New York, London, LA, Miami, and pretty much anywhere else people age. Needless to say, I was terrified. I wanted to hit the right note but knew Fred would be watching and would hate if I made it too somber. Luckily, my speech was well received, and afterward people were filing past me to say how much they enjoyed what I had said, and how funny they thought it was, and how much Fred would have liked it.

I stayed until just about every person left, as I was waiting for the endless New York City springtime rain to cease, because naturally I had forgotten my umbrella. As I was walking out of Alice Tully Hall at Lincoln Center, I saw a woman approach me. She was familiar to me, but for the life of me I couldn't remember her name. That always happens to me. The woman had a sheepish smile on her face when she got to me, and so I had to fake it. "How are you?" I asked hoping the name would come out of my mouth at the eleventh hour.

"Oh, Kelly, you probably don't remember me, but you saved my life a few years ago at Jane Buffett's house." ("WHERE THE EAGLES FLY ON MOUNTAIN HIGH!")

I looked around hoping against hope that anyone else I'd told this story to, which is everyone, had overheard, but we were the only two people left. "Well, you look great," I said. "I should have known you were a patient of Fred Brandt's, Richard Gere and I could not figure out your age to tell the paramedics."

And, this woman, whose name I never learned but I now love with all my heart, asked the perfect question: "He was there?"

"I know who I was this morning, but I've changed a few times since then."

—ALICE IN *ALICE IN WONDERLAND*

CHAPTER THIRTEEN

I MIGHT HAVE BEEN HIGH, POSSIBLY, MAYBE

I might be high. Right now. I say I might be high because I'm not entirely sure. I don't take drugs, so an extra-strength Tylenol makes me appear like I've mainlined . . . something one would mainline. Again, not sure what mainlining is, but I heard the phrase used once in a movie in reference to what I think was drugs. I can't be sure, maybe they were talking about a fancy part of Philadelphia. It isn't my area of expertise, and like I said, I might be high.

It has suddenly occurred to me that maybe you have no idea who I am. You may not be a TV person. Maybe you don't own a TV. Maybe you just grabbed this book in an airport. I get it. The skirt on the cover is electrifying. Maybe someone gave this to you as a gift. Maybe you thought this was a book about Sarah Jessica Parker because, let's face it, my hair does fall in soft waves around my face just like hers. If you aren't familiar with my talk show, I don't recommend you start viewing now. Wait until you're hospitalized. That is how most people find me—when they are hospitalized and can't change the channel. But, if you do watch my show, you will know I don't do well taking pills. Advil to vitamin C makes me feel loopy. I am willing, however, to take the risk of pills for the sake of my neck. And public speaking. But that was an accident.

You should know, as I am writing this, I am recovering from a mild form of plastic surgery. "Mild" meaning, no aftermarket parts were added. I don't necessarily believe in changing the bones of a fine house—just now and again rehanging the curtains. I had been feeling bad about my neck, or, the appearance of my neck, I should say. Is a turtleneck really meant to go all the way over the chin and lower lip? I don't think so. Well, guess what? After a year and a half of office Zooms, school Zooms, family Zooms, and broadcasting a nationally syndicated talk show through a computer hole, I only wanted to wear my turtlenecks pulled up over my entire face. My neck had become a source of deep self-loathing. The appearance of it, I mean.

Don't get me wrong, I'm eternally grateful that my neck does everything it is supposed to. It holds up my head, it makes it move left to right, and up and down. I mean, it helps me dance if the music is good. It whips my hair back and forth. It does all the stuff. It does all the neck-y stuff. But I am currently faced with two issues: One is physical pain. The other is emotional.

For reasons still unclear to me, I thought it would be a productive distraction to write a book, in the middle of the universe falling apart and between my hectic Zoom schedule and on the precipice of menopause. I was wrong. I thought it would be easy, frankly, because I know some real dipshits who have allegedly "written" books. Now that I'm in the process of actually writing my own, I realize that they obviously had a ghostwriter, or more likely, dug up an entire graveyard of ghosts to help them write their books.

Writing is hard. It's hard on the brain, especially since I never worked up to my potential in school, according to all of my teachers back in South Jersey. I used to think that was just a load of bullshit, but now, as I google when and how to use a semicolon, I realize that they had a point. I also still have no idea when or how to use a semicolon, even after googling. But as hard as it is on the brain, it's even harder on the neck. In particular, the back of my neck. Writing leads to a lot of stiffness, soreness, and whatnot as I crane over my laptop trying to figure out what tense is the right one and whether what I am writing will actually be interesting to anyone besides Mark, who has to say nice things.

But the front of my neck? The front of my neck hurts my eyes, and I suppose, hurts my ego. I will log on to a Zoom meeting, and immediately be greeted by the Crypt Keeper in the form of my face being kept in the digital waiting room. Because I loathe Zoom tardiness, I'm usually the first person to log on, giving me plenty of time to drink in my own appearance. Not to mention, plenty of time to focus on troubleshooting. I started doing practical things, like adding a ring light. Then a second ring light. Then a third. My home office/bedroom took on the ambient lighting of an amateur porn set, minus the tacky furniture and fake orgasms. It wasn't enough. The neck was still an issue. So, I started stacking my computer on top of my old encyclopedias, to get a faraway angle and to force me to look up when on the Zooms. UP! That way my neck, jowls, and subsequent folds of skin could fall back and away. Still, not enough. Then, I resorted to DEFCON 5—toupee tape at the nape of my neck, because from experience I can tell you that masking, duct, and electrical tape will result in severe skin and hair loss. I taped my excess neck skin behind me, which was way more comfortable than the chip clip I had tried first. (Relax, I didn't put it back on the chips.) The truth is, my neck was aging in dog years compared to my face, and the amount of Botox required to make my neck match my face would have resulted in a complete inability to . . . breathe. But, I tried, I tried everything because I always think surgery should be a last resort to repair one's vanity. Don't forget, you are reading the book of a woman who refers to her bosom as a 32 AA long . . .

Now, here, I would like to take a minute to pause and contextualize my neck issues as revealed during the global pandemic. I realize that in the grand scheme of all the human suffering experienced due to COVID-19, my neck is a minor thing. I already know that I'm lucky. Mark reminds me often that I have three healthy children. My mother reminds me that I am lucky in general, and, if I don't like the way I look, I should just take off my glasses. I'm very fortunate to have people who keep me grounded. But it really is the audience at home that keeps me the most grounded, and by grounded, I mean stomped into the ground. Just take a look at the comments on my Instagram pages. While I don't take comments on social media very seriously, there was a recurring theme that my neck was starting to resemble a vagina. It can't be said enough, no man is dealing with those comments no matter how many labia folds his neck features.

I started doing that thing women, and I suspect some men, my age, do. I began comparing my neck to other necks out there. This is particularly hard to do nowadays because we mostly only see one another on social media, and I think we can all agree that there is some optical illusion filtering going on there. I don't like to edit my photos. I feel like it's false advertising. That's what cosmetic dermatologists and plastic surgeons are for. They are the lord's filter. That's also why I keep the holy trinity on speed dial: Dr. Robert Anolik, Dr. Roy Geronemus, and Dr. David Rosenberg. Why would I falsely edit a photo on FaceApp, when I can have Dr. R do the actual work? I talk the talk, and he lifts the neck.

Also, like social media, plastic surgery should be used sparingly. If your house needs to be painted, you wouldn't burn it to the ground, you'd paint it. And my neck needed to be painted.

In terms of necks needing work, mine was at the very low end of the neck spectrum, the necktrum, if you will. Listen, compared to some necks I've known, I felt okay about mine. But soon, I started noticing necks that appeared to be aging in reverse. How could this be? These are the same necks who claim they only meditate and drink water and have never ever tried Botox. I think those necks are full of shit. Although, in fairness, my mom is in her eighties, and has a long, line-free neck, and has never had any help whatsoever. No Botox, no nothing. But she also doesn't wear makeup, hunch over a computer, or do anything I would consider remotely stressful.

So after more comprehensive research, 750,000 Zoom meetings, and deep comparative analysis with other necks, I saw where things were headed. I'm all about being proactive with small, incremental, and preventative changes, rather than the full *Silence of the Lambs* situation down the line.

Also, I know what I look like. I'm not delusional, and I don't fuck with things that aren't asking for it. Do I wish I had bigger boobs? Of course, but unless my boobs are going to interview Hugh Jackman, they can just stay trapped in their 32 AA bra and pipe down. Luckily, the vast majority of the universe pays me no mind. Talking about my boobs interviewing Hugh Jackman reminds me that I might be high.

Which brings me to a recent family trip.

Our family traveled to Europe together this past year. It was a graduation gift, originally for our son Michael, who got a BFA at NYU film school, and our niece Isabella, who graduated high school. When the pandemic happened, naturally the trip was postponed, like everything else for everyone else. I use the word "trip" deliberately. I do not use the word "vacation." Remember, any travel involving more than one person needing diapers and/or a tackle box of medication is a trip, NOT a vacation.

The reason I bring up the trip, not vacation, is because *Riverdale*, the show in which Mark played the divinely evil Hiram Lodge, is extremely popular in Europe. Well, the show is extremely popular everywhere, but not popular enough for me to live the life of a spoiled Hollywood wife, which is all I really want. It's what we all want, isn't it? When Mark's Apple/Netflix/Hulu/Quibi pilot gets picked up for ten seasons . . . bye guys, I'm off the air faster than an ABC sitcom. I am completely prepared to rest and spend Mark's money. Just kidding, I've been doing that all along.

Anyway, back to me possibly being high. No wait, back to my neck. No wait, back to Europe, which will eventually bring me to my neck, and then to me being potentially high. Still with me? Good. Let's proceed.

I have mentioned this before, but it bears repeating that when we are together, Mark is always the one who gets recognized, not me. This is especially true in other countries, and especially now with the whole RP (*Riverdale* phenomenon). In any little town, in Italy, Greece, France, or really anywhere young people are congregating, there comes the familiar look of shock when they see Mark, followed by hushed squeals, some sort of ARB (all *River-*

dale bulletin) sent by Insta-Snap-TikTok to any and all people under the age of twenty-three in a twenty-mile radius. Sometimes the only English these fans know is "Hiram" or "*Riverdale.*" With shaking hands, they ask for "un foto?" That's when I heroically step in, because a good Hollywood wife knows the importance of well-documented fan interaction and appreciation. And, if a fan can't post their encounter on social media, then it didn't happen. I should point out that in this new era of everyone being connected to their phones/cameras at all times, fan snaps are quick and easy. Once upon a time, a fan photo took an eternity. From the wife yelling to the husband in another terminal, who had the camera somewhere in his luggage, to the turning on of the flash, to the winding of the film, to the needing to take a second shot because someone was certain they blinked. Now it's easy breezy. Just, "Here lady, un foto with Hiram," followed by a cell phone being thrust in my direction. What I'm never prepared for, however, is the face staring back at me on the phone screen. No, not of my husband or the group gathered around him, mind you. Oh no, what I see is myself, at a horribly close angle. Due to CSM (chronic selfie mode, a modern affliction we all suffer from. Admit it.), I am always faced with the reality of my face. Which is fine, but only when I'm expecting it. The look of my neck on selfie mode sucks the joy right out of the moment. Instead of Hiram Lodge, these fans get Dobby from *Harry Potter.* Un foto from hell.

So, with all the neck issues staring me in the face, I decided to get to work. Or to get the work. And afterward I took a Valium, as prescribed by my doctor, to calm my neck muscles enough to swallow . . . mostly my pride. I was supposed to take Percocet, but

I had that after my first C-section, and all that did was make me constipated. So, my plan was the Valium and then a Tylenol. Remember, I don't take pills. Ever. Not even Advil. So, I was a little worried about the Valium. But I took it, and then I started writing this chapter. Lucky YOU! As you can tell, I'm not great with downtime.

There was only one other time I took a Valium—although, now that I think about it, maybe it was a Xanax? Are they the same? Or wait, was it a Klonopin? I don't know for sure, but I took something. It was actually only a half of whatever pill it was, because again, I don't take pills. But I'm pretty certain I was high then. For sure.

Here's why I took that pill, whatever it was. I AM TERRIFIED OF PUBLIC SPEAKING! Funny, right?

I know. It doesn't make any sense. How can a talk show host be afraid of public speaking? It's more common than you think. We should all start a support group. Also, I don't really think of myself as a talk show host, or a "TV presenter," as they say in the UK. (I like that better. They also call talk shows "chat shows." Not sure how I feel about that. Chatting feels comfortable and something done between friends. While I am friendly with many of the guests on *Live!*, and certainly with Ryan, I would not say that the atmosphere is all friendly, all the time. They also call them "breakfast shows." That I don't mind as much because it implies that food might be served.) In my nonwork life, I go to great lengths to avoid speaking engagements. Hosting events, other than my own talk show, fills me with a level of dread that I cannot explain. Even doing other talk shows, hosted by my friends, renders me unable to eat or sleep. I'm ashamed to admit that I've turned down incredible opportunities that other more outgoing hosts would and have jumped at. I kept at it for so long, trying and trying, thinking exposure therapy would cure me of my public speaking fear. I figured I'd eventually outgrow whatever form of stage fright this was. But let's face it, at my age, I'm done outgrowing.

I do make exceptions, occasionally, to present an award to a friend. Or participate in a roast, or moderate a book event, but it is always for someone I love more than myself. And it always takes at least a year off my life.

It was May 9, 2015, and I was being honored with the GLAAD Excellence in Media Award. I certainly didn't feel worthy of such an honor, but certainly knew the importance of GLAAD and all the work the organization does to promote positive LGBTQUIA representation in media. So even though I have a horrible fear of public speaking, I agreed to accept the honor and say a few words. Plus, I welcomed the opportunity to acknowledge *Live!* as well, for allowing open and normal on-air conversations with and about gay people on morning TV, which I didn't realize was a rare thing, until it was pointed out to me by everyone.

Making matters better and worse, one of my dearest friends, Anderson Cooper, would be presenting me the award. The last thing I wanted to do was put more on Anderson's plate. I was, and am, always mindful of Anderson's plate. For it is perpetually loaded with the weight of the world, seriously, and his plate does not need any extra helpings from me. The good news was that a ton of my friends would be attending in addition to Anderson, as well as my kids. It was to be their first ever, nonschool, fancy event. Even though they were confounded by the fact I was getting any kind of award at all.

As I sat in a chair in my bathroom, which had become the de facto makeup and hair station for the evening's festivities, Joaquin had some questions. "Why are you getting an award for being friends with Anderson?"

"She's GETTING an award from Anderson," corrected Lola.

"Okay, but . . . Why?" demanded Joaquin.

Yeah. Why? demanded the voice in my head. I sat waiting for Lola to answer our questions, but she just eyeballed me instead, as if to say, "Go ahead, lady, we're all waiting . . ."

I struggled to formulate the correct response. We have tried to raise our kids with the foundational belief that all people are created equal. I know, now, that my naïveté sounds preposterous. I just wanted to lend my voice to protect the marital and employment rights of LGBTQUIA people, which were at the time, and are perpetually, on the chopping block. My kids have always had gay and lesbian people in their lives. Not just family and friends, but teachers, doctors, and their friends' parents as well. I didn't want to say something that would give them the idea that being a member of the LGBTQUIA community was somehow a problem.

"Well, I . . . you know, when people . . . when people . . . um . . ." I searched for words, filling the space in the hope that maybe they would fall asleep.

At this point Michael entered the room, because, apparently, we were having a contest to see how many bodies we could fit into our bathroom. "Will there be a trophy?" Michael asked. This caught everyone's interest. The idea of a trophy canceled out all the chatter about why I was being honored.

"I don't know. Maybe? I assume, but I don't want to say yes

because I really didn't ask." Forget about equality, folks. Just tell me if there is a prize. Could you imagine?

I wrote my speech for that night several times. After every draft, I'd rehearse it out loud with Albert Bianchini, my producing partner, and the brother I never had, timing me. I'd been told that the speech should be between two and five minutes, but no longer.

I would have preferred the speech to be no longer than five seconds, or however long it took to say, "Thank you!" and walk off the stage. Eventually, and with much anxiety and hand-wringing, I got it to a place where I felt as comfortable as possible for me. The speech was two and a half minutes long, with me speaking at my normal pace. I knew, however, that once I took the stage, my nerves would kick in, and my mouth would start to move at lightning speed. At least twenty seconds would be shaved off my time. This could be problematic.

"Kel, you should take a Klonny," Albert advised. Because Albert knows me better than most people, he had been watching my anxiety level build slowly over the weeks leading up to the event. Now, there I was standing before him, at the cocktail hour before my big moment, with shaking hands and cottonmouth.

"I don't take drugs, Albert. Maybe just grab me a vodka." I decided to focus on my kids, who looked so beautiful, the boys in their suits and Lola in her dress. "Guys, you look great! Isn't this fun?" Lola and Michael enthusiastically agreed that it was so fun, but Joaquin confessed he was feeling sick. "What kind of sick? Do you have a fever? Do you need to leave?" That's when the kids told me about the sushi they had ordered for lunch, that didn't look right, but Joaquin ate anyway. I watched Joaquin dissolve very quickly before my eyes. He started sweating profusely, and then doubled over in pain. Michael volunteered to take him to the bathroom. I volunteered to take him to the emergency room.

"No, you stay, I'll take him home," my long-suffering chief of staff, and only staff member, Lauren Travaglione, chimed in. I considered firing her on the spot for insubordination.

The dinner bell rang, letting the crowd know they had ten minutes to grab a decent Ketel One cocktail. (Thank you, sponsors!) That bell also meant that in a matter of minutes, I would be paralyzed with fear in front of the chicest group the Waldorf Astoria had seen in years, and my friend Anderson Cooper.

Cue the cottonmouth and add in flop sweats.

As the speech approached, so did my thirst for that vodka martini. Albert had a supernatural ability of knowing exactly when I needed a drink, and right on cue, procured one and walked it to me. "You okay, Boo?" he asked. I didn't answer, and instead attempted to peruse my speech, which Lauren had printed out on note cards, while gulping down my martini. Despite the booze, my mouth was far too dry for talking anyway.

At first I thought my speech was written in another language, as I couldn't read the words. But then, I realized it was just because my hands were shaking. Anderson, his then partner Benjamin, and Mark walked over to see if I was ready to go into dinner, since the kids, minus Joaquin, were already at our table along with a few close friends who had come to lend support.

"She's freaking out. I think she should take a Klonny. You want a Klonny, Kel?" Albert asked. I shook my head. I didn't want to waste my limited amount of saliva on idle chit chat.

"If you're nervous, a half a Xanax won't hurt," Anderson

agreed. Then Mark agreed, then Benjamin. My girlfriend, Rachael Harris, one of the funniest, brightest, and most intuitive actors on earth, came to check on me. Upon seeing me try to suck the vodka off my note cards, and hearing the discussion of nerves, she began searching her purse for said Klonny, while the men attempted to procure a Xanax from somewhere. I was left to wonder if the swag bags contained benzos. In all the commotion, panic, and frankly vodka, I felt a half of something pill shaped slip into my cards-free hand. Without thinking, I slipped that half of whatever it was into my bone-dry mouth and washed it down with the rest of Albert's gimlet. On an empty stomach no less. What could possibly go wrong?

After a beautiful introduction from Anderson, I gave my speech. I think. You see, I was immediately high, so I have no recollection of it whatsoever. Through the miracle that is YouTube, I've been able to piece together a sequence of events. If you want a laugh, now that you have the backstory, I invite you to travel on over to YouTube yourself for a real treat at my expense.

What I will tell you is this: I don't know how I got to the stage. I assured Michael that I did, indeed, get a trophy, which I am sure the folks at GLAAD found as gauche as it sounds now and was a complete ad lib and deviation from the speech I had worked and reworked with Albert. Perhaps I have a side hustle in improv?

I know that I began to slur my words. I am not proud of this. I am also not proud that I made a great big deal out of how good-looking my friend Anderson Cooper is. Everyone knows Anderson Cooper is insanely handsome. He's on television every night. He's a best-selling author. His mother was Gloria Vanderbilt. Did he need my drug-addled self to say how handsome he was? Also, why did I keep with the ad-libbing? This was clearly going nowhere fast.

Anderson, I am sorry.

When I finally managed to get it together, I made it clear that I knew what a difference that Anderson had made in my life. How he had given voice to so many voiceless people in society. I talked about how those who had felt marginalized or threatened in any way needed to be championed, and that Anderson had done that. I talked about Matthew Shepard and Tyler Clementi and how we all needed to remember those who could not fight for their basic human rights any longer.

Then, I decided to remind the room that Mark and I had recently celebrated our nineteenth wedding anniversary, and that we were lucky to have spent our entire marriage surrounded by, loved by, and influenced by the LGBTQUIA community. Which is true. And I do feel fortunate. Then from the stage, I used my psychic powers to will Albert Bianchini to read my mind, and bring me a glass of water, as my mouth was turning into paste. But I guess we know who took the other half of the Xanax, because he was picking up on nothing. So, I needed to loudly instruct him from the stage to bring me a glass of water. Which he did. I only know because I watched it on YouTube.

In case you missed it, I was high.

I prattled on, paste mouth and all, eventually rambling to the end when I felt the need to close with a confession. That's right folks. I confessed to everyone that I had chomped down half a Xanny. My two and a half minutes had morphed into seven. I was honored, but I was also HIGH. I think.

That was my last experience with loopy-ness. Until now. Public speaking and neck reconstruction, both extreme and necessary measures.

In closing, they haven't come up with a pill to cure the fear of public speaking, nor a pill to relieve the dreaded beaver neck. But I guarantee you, when they do, those pills will just make me high.

"You see much more
of your kids when they
leave home."

—LUCILLE BALL

CHAPTER FOURTEEN

THIS NEST IS CLEAN

I remember the exhaustion being overwhelming, but not as over-whelming as the sense of joy, purpose, and the intense love that overrode any need for sleep, or clean clothes, or a hot shower.

Although I still desired basic hygiene, it suddenly and eternally took a secondary role. I just wanted to look at them all the time. Stare at them all the time. Watch them change minute by minute, while simultaneously willing them to stay exactly as they were, right then and there.

The them being our children.

The me declaring every single phase my favorite.

Each of them.

Every second.

It never got less exciting.

But . . .

It never got less exhausting. Everyone told us to cherish those moments because they'd grow up and be out of the nest in the blink of an eye. Our parents told us. Our friends with grown kids told us. Strangers told us. They tried to prepare us.

They warned us!

However . . .

Bestowing that advice on people who haven't slept in five to eighteen years isn't helpful in real time because to the tired people, anything positive seems impossible to believe. But those words did come back in waves as the deadline drew ever nearer to The

Emptying, with each little chicken leaving our nest in the order in which they arrived. With each departure, Mark would comfort me that we still had two more in the nest, then, one more in the nest. Then, he started thinking of ways to distract from the impending empty nest. I started thinking how the phrase "empty nest" sounded like the word "emptiness." Was reality trolling us?

As my kids left, the anxiety attacks started as I thought back on all the things I should have paid more attention to. Did I drink in the baby smell enough? There is nothing quite as intoxicating as the smell of a baby. Could I conjure it now? Did I kiss the boo-boos away enough? Did I teach them how to kiss away their own boo-boos when I wasn't nearby? Did I listen to their laughter enough? Could I recall each giggle when I needed a pick-me-up? Did I give them enough reasons to laugh? Did I listen to their sorrow enough? Or did I tell them to suck it up? Was I nurturing enough? Was I protective enough? Was I mommy enough? Was I enough, enough?

And so, I kept dwelling on all the things that I missed or forgot or left undone—all the morning drop-offs that I missed, the permission slip I forgot to sign, the homework I didn't check, and then found in my purse days later. The special after-school snack I was supposed to include in the lunch box the day the kids had play rehearsal. The day I forgot to bring the costumes to play rehearsal.

All the wisdom I sort of half instilled in my kids because taking the shortcut to wisdom was easier at the time.

I began reminiscing scenes from their childhood, including the many nights we crammed together into one little bed because my kids loved to sleep like a pack of kittens when they were young. I have vivid memories of reading "Hansel and Gretel" to them over and over, as for some reason, it was their favorite. It was a story I had also loved as a kid, because I found the pictures of the gingerbread house to be enchanting, and my children were also enthralled by the whimsical fantasy cottage made of sugar and candy. To them, and my childhood self, that was to be the focal point of the entire book. But reading that story as an adult, I saw it differently. That is some dark stuff. Even the updated, less horrifying version, is still rather horrifying. So, I started making small edits here and there to make it a little more "child-friendly." I would change a word, or gloss over something sinister. I would skip an entire page if it was potentially nightmare inducing.

There was an unmistakable and troubling trend in most of the stories I read to my kids, be it the Brothers Grimm, Charles Perrault, or Hans Christian Andersen. It was as if these authors all worked from the same playbook. The mother is almost always missing—dead, or mysteriously unmentioned, or generally not present—and in her place is an evil stepmother, or an evil stepsister. Or an evil queen. Or an evil witch. The fathers are almost always benevolently present and hapless and more often than not, inert. They are powerless to stop the wicked female from torturing the children, and usually complicit in the evil deeds she commits against the creatures she deems so burdensome. So, the moral of these stories was, it's never too early to start conditioning the children of the world to be little misogynists.

But I didn't mention any of that at the time. I didn't say, "You know, Joaquin, the house may look delicious, sure, but why is every woman in this story portrayed as an evil witch? What do those Brothers Grimm have against their mother anyway?" Or "Lola, listen, I'm not sure where Snow White's mom is, or why her stepmother is completely homicidal over her young stepdaughter's looks, but comparing your looks to anyone else's is a fool's errand, as is sitting around waiting to be rescued by some prince." Or "Michael, just because a young woman seems trapped in a tower and in desperate need of a haircut, doesn't mean she's actually trapped. It's more of a metaphor for the struggle women face in every aspect of life. Especially in finding a good, reasonably priced haircut."

But I didn't say any of that, which in hindsight, was the right call. The kids probably would have thought I was having a nervous breakdown. And maybe I was. Thinking about those nights of bedtime stories now, I laugh at the way I tried to edit the world for my children. This was my attempt to make them feel safe, like the world outside our front door was not going to be tricky, or dangerous, or scary. I wanted them to feel as safe and as cozy as we all did those nights, bundled up in that bed, reading books. I certainly never wanted them to know how I felt when I woke up with a kink in my neck from falling asleep, surrounded by my kids and books and stuffed animals. Exhausted to the point of tears, but with no time to cry because I had to get ready for work. And work. And work.

Those days felt so long, like they'd last forever.

It was one of those long days when a woman approached me in the Fairway near our apartment as I was attempting to push a double stroller with a child skateboard attachment on the back, down one of the aisles. If you don't live in New York City, you might not understand what a preposterous feat that was. We have no mega stores in the city. No Costco. No Publix. We recently got a Target on the Upper East Side, but I hear it sucks. So, there was no space for one human being in the aisle, much less one pushing two kids in a double stroller, with a third behind the stroller on a skateboard.

As the woman approached, I remember the feeling of dread, and started to mentally prepare to defend myself over having an obstructive Land Cruiser in such a prohibitive space. I reminded myself that I had just as much right as she did to pay quadruple the price for my broccoli as she did, even with my kids in that stroller.

I squared off, pulling the stroller back and attempting to turn it around in case some shit went down. The entire movement turned into a thirteen-point turn—which was very irritating, if not exhausting. Then, the woman did something I never saw coming, she smiled at me and said, "Just remember, sweetheart, the days are long, but the years are short." Then, she leaned down and cooed at the kids, who were sleeping, and told Michael she could tell he was a good big brother. Michael puffed up at the compliment.

I focused on her words.

The days are long, but the years are short.

Of course, at the time, those words were like a foreign language. I wanted to say, "Listen lady, the years are long, too. Wanna know the last time I showered all my body parts at the same time?" But instead, I said, "Oh yes . . . Sorry about the stroller . . ." I was in that place of the forever apology, whether or not it was warranted. I was so tired and brittle. But I was also incredibly relieved to be given words of kindness and attempted encouragement that I may have cried but pretended it was allergies.

Moments like these played like a loop in my mind, over and over, as I watched my children prepare to go into the world beyond our door, and set up for the life I would have once they were gone. Mark and I had no idea what was before us. Just as we were the first in our peer group to have kids, we would be the first to face the inevitable emptying of the nest.

When Michael decided to go to NYU, Mark and I actively attempted to change his mind. "You can't go to college here. You grew up HERE! Go to UT, you loved Austin. Or go to USC, or to Chapman in California. You loved all of their film programs.

Go to one of those schools, but don't stay home." This became our mantra. "Go to Emerson! You liked that school. Remember?" But Michael was determined to go to NYU and enter one of their creative arts programs at Tisch. He wanted to be a storyteller like all the filmmakers he admired: Oliver Stone, Spike Lee, Martin Scorsese, and M. Night Shyamalan. This was exciting for him, and for us, but we encouraged him to apply to television and film programs all over the country. And when he was accepted, we encouraged him to attend the orientation days for incoming freshmen at those schools, to see if he could visualize himself living somewhere, anywhere else.

He did, in fact, love the food in Austin, Texas. He also showed a great affinity for the comic bookstore in Orange, California. He even indicated a deep appreciation for the architecture of Los Angeles. And he simply raved about the water pressure in the hotel shower, in Boston.

But we kept asking the question: Can you picture yourself here?

And we kept getting the same response: Um, I don't know.

Definitely not definitive.

Were we asking too much of an eighteen-year-old? How can young people be expected to know what they want to do for the rest of their lives at that age? I wondered about the stories I'd read, or documentaries I'd watched, or even people I'd interviewed, who said they always knew, since infancy, what they wanted to do for the rest of their lives. How can that be? I still don't know! But after this book hits the best-seller list, I think we'll all agree that I should become an author.

When we attended Accepted Freshman Day at NYU Tisch School of the Arts, we were genuinely impressed with the extraordinary welcome presentation, and the overall seamless organization of the various tours at the many different departments. Even if it was right down the street from where Michael grew up in SoHo, it stood out as an exceptional program. Michael even bumped into a group of kids he attended film camp with in Brooklyn when he was a middle schooler. As we stood in a hallway outside one of the administrative offices, waiting for our tour, we heard our name being called. The voice sounded oddly familiar. "Consuelos!" Mark and I both turned to see who was calling us, but the familiar voice wasn't calling us at all. The voice was connected to an even more familiar face and was headed toward Michael.

"You have to come to NYU because I am responsible for you being here, so . . ." beamed Chris Goutman, an incredibly gifted, five-time Emmy Award–winning director at *All My Children*. This was the man who directed the screen test between Mark and me, so as it turned out, he was responsible for Michael being here. At least theoretically. Chris, who has a megawatt smile and perfect bone structure, began his career as an actor. He then moved into directing and writing at several soap operas, including *All My Children*, *As the World Turns,* and eventually *Another World*. And now, our paths were crossing again, with Chris assuming the role of academic director and associate professor at NYU, Michael as aspiring actor/writer/director, and Kelly and Mark in the roles of supportive parents.

Chris remarked that he knew our son as soon as he saw him, because it was like looking at Mark all those years ago. He told Michael about the hands-on approach at the school, and how even the freshmen got to work on student film projects right away. We kibitzed for a few more minutes, catching up and reminiscing. Before saying goodbye, Chris turned to Michael, leaving him with some words of encouragement. He then turned to us one more time, flashed that megawatt smile, and was gone.

Then, it was time for us to explore the campus grounds. We strolled the streets around Greenwich Village with our third-year film student tour guide cast as our intrepid leader. This was an unmistakably non-campus-y campus, and basically the neighborhood where our kids grew up. But for the large purple-and-white NYU banners hanging from certain buildings, and balloon sculptures of the same color scheme adorning specific dorm/apartment housing, and our tour guides in their NYU T-shirts, one would never know we were on a college tour. We just looked like any other large group of tourists wandering aimlessly behind a purple flag.

Mark and I were struck by how terrified the other parents on our tour were. We couldn't help but eavesdrop as their questions of campus safety and police presence were stifled by their mortified children. I felt relieved knowing we weren't the only parents who embarrassed our kids. It was when we walked through the "quad," which was really just Washington Square Park, that I thought one of the moms from somewhere in the Midwest might actually die from an anxiety attack. I turned around to the mother, who nearly jumped out of her skin, and said, "This is a really safe city. I raised my kids here, and this park is where I took them every day. It gets a bad rap, but it's safe."

I began dragging this poor woman back in time with me, regaling her with stories of how different the city, and Washington Square Park, was when I was our kids' ages. How I was glad I persevered when it seemed like I was living in hostile territory. And that I was equally glad to have stayed the course when our family went from two to three, to four, to five. Although, we did make a short-lived and halfhearted attempt to retreat to the suburbs when Michael was a baby. It seemed like something we were supposed to do. But no amount of extra square footage or lush front lawn was worth the time spent commuting to and from work each day, and we quickly returned to the apartment we kept, just in case we changed our minds. As it turns out, the grass may be greener, but it's a pain in the ass to reach after 5:00 p.m. And nothing was more invigorating than raising kids in the city. That's when I noticed the lady's eyes started glazing over, and her husband finally came over to rescue her.

Long story longer, Michael chose NYU, and we were happy for him. We understood why it appealed to him, and we agreed that for what he wanted to study, and how he liked to learn, it was the best environment for him.

Lola, of course, began with a campaign of relentless haranguing. "Michael, are you nuts? You should go out to California. Who stays home? What is wrong with you?" Mark told Lola that if she thought California was right for her, then she should go to college there. "Oh, don't you worry, I will. There's no way I'm staying here. I'm either going to USC, or UCLA, or UC Irvine, or UC Santa Barbara, or UC San Diego, or Miami, or Hawaii. Does Hawaii have a college? You know Michael's going to be home every weekend. You know that right? You won't have to worry about that with me!" As unclear as Michael was about where he could see himself, Lola was crystal clear—she saw herself somewhere sunny and warm.

We pulled up one hour before our assigned drop-off time because Mark can't help himself. I was impressed by the organized chaos of it all, and equally impressed by the fabulous location. I couldn't believe they were giving first-year students, park-front housing at Washington Square West. The building housed approximately 700 students, and was ominously called a FYRE, but unlike the festival, this First-Year Residential Experience lived up to the hype. The former Hayden Hall was sparkling new, with a gut renovation generously sponsored by and renamed after Martin Lipton, a prominent alumnus of the School of Law who I assume is filthy rich. With common entertaining areas on several floors, party rooms with complete kitchens, and rehearsal and study spaces, the building was completely self-contained. It was secure and spacious, like a luxury condominium with what is known as the best dining hall on campus. It was also walking distance from the Kimmel Center, where many of Michael's classes were.

Michael lived in an air-conditioned, park-facing corner room on the fourteenth floor. He had two roommates, a kid from Singapore who lived in the single bedroom, and a kid from Mexico who shared a slightly larger room with Michael. All three of them shared a bathroom. I couldn't believe how big their dorm room was. I had always heard about the dire conditions of college dorm room life, not having gone to college myself. The small, cramped, and dank spaces, with communal, moldy bathrooms. I actually thought that dire conditions might be a good thing for the kids of this generation of participation trophies, without ever having to participate. Kids who had never held down part-time jobs and were heavy on social media and light on social skills. And yet, here I stood in a dorm room that was at least four times the size of my first three apartments. With air-conditioning and a park view!

Maybe the world outside our door didn't need much editing after all.

This room is too nice! This is so irritating! How are these kids ever going to learn anything if they don't experience hardship?!

Who said that?

I realized the voice in my head was beginning to sound an awful lot like my parents.

Mark got to work right away. With military precision, he somehow produced bed risers out of thin air and raised Michael's bed an additional two feet off the ground, providing plenty of storage space underneath. Michael, with the same task-oriented speed, began unboxing the mini fridge, microwave, and computer printer. He then stacked them in a diabolically genius way, for prime functionality and spatial efficiency. *He gets this from Mark's side of the family*, the voice in my head reminded me.

Meanwhile, I began the futile attempt to interior design a dorm room for three boys. I put down a fluffy bathmat in the bathroom and coordinating area rug in the small common area. Michael immediately rolled up the rug and handed it back to me. I unfolded a three-way dressing mirror and placed it in the corner. Michael refolded it and told me to save it for Lola's future dorm room. I pulled various objets d'art from a box that I had been saving for this day and placed them thoughtfully on his study desk. He followed behind me, and using his new Swiffer, swept them back into the box in one fell swoop. Mark handed me a list of things we still needed, and sent me to The Container Store, with the rest of the lesser parents who were obviously just getting in the way.

I was at The Container Store only an hour. Maybe two when my phone started buzzing. A text message from Mark read: *ARE YOU COMING BACK???? HELLOOOOOO??????* I knew that meant the other parents must have shown up and he was running out of small talk.

At least I was useful for something. I made it to the fourteenth floor in about ninety seconds because I'm really good at climbing stairs. I walked through the open dorm door in a full sweat and realized that the air conditioner in the room was clearly on the fritz. Good! I was warmly greeted by Omar, Michael's roommate, and his parents, whose names I immediately forgot. Mark and Michael were helping Omar and his father raise his bed two feet off the floor when their other roommate showed up.

Jun from Singapore arrived sans parents, and like a boss, fixed the broken air conditioner in less time than it took me to climb the stairs. I was impressed by his independence and his ability to problem-solve using nothing more than an Allen wrench, so I decided to spare him my hardship speech. Mark asked Jun if he needed any help lifting his bed with risers, but Jun politely declined and closed his door. Four minutes later, Jun reappeared in the open doorway to reveal a bed that was somehow lofted off the floor, using nothing more than his desk and the wrench. On the opposite wall, Jun displayed the most impressive sneaker collection I had ever seen, outside a Flight Club, which I am told is a cool version of Foot Locker. I'm sure Jun knows it.

As we were saying our final goodbyes, we pulled Michael into an embrace and told him all the things that parents tell their kids. How proud we were of him, and all his hard work, and his creativity. We didn't ever want him to lose his sense of compassion and kindness. And we reminded him to continue to use good judgment and make smart choices. Then I pulled him outside the door for a one-on-one and beseeched him to try to wash his dark clothes separately, and on cold. I gave him one final hug and said, "Just remember, if anything happens, or if the shit hits the fan, find Jun. He seems really capable." Michael agreed. Then, Mark and I did what almost every parent inevitably must. We walked away.

Standing on the edge of the quad/Washington Square Park, we embraced each other. "Good job, Mom. One down, two to go," Mark said.

"Do you think he'll be okay?" I asked Mark, looking up toward his building, trying to count up to the fourteenth floor, which was really the thirteenth, but why tempt fate?

"Babe, he's gonna be great."

We hit our favorite brunch spot, Lafayette, on the street of the same name, for some good old-fashioned carb loading. We distracted ourselves with their famous bread basket and salted butter while we ordered. I had a Croque Madame with frites, and Mark had the French toast with frites. We also ordered an extra side of frites, and some bread pudding, because something had to soak up the mimosas.

We looked over the schedule of student activities that NYU had planned for the incoming freshmen, and quickly deduced that Michael would not have the time to miss us. We relaxed knowing his first week on campus would be well occupied with student mixers and school-sponsored distractions. Or maybe we relaxed from the alcohol.

When we walked through our front door on the Upper East Side, both exhausted, and both in desperate need of a shower, we were shockingly greeted by Michael. You know, our son? The one we just dropped off at his dorm? "Did you forget something?" Mark asked.

"No, I just thought I'd spend the weekend with you guys since it's just a bunch of welcome to the city activities," Michael answered, without hesitation. We stared at him in stunned silence. I could feel my mouth hanging agape. I knew he would push the boundaries of the visitation agreement we had created, which was that he could only come home on holidays, but I thought we'd at least get through the first day, or possibly week without said attempt. I formulated a measured response.

"No, honey. Those are activities designed to help all the kids get to know one another. To help all the roommates get assimilated. Plus, you know the city, so you can show your roommates around. Dad and I looked at the schedule. They have so much planned for the incoming freshmen, you should take advantage of all of it." Just as I was finishing my sentence, Lola and Joaquin came downstairs. Their reactions to the developing situation could not have been more divergent. Joaquin ran into his brother's arms, as if they hadn't seen each other in years.

Lola, on the other hand, moved in for the kill. "Are you kidding me right now? Is this a joke? You're home already? What did I say? What did I tell you? He couldn't stay away for five hours!" Mark sent Lola and Joaquin out of the room.

"The first child is not unlike the first pancake," my friend Finola Hughes once dryly remarked, which really made me guffaw for its complete accuracy. I've since repeated that phrase at least ten thousand times. Only when I say it, it lacks the charm without Finola's British accent. It's always resonated with me over the years, and never more so than on that first college drop-off day.

The first child is not unlike the first pancake.

It's hard to know when the griddle has achieved the perfect temperature. Or how much butter to use so the batter doesn't stick. Or when the time is right to flip the pancake, so it's not burned on one side and raw on the other. So, the first pancake is neurotically hovered over, constantly having its edges prodded by the first-time spatula, in the hands of the first-time chefs who have no idea how to cook but are somehow learning while working full-time in a restaurant.

It's hard to know how to respond to certain scenarios, when encountering them for the first time. It's hard to do and say the right thing all the time. There are no crystal balls for pancakes or children. Should we have forced our pancake onto a griddle in another state for forced independence?

Michael was once again pancaking a new trail. Boldly going onto the griddle first and gauging the temperature and slipperiness of the nonstick surface, so that his siblings didn't ever have to get burned. It was all melted pats of butter and maple syrup for those next two pancakes. They could thank their brother for that. But the one thing I knew for certain, was that there was no way I could allow this smart, funny, kind, and perfect pancake to flip himself onto the home plate right now. So, we hugged our pancake and flipped him back downtown.

And then, in the blink of an eye, we were doing it all again with Lola. California-bound Lola. But first, we would have to repeat the same conversations we'd had with Michael, and the days spent sitting in the office of the high school college adviser, listening to his list of schools he thought might suit our child. Lola, of course, pushed back against any school in the Northeast. Lola pushed back against any school that didn't feature palm trees, actually. She had chosen to pursue a career in recorded music, so wanted a school with a great music program. Lola is a fabulous singer and songwriter, although I'm her mother, so she would say I'm biased, but other people who are not her mother have said the same thing. She was in the Advanced Vocal Technique program in high school, and, therefore, forced to perform in the school opera—a genre she did not enjoy—but on the flip side was able to sing the song of her choice at the spring concert. She always chose jazz or blues, two genres she loves.

Lola had already recorded several songs with the help of one of our dearest friends, Jason Sellards. Jason, who also goes by the stage name Jake Shears, is a founding member of the band Scissor Sisters. Jason/Jake is a prolific singer/songwriter and collaborator, and easily the most electrifying performer I've ever seen on stage. After completing his Broadway debut, starring in the musical *Kinky Boots*, Jason relocated to New Orleans. Packing up his apartment, and driving himself down to the Big Easy, where the air hangs wet-hot like jasmine soaked in brandy and rolled in powdered sugar. It was there, in the heart of this cultural-musical hub, that his creative juices flowed like Cajun jambalaya during Mardi Gras (He will hate this description and categorize it as basic, but I'm not the gifted writer he is.), he wrote an incredible solo album, dropping his first single, "Creep City," which you should download after you finish this chapter. You're welcome. During this time, he was also composing several musicals, and completing his brilliant book, *Boys Keep Swinging: A Memoir*, which you should also order after you finish this chapter.

Much like the process of applying to college for Michael, who had to create a student film sample, Lola had to send sample recordings, both covers and originals, for a total of five music submissions. I had to video her recording the music, to assure live singing without Auto-Tune or other production tricks for the submission. This might sound simple enough, however, Lola has a "no mom in the room" rider in her contract. So, I enlisted some outside help—friends of mine who Lola didn't resent.

Once her recordings were finished, we started setting up the college tours, which were mostly held during spring break. This was convenient for me since our show has a two-week break in the spring, coinciding with all of our kids' times off from school. That is unless they played sports, which Lola very casually did, but we all agreed that the chances of her becoming a college field hockey or lacrosse player were right around zero percent. Equally slim were her chances of getting any playing time. So, we skipped whichever sport with a stick that happened in the spring tournament and hit the road.

Quick parenting note here: I'm not big on giving unsolicited advice, but if you're reading this, you might not mind. If you take a college tour with your child and you think that the (insert university name here) is the BEST, and that your kid would excel there, resist the urge to say so out loud. Especially in front of your child. I guarantee that your kid, yes yours, will develop a sudden aversion to the very school they at one time adored. I made this mistake . . . several times.

I loved USC and found it to be positively glamorous, mostly because I'm a sucker for a palm tree, but I also liked the music department, and the convenience of the new shopping and living center the university recently built. But I could tell Lola was bristling. She suddenly seemed overwhelmed by the tour. Even when the kids and parents split off into small groups based on their individual majors, Lola appeared to be intimidated. By what, I wasn't sure. When the kids were asked to introduce themselves and say where they were from, Lola looked at me with terror in her eyes and pleaded, "Mommy, what should I say?" I stared at her in utter disbelief.

"Do you know your name and where you're from?" I said under my breath. I had never seen my daughter like this, ever. Lola is confident and self-assured and the opposite of everything that she was exhibiting at that moment. And it didn't end there.

Same thing happened at UCLA, and UC Everywhere. California Lola seemed to be entering a fugue state. Then we headed to New Orleans, a city every member of our family adores. On this trip, however, it was just Lola and me, not the whole crew. We planned to have dinner with Jason in the French Quarter at a super swanky place called Restaurant Revolution, when we arrived. He came directly from the set of his new music video for "Big Bushy Mustache," which was to be his next single. He was resplendent in a head-to-toe black-and-white hand-painted leather getup, complete with platform boots, biker cap, and—you guessed it—a big bushy mustache. We sauntered in looking . . . unusual, even for the area. Jason approached the host station and declared that he was there to put the "revolution" in the restaurant. Not one person batted an eyelash. Nor did Jason, even when the maître d' referred to us as Mr. and Mrs. Consuelos.

The next morning, we toured Tulane University, which Lola absolutely loved. Until I did, too. Then, just like that, we were headed to schools in the Northeast. Goodbye Café du Mond beignets. Goodbye French Quarter jazz. Goodbye Garden District and Mardi Gras and Commander's Palace and The Spotted Cat and king cake and voodoo. Goodbye Audubon Park. Goodbye Restaurant Revolution!

Hello, NYU? No way. NO WAY! There's absolutely no way that Lola, California Lola, good-time-Charlie-warm-weather-super-independent Lola, was considering the same NYU attended by her brother. What happened to her desire for a real campus experience, with a real quad and real Greek life? What happened to me getting to visit a warm climate once in a while? What happened to me having less laundry to wash?

To hear Lola tell it, she wasn't going to the same school as her brother. She was going to the Clive Davis Institute of Recorded Music at NYU, and therefore, studying in Brooklyn, and eventually abroad in Europe, whereupon she would learn the underground music scenes of Berlin or London and potentially apprentice with a world-renowned deejay, or busk on the metro. The only thing I heard during her soliloquy was that she wanted to study being unemployed for a living. Honestly, didn't any of my kids want to be a plastic surgeon?

Ultimately, after much deliberation and carefully weighing her options, Lola chose NYU, too. My first two pancakes landed on the home griddle. When it came to Michael, the decision to stay local didn't surprise me in the least, but with Lola? I was absolutely stunned. I was beginning to think maybe we made things too comfortable for our kids. We had coddled them too much. Lola was always my most adventurous and social kid. She craved freedom at four the way I did at eighteen. She went to day camp in the summer as soon as I would allow it. I remember tiny Lola excitedly climbing the steps of the Ramapo Country Day Camp bus with her big brother, and her even bigger backpack. If you had seen her from behind, she looked like a backpack with legs. Lola always made the most of everything camp had to offer. At the end of a long day, Joaquin, Chewie (our dog), and I would wait at the corner of Spring and Crosby, across the street from our apartment. As soon as the bus started turning the corner, Joaquin would vibrate with excitement. He was too young to go to camp with them, and their return trip home became the highlight of his day. Lola was always the first one off, bounding down the stairs, with her face painted and eating an ice cream. She would regale us with every single detail of the day, then give Joaquin the lanyard she made just for him. Then I would ask her about Michael's day, because the most I could get out of him was, "It was good."

It was at Ramapo that Lola first heard about sleepaway camp—the holy grail of summer in her mind. Sleepaway camp for us as parents was a hard no. We didn't go to one as kids, so we didn't understand it. We felt like we only got about eighteen to twenty summers with our kids before they started their own lives, so we weren't willing to sacrifice a single week, much less seven.

I had no idea that sleepaway camps offered endless adventures and options for all sorts of individual kid interests. Especially for city kids, where outdoor time and space were so limited. Camp in the Adirondacks or Maine or wherever was a welcome respite from the traffic and noise and unrelenting heat of New York City, or any city, in those summer months.

There were specialty camps of every sort as well. Theater, sports, culinary, and film camps. Even the basic sleepaway programs offered a combination of everything. I always thought camp was a place where kids were sent when they were troubled or unwanted by their families. I probably got that idea from my mom, who used to threaten to send my sister and me away to camp if we didn't behave.

Eventually, Michael aged out of Ramapo, and his best camp friend Robert's mother reached out to me about looking into some sleepaway options. Our kids had strikingly similar mannerisms and personalities. They liked the same food. They liked the Tasmanian Devil cartoon character. They were both introverts. They even dressed alike. And they both had reservations about sleepaway camp, although Michael more so than Robert. Rosalyn found a fabulous place on Little Bear Pond in Maine called Camp Wekeela for Everyone. As I watched the DVD included in the information/application package, it was obviously one of those camps that had everything, and by everything, think Club Med meets everything. Arts and craps, culinary classes, outdoor adventures, land sports, water sports, performing arts. You name it, Wekeela had it. They even offered a two-week option, for first-time campers.

Michael seemed completely disinterested, unlike Lola, who watched the DVD over and over. She carried around the map of the camp everywhere she went. She begged me to enroll her. I told her she was below the age they allowed. (I lied.) Although Michael was reluctant, I realized that all of his friends in the city, and now his best friend, would be going to sleepaway camp. So, for the sake of having social interactions with peers and outdoor adventures in the country, I signed Michael up for the same two weeks in Maine as Robert.

Lola chomped at the bit to have her own outdoorsy lakefront experience. Every night she would log on to the camp website, in search of pictures of her brother having the adventures of a lifetime. She would drag me to the computer screen to show me all the kids who, she was certain, were her age or younger. As luck would have it, Lola would get her chance to spend one night at Wekeela when we picked up Michael after his two-week stay. The famous sibling sleepover, which became so because it turned into a nightly talk point when I tucked Lola in bed. She would reiterate that she most definitely wanted to attend that sibling sleepover. Lola stayed with a group of girls her age that she didn't know, while Joaquin got to spend the night in Michael's cabin, with all of his new friends and their siblings. That cabin smelled of urine and the sweet odor of rotting armpits and unwashed feet. There are certain things you can't unsmell.

It wasn't long before Lola went off to a sleepaway camp of her very own. She chose the all-girls Camp Tapawingo in Sweden, Maine. It wasn't very far from where Michael was located, however he only went away for one other summer. Lola proved a much more intrepid camper. Even though her camp didn't have all the bells and whistles of Wekeela, Lola dove headfirst into everything, including the snake-riddled lake. She found her adventures away from home liberating. As the only girl sandwiched between two brothers, she absolutely relished her sisterhood summers. There was a dull quiet in the house, and a lack of discourse between the siblings that we should have reveled in, but instead, we found ourselves longing for the liveliness Lola provided. I missed her conversations, even the combative ones. Being at home without my daughter was like working in a library. I had a whiteboard calendar with Lola's return date circled in red. I counted down, anxiously crossing off each day as it passed, until the long-awaited day finally arrived. Lola sobbed when we took her home. She would beg and plead with us to let her stay for the full seven weeks of camp instead of the half-session. Eventually, after a few years, we caved in. For seven summers, we endured the deathly tedium of life without our daughter. Seven summers. That was a total of forty weeks. That's 280 days.

I wanted those 280 days back when it came time to move Lola into her dorm room. We returned to the very same building Michael resided in his freshman year. This time we were headed to the fifth floor, where Lola would live with her four roommates. The thought of five girls sharing one bathroom sent a chill down my spine.

The move-in process was much less emotionally taxing the second time around. We were uncharacteristically late, meaning we were only forty-five minutes early, which felt relaxed. Joaquin came with us this time, to help Mark raise the bed, while Lola tricked out her corner of the shared space with color-coordinated bedding, area rugs, and assorted dorm room accoutrements. Once again, I marveled that college students were living in park-facing real estate in a space three times the size of the average New York City apartment. When the other girls/women arrived with their parents in tow, I could tell they, too, were shocked about the size of the dorm, but for the opposite reason.

We hugged and kissed Lola goodbye and gave her basically the exact same talk we gave Michael but added warnings about protecting herself at parties and going out at night in groups and never being on the subway alone. And before you tell me that changing aspects of the talk for my son and daughter with regard to campus safety is sexist, I have several books and newspaper articles I can recommend for you that back up my reasoning.

Lola told us that she'd see us on Thanksgiving, and not a day before. She told us we had a zero percent chance of finding her standing in the foyer when we got home. I told her she was 100 percent correct because we were going out to Long Island for the weekend. I also reminded her that Michael now only lived a few short blocks away should she need anything, but Lola was adamant about her independence. "This is not a Michael situation. I don't want you thinking I'm coming home for Sunday dinners, so don't get your hopes up."

So, Mark, Joaquin, Chewie, and I loaded into the SUV and headed out to Long Island for the weekend. Summer was drawing to an end, so every weekend warrior in the Northeast had the same brilliant idea: sitting in bumper-to-bumper traffic for three and a half hours.

The thought of spending one more second in the car to go to a restaurant was as out of the question as me cooking dinner, so we came up with a livelier plan once we finally arrived. We ordered in dinner and invited our friends Albert and Kyle to come eat with us. Albert, who went to NYU, was well pleased that now two of my kids had chosen his alma mater. Kyle, however, who not only was a proud USC Trojan but also Mr. USC, was less than thrilled with their choices. We spent the entire meal debating the virtues of both schools, with Kyle and Albert attempting to entice Joaquin to their place of matriculation, and me trying to entice Kyle into finally telling us what year he graduated, and by deduction, his probable numeric age. An enigma so closely guarded, not even the most clairvoyant prognosticators at SAG-AFTRA know for sure.

After the guys left, exhaustion took hold of us. Joaquin headed to the TV room to play some video games while we cleaned up the kitchen, then dragged ourselves upstairs to bed. Like zombies we stood, undressing, but not in the sexy way, and brushing our teeth, when the first alert popped up on Mark's phone. He looked, then hit ignore, assuming it was a false alarm, but then another one came. Then another. And another. I looked at him expectantly, while he stared at his phone. "The motion detector is going off on the roof," he said in disbelief. Motion detector? Who even knew we had a motion detector on the roof?

"Maybe it's a pigeon or . . . You don't think it's a rat, do you?" These were and are my primary concerns about having green space at our house. On the one hand, having outdoor square footage in the city is a relatively rare luxury, and we were so grateful to have it. On the other hand, I had a preoccupation with rats, mice, pigeons, and cockroaches, and how to effectively keep them outside the outdoor space.

"I don't know, I'll turn on the cameras," Mark said. Cameras? We have cameras AND motion detectors? Who was this man I married?

"We have cameras and motion detectors?" I asked.

"No, we have cameras IN the motion detectors, one and the same," Mark said matter-of-factly. He was definitely in the CIA, like his father before him. Probably grandfathered in, by his actual grandfather.

A shocked expression moved across, and eventually hardened, on his face. "What is it?" I begged, the sound of fear making its way into my throat.

"Lola is throwing a party on our roof! With a group of kids. There are one, two, ten, no fifteen kids on our roof! She's throwing a rager!" I heard what Mark was saying but couldn't understand what he was telling me. I grabbed the phone out of his hand and stared at the black-and-white image looking back at me.

Instinctively, I started screaming into the speaker, "What happened to 'I'm not coming home before Thanksgiving'? Who are all these people?"

Mark snatched his phone back. "You're wasting your time. She can't hear us." We watched the small night vision footage on Mark's screen, as I called her cell phone from mine. Then, we watched her pick up her phone, look at the number, and ignore the call. Like the badass, parent-defying, independent, the-force-is-female-warrior woman her mother had raised. Dammit. It took.

I started screaming into Mark's screen again, "Pick up the phone before I call the police on your new friends!"

Mark jumped up. "Stop being ridiculous, she can't hear you! I'm driving back to the city." He started putting his clothes back on and searching for his keys. He wanted to drive back to the city, and I was the one being ridiculous?

"You're not driving back to the city. You'll fall asleep at the wheel. You were almost asleep at the sink." We decided a better plan would be to bomb her with phone calls and text messages. And when that didn't work, Mark decided that Lola's flagrant disregard for our home meant that she should be punished by living at said home instead of her dormitory for her freshman year. I explained to Mark that his idea only punished me, since he lived in Canada most of the year for work and wouldn't have to deal with the emotional fallout. My plan, however, was inspired!

"Let's change the locks, that way she can't throw parties the second we're gone."

Was Lola's party really that big a deal? No. In the grand scheme of what young people can do when their folks are gone, this was hardly a thing. But, in the context of her relentless browbeating of Michael, and lecturing us about how we wouldn't see her until Thanksgiving, I felt like a boundary reset was necessary, and that reset would begin with a locksmith.

Just as we started to get comfortable with the feeling of an emptier nest, as parents of independent children, the universe chimed in. Unbeknownst to us and the rest of the planet, a global virus was readying to rear its hideous and destructive head, separating some family members for eternity, and forcing others together, all across the globe.

And so, our emptier nest had a short reprieve, albeit one filled with uncertainty, anxiety, and depression. We were together. And we were healthy. This was our good fortune, and we knew it. But that good fortune was met with guilt—we were not with our parents, siblings, and most of our extended family. We were able to be with one nephew, but not the other. So, our nest was not full.

Michael graduated, not in famed Yankee Stadium, as my dad was so looking forward to, but on the computer screen. So, too, was his film school graduation at Radio City Music Hall, replaced by a Spike Lee Virtual Joint. Lola never went back to her dorm room, as it was needed for emergency services, due to the unimaginable number of people lost during the pandemic. She and a friend from the music school moved into an apartment near campus. They recorded their song projects in the bathroom for the best possible acoustics, since the recording studios were all closed. And then there was Joaquin. The last one in the nest, who would never get to tour schools in person like his siblings. There were no welcome freshmen tours for him to attend and try to figure out where he might fit best. He had to tour virtually and visualize. As a wrestler, he interviewed virtually with athletic coaches. And as a burgeoning actor, he auditioned for the various drama departments, virtually. He also solidified my claim that our children all chose careers of unemployment for their futures.

Joaquin has always been different. Braver than most kids, certainly the ones I knew. I don't know if it is a birth order thing, or a nature/nurture thing, but he always possessed a sharp focus. Maybe it was the dyslexia and dysgraphia that forced his focus. Maybe it was being diagnosed with those learning disabilities at an early age that made him such a hard worker. Or maybe it was the remediation he received in school that made him a self-assured self-advocate.

Perhaps it's just something undefinable that gave him that special sauce they call the X-factor. He is a person who is able to draw the eye of a crowd in his direction and knows how to read the room. He is steadfast in his beliefs, and unmoved by peer pressure. He doesn't care about being cool, which inadvertently has the reverse effect. And so, he is cool. But he is kind-cool, not asshole-cool. Joaquin had that magnetic energy from day one.

As only the third child could, Quino slept through the night immediately, and walked and talked early. He didn't bother babbling like a toddler. He had things to say, and the only way to be heard above the racket of his older siblings was to declare, "I AM HUNGRY!" He didn't mess with those push toys that help teach kids to walk, he pushed five-gallon water bottles around the hardwood kitchen floor. He always smiled. My friends started referring to him as Bam Bam, since he possessed a freakish level of physical strength for a baby. He went from pushing the water bottles one month, to waddling around carrying the empty bottles the next. Empty but still heavy for a one-year-old to carry around. Bam Bam was soon known as Tarzan when he began climbing . . . everything. The walls, the staircase, the kitchen cabinets, the trees in the park, the fence on the rooftop gymnasium. I know this is going to sound braggadocious, but he potty-trained himself, although he did use the floor instead of the toilet for a spell, but he understood the basic principles. He loved to sleep. And every time he woke up, it was like a beautiful rebirth. He would somehow metamorphose to some newer, better, more interesting version of himself. Curiouser and smilier, he would emerge from his crib looking noticeably different. His shoe-brush straight, jet-black hair was beginning to shed with each bath at night. Every rinse of baby shampoo revealed a soft, white-blond downy fluff. By the time he was two years old, Joaquin, with his thick black hair and eyes of ambiguous darkness, had transformed into a cherubic toddler with curly platinum ringlets and electric green eyes who was constantly mistaken for a girl. "You know you're lucky he wasn't born looking like that, or we'd be taking a paternity test." Mark laughed one night.

"Born looking like what? You mean born looking like me?" I said not defensively, but not NOT defensively.

As Joaquin grew, so did his sense of adventure, as well as his athletic abilities. This third kid, the one I mistook for a flu, was absolutely the center of attention wherever he went. He had a packed social schedule thanks to his siblings, and frequently got to experience events that showcased his promising athletic abilities. Lola's birthday party, at Elite Gymnastics in Tribeca, was Joaquin's first exposure to tumbling, and right away it was clear that he had a level of strength and flexibility uncommon for a novice of his age. One of the trainers pulled me aside and asked me if Quino was potty-trained. "Yes!" I bragged, carefully leaving out the very real possibility of him shitting on the floor. Then, the trainer told me about an "invitation-only" comprehensive they had, for preschool-age kids, five days a week. He said that Joaquin had the dexterity and overall body type that is conducive to gymnastics. To me he looked like he had the body type of every three-year-old in Manhattan, although he did seem to be able to walk on his hands more than most and was excessively bouncy. But I demurred at the idea of someone so little having to deal with such a big commitment. I told them we'd consider it, maybe down the road. I wanted him to stay cuddly.

As a person being constantly doted on, and cuddled and carried, he responded with reckless joy, and wanton adorableness. His optimism, utterly contagious. His smile, lighting up every room. And because this third newborn, not the flu, pancake of mine came in this order, he benefited from having a trained chef at the griddle, which was usually at the perfect temperature. I was not going to flip him too early. Or burn him on the sides. I was not going to hover over him, looking for bubbles.

So, it was with this knowledge that I went into the kindergarten classroom of his school, the same school attended by his brother and sister, to talk to his teacher. The same kindergarten teacher the older two had. She was a great teacher. Loving, low-key, and devoted to filling her students with an excitement for learning. I told her of my suspicions regarding Joaquin's comprehension of the alphabet. Or rather, his lack of ability to identify letters. Or numbers. Or symbols. Shapes, signs, and anything written or drawn on paper were out of the question. She reassured me that it was a maturation thing, and probably being the youngest of three meant he didn't get the same level of attention. She also reminded me that the school was progressive, so they wouldn't be introducing a reading curriculum yet. Progressive education, at that time, meant students called their teachers, as well as the other parents, by their first names. They also didn't learn the Pledge of Allegiance, reading or writing, and writing, I mean printing because they would never be taught script, and would not receive grades, until it was time for middle school.

But, grades or no grades, I knew something was up. I had two comparatives living with me for reference, so I knew what was scholastically "typical," even for that school. I knew something was different about the way Joaquin saw things. And because of his perceptive nature, he understood this, too. I knew he knew I was spending too much time trying to teach him the letters of the alphabet. He knew I knew he was getting frustrated that we couldn't get past the letter *A*.

It wasn't until the middle of first grade that I decided proactivity was in order. It was the annual classroom library day for the parents. The students wrote and illustrated their own storybooks, based on anything they wanted, then displayed them like an in-class library. All the kids proudly stood by their books and showed their parents, and then all the other parents as they came to each table to see the other kids' books. Some of the kids were able to print actual words. Some were not yet able but drew pictures to tell their stories in lieu of words. Joaquin bounded over to us with his characteristic excitement and immediately took us over to one of his friends' books. It was a story about a shark, and Joaquin couldn't wait to show us the drawings. Then he showed us another student's book, then another. "Where's yours, buddy?" Mark asked, but Joaquin kept showing us all the other books.

"These are great, Quino, will you show us yours now?" I asked, squatting down to face him, hoping my slacks didn't split. He started rubbing his eyes, like he did when he was trying not to cry and put his forehead against mine. "Okay, you better not show me your book because I won't look at it," I said to his immediate giggle.

"Yes," he replied with a sparkly grin.

"Nope. No way, no how. I won't look."

He began pulling on my arm and laughing, and Mark joined in. "You better not show Daddy because I won't look either." This was almost too much excitement for Joaquin, who was now jumping up and down and pulling us both over to his book. He grabbed it and handed it to us, looking up expectantly.

"Wow, honey! This is so great! We love it, don't we, Daddy?"

And Mark turned the pages with great fanfare, "I think this is my favorite book ever. Son, can you tell us about the story?" He told us the story of a king in a faraway land called Joaquinian World. He went into great detail about the LEGO village, and a thief stealing the children's toys, and the king floating up and away from the trouble. We listened as his voice became more animated describing how the king saved all the children's toys and floated back down to his world. Mark and I glanced knowingly at one another, as we turned the blank pages of his book, closing it and looking at the faint lines, drawn erratically in pencil, on the cover.

Before long we were given a formal diagnosis. Joaquin was

profoundly dyslexic and dysgraphic. Alternately, his reading comprehension, when read to, was off the charts, high-functioning. As was his vocabulary, memory, and recall of details. His scores were incredibly high, in every area tested, except for reading and writing. The evaluator told us she thought the best course of action would be to switch to a school that specialized in learning differences. We had no idea what that even meant, but we faked it by nodding in the affirmative, and asked if she had any schools that she preferred for this sort of thing. (We never would have been this proactive with the first two pancakes.) She then provided us with a list of her favorite schools catering to Joaquin's specific challenges. I couldn't believe how few of these schools there were, and how many students were waiting for a spot.

Flash-forward to 2017. Joaquin graduated from the Stephen Gaynor School in the eighth grade. It was this school, and the teachers, administrators, and learning specialists, that set him on his path to not only loving school but excelling at it.

Yvette Siegel-Herzog, who founded the school back in 1962, and is still one of its dynamic leaders, coined the phrase "Every child can learn. Not every teacher can teach." It is with that spirit that every learning specialist taught each student. The years we spent as a Gaynor family were our favorites. We were involved in as many parent activities as our schedules allowed. Joaquin signed up for absolutely everything. School dances, bowling tournaments, and the dreaded, yearly school ice-skating night. I say dreaded because Joaquin always invited me as his "date" and ice-skating is not among my skill set, at least not the kind on actual ice.

After Gaynor, Joaquin was accepted into every high school where he applied. Now he had to make the decision. There were two schools I was leaning toward, one was a school specifically for kids with learning differences, the other was a hybrid school, meaning it was mainstream, but offered a separate IEP track as well. Coincidentally, Joaquin vacillated between the same two schools, but the choice was his to make.

He chose The Churchill School, which was the perfect choice. It offered a rigorous class schedule, but also allowed academic support, and a small student-to-teacher ratio. All of his new teachers recommended him for the honors program, and Joaquin, knowing himself, started out with just honors English. Then, as the semesters continued, he added himself to honors math, science, history, and writing. He thrived at Churchill the way he did at Gaynor due to the dynamic instructors, who specialized in teaching to the individual. Characteristically, Joaquin signed up for everything the school had to offer. He really took to student government and volunteered to be part of a four-year community service–based student program. He also founded the school wrestling team and dabbled in theater, playing the role of Lord Capulet in *Romeo and Juliet*. From poetry slams to art project showings, he did it all. Mark and I attended parent-teacher conferences, marveling at his grades and his teacher write-ups. After a while, we started looking for problems, something, anything. But Mr. Murphy, Joaquin's adviser, found our insistence that something MUST be wrong amusing.

The four years passed in a flash, and despite the respite of having all of our kids home for those COVID-19 lockdown months, we knew the inevitable was approaching. Joaquin spent the majority of his senior year learning remotely. He went to prom, which almost looked normal, but for the face masks matching the tuxes and gowns, it could have been any other year. We went to his graduation, which was an outdoor affair in the Brooklyn Botanical Gardens. Only four tickets per family were granted due to, you guessed it, COVID-19 restrictions, so Mark and I attended alone. We couldn't figure out how to invite one sibling without the other. So, they watched online, as did their grandparents and cousins.

Witnessing our son, the one we initially worried would never find a place that could teach him or reach him, walk in his bright blue cap and gown, adorned with his gold Honor Society tassel was a moment we will never forget. Knowing that he won achievement awards in math and art and science, was accepted to almost every university he applied, and offered academic achievement scholarships, was a reminder that indeed every child can learn. We may have suppressed ugly cries that day.

As festive and celebratory as the graduation was, I couldn't silence the ticking in my head and heart.

The moment had finally come. The emptying was imminent.

We had a family dinner that night, and everyone gave a speech about Joaquin, what they loved about him and what they were going to miss most when he left for the University of Michigan in August. That's right. My newborn baby, the one who never went to a sleepover, much less a sleepaway camp, was headed to Michigan. *Tick, tick.*

Joaquin started asking for things that summer that had long been forgotten. Back tickles. Head scratches. Tuck-ins at night. Extra hugs. Pancakes from the mix, not from scratch. (He did not enjoy healthy pancakes.) *Tick, tick.* Lola and Michael moved back home to spend the last few weeks with their brother before he left. There seemed to be an unspoken group regression. The kids would all congregate together in one room, and because they went to bed way later than I did, I would "tuck them in," but I would be the one who went to sleep first. "Mom, do the thing you used to do. Where you leave and come back for one more cuddle," Joaquin asked. *Tick, tick*. I honored the request that night, and all the others.

Night after night, just like we used to, I would tuck the kids in, give them cuddles and kisses, then leave ... only to return again for one more cuddle. When the kids were tiny, they would squeal with excited laughter and joy, every time I reappeared in the doorway for one more! One more! Now the reaction was still laughter, but more of a knowingly limited kind of joy.

Those weeks from graduation until drop-off day felt like they passed in three seconds. There was an unmistakable tension and dread in the house that no amount of cuddles or tuck-ins or one mores could dissipate. I could feel Joaquin pushing away from us. Sometimes in a lashing out kinda way. Mark told me it was normal for Joaquin to make it better for himself by detaching from us little by little. I told Mark to shut it.

Tick, tick.

I found myself checking into the Graduate Hotel on August 24, 2021, along with Mark, and our newborn baby, the night before the official move-in. The city of Ann Arbor, Michigan, is spectacular in every way. A true college town. With stately manors that housed fraternities and sororities. All within walking distance to fabulous restaurants, bars, and shopping centers that have absolutely everything. EVERYTHING! They have a Target next to a Michael's next to a Whole Foods across from a Walmart, which is next to a Bed Bath & Beyond. Each megastore is the size of a small airport. I felt like Dorothy in *The Wizard of Oz*. "You gotta love Michigan. Where else can a person buy slacks, almond milk, a rotisserie chicken, and a reading lamp in one place?" I said in the parking lot.

"Literally everywhere else outside New York City," Mark reminded me.

We walked into Target to get essentials for Joaquin, who as the third pancake, had parents who FORGOT THAT HE MIGHT NEED SHEETS TO GO ON HIS BED! But as soon as I walked in, I was quickly overwhelmed and started picking up Halloween candy and Christmas lights, which Joaquin removed from my gigantic cart and returned. "Try to stay focused, Mom." I wanted to search up and down every aisle for things we might not have thought of getting. I was rebuffed by both Mark and the newborn, who insisted we stick to the list.

"But look at that two-thousand-piece thumbtack set. Don't you think you'll need those?" Silence. As we were checking out, I got my revenge by throwing a twenty-six-pack of spearmint gum and three pounds of sugar-free salt-water taffy onto the conveyor belt. As we were marching through the parking lot at a pace I still don't understand, a car full of girls pulled up to Joaquin and handed him an invitation to a party that night. I could tell Mark was hurt that they didn't include him, but Joaquin definitely puffed up a little bit.

The move into the dorm was seamless. The freshmen on the wrestling team all lived in the same building, and all helped one another out, either carrying things, or assembling things, or just pointing parents in the right direction. Joaquin and Mark set a personal record for getting the beds raised, the bookshelf set up, and the fridge stocked. I started unpacking Joaquin's clothes for him and didn't recognize anything in his suitcase. White linen trousers. Cashmere sweaters. Odd fashion-y jackets. At first I thought we mistakenly took the wrong bag, but it had his initials on it, and I knew the suitcase because we bought it for him, for just this occasion.

"Joaquin, are these your clothes?" I asked, still expecting him to tell me that I had mistakenly taken the wrong bag.

"Yeah. Lola took me shopping for stuff she said I needed," Joaquin said, in the defeated tone only someone who has shopped with Lola could possibly understand.

"Honey, you're never going to need any of this stuff," I said. Unless he was going to school in a Duran Duran video of the eighties, I didn't see him ever having an occasion to wear the outfits I was hanging.

"It's okay, babe. The team gives him most of his stuff, and he's got jeans and T-shirts for the rest," Mark reassured me.

Just as I was finishing hanging a confounding fishnet trench coat, Joaquin's roommate walked in. A fellow wrestler, who had a twin brother, who was also a wrestler. Twin wrestlers! I wondered how many at-home wrestling matches their mother had to break up between them over the years. I was dying to ask them if they had mental telepathy, or could feel it when the other got pinned, but Mark must have sensed stupidity brewing within me and started to suggest we go back to the hotel. There was a wrestling team dinner for the freshmen and their parents that night. Joaquin walked us out, and suddenly looked noticeably large compared to both of us. *HE'S THREE!* I shouted internally. We shared a group hug and told him we'd see him at the dinner. Then, I pulled him into a separate hug and whispered, "Ask Christian if he and his brother have mental telepathy, but wait till you know them better." And with that, Joaquin laughed heartily, like I hadn't heard in a long time.

That evening we went back to the wrestling facility, where we met the other freshmen team members and their parents. We all gathered into the locker room and got to see our son's names emblazoned on their lockers, which were stuffed with regulation wrestling team gear. We took pictures of Joaquin in front of his locker, but only when we saw the other parents doing it as well. Then Sean

Bormett, the head coach, gave a rousing speech about the significance of this particular team, being the 100th wrestling team for Michigan, or Team 100 as it's known. So uplifting and inspiring were his words that I was certain I would become the first parent, walk-on team member to represent America in the Summer Olympics in Paris. "Ooh la la!"

Mark snapped his head around and scowled at me.

"What?" I said.

"Shhh, keep it down," he softly barked.

"I didn't say anything," I whispered, baffled.

"You said 'Ooh la la,' and whatever you're up to, get un-up to it," he warned.

I was certain I had only thought *Ooh la la*.

We dined al fresco, next to the wrestling facility, under a beautiful late sunset. Mark and I sat silently looking across the table, watching Joaquin fit right in, knowing that we were facing the inevitable. Knowing that we had that meal, and then hopefully breakfast the next morning, before we flew home, alone. It's a strange thing, to show up as three and leave as two. *Tick, tick, tick, tick.*

We went back to our hotel room and stopped in the lobby to purchase some candy and other refined sugar–based carbohydrates, because there has never been a sadness that can't be cured by Twizzlers. We crawled into bed, cracked open the candy, and an apple pie, and dug in. And before you get judge-y, I know you've eaten in bed once or twice, so SHUT IT.

We were just settling down to watch Hulu when Joaquin FaceTimed to let us know he was going to a party with the other wrestlers. We were relieved that he was feeling social, and a part of things. We told him to have a great time, to make smart choices, and not to worry about breakfast in the morning if he was going to be out late. But Joaquin was insistent that he would be at the hotel in the morning, for a final breakfast.

The next morning, we woke up to the ding of a text message. Fully expecting to find Joaquin canceling our breakfast, we were instead pleasantly surprised to find a text saying he was on his way. We finished packing just as he knocked at the door.

"Hi! How was the party?" I asked, trying too hard and too loud and too upbeat.

"Mom, calm down," he said. He was salty. We knew that this might happen, the cloud of doom that hangs over the last hour of college drop-off. We went down to the hotel café and ordered breakfast sandwiches to eat outside. We asked Joaquin questions about his night, hoping to spark a conversation but received mostly one-word answers. He barely looked up. I knew he was in pain, because we were, too. I instinctively reached out and ran my fingers through his thick, wavy hair. "Mom, I'm gonna need a back scratch, too," he said, almost sounding like himself.

I slid my chair a little closer to his. "You okay, honey?" I asked. But he just leaned into the back scratch and didn't say a word. Mark and I looked at each other across the table, and I knew he heard the ticking, too.

We slowly walked to our rental car with our arms wrapped around Joaquin. I silently replayed pieces of his life in my head. I watched him sleeping in his bassinet. I could almost feel myself holding tiny him again. I watched him crawling in his diaper. I could see him climbing into our bed early on a Sunday morning. I saw him go to nursery school, proudly carrying his backpack. I watched him catch a fish. I could feel his little hands holding mine while we danced at a Bat Mitzvah. I watched him blow out the candles. I heard him find the presents under the tree at Christmas. I watched him crying in agony, begging me not to take him out of his school, to a new and an unknown one. I watched him find his way and grow and thrive and lead and succeed. I watched him graduate with honors. I witnessed the transition of him sitting on his grandfather's shoulders, to carrying his grandfather's bags through the airport. He went from riding a trike to a bike to a scooter, to driving a car. He grew up. I thought of all the things I would give to go back in time, for only an hour. I told him as much as I pulled him in for a hug. "I really didn't know it would go so fast." I stopped talking because I could feel myself getting choked up. He felt, at once, giant and small.

"We are so proud of you, Joaquin, and so excited for this next adventure," Mark said, leaning into a group hug. I gave him a final kiss on both cheeks and his forehead, then we rubbed noses, like we used to when he was tiny. He turned and started walking away.

"Wait, Joaquin! One more . . ." I said, thinking he would laugh and come back for one more, but he didn't. He walked away and kept going.

Our ride to the airport was silent, and our flight home lonely. When we walked into the empty house, we found Lola, bringing home our dogs that she cared for in our absence. "How was it?" she asked as the dogs ran around us like we had been gone for six years. Instead of answering her, we pulled out a bag of Michigan merchandise that we had picked up for her as a thank-you. Lola immediately went to try on the cutoff hoodie and cutoff T-shirt that went with the cutoff shorts and cutoff sweats. She looked super cute in everything and said she couldn't wait to go visit Joaquin. Then, she whipped out her cell phone and showed us a bunch of photos of her brother at various parties.

"Where did you get these?" Mark asked.

"Sibs sent them to me. How funny is that? Notice how boring Joaquin is holding a water bottle?" Lola declared. Sibs is one of Lola's best friends since her first day of pre-K, who also attends Michigan.

"He should be holding water, he's eighteen," Mark responded to Lola, who looked at him like he was speaking another language.

"Hey, do you want to have dinner with us?" I asked, thinking it would be nice to catch up with our most elusive child.

"Oh, I wish I could, but sadly no. I've got a party tonight, so I've got to bounce, but try to have fun without me, you two lovebirds." Then she made a gag face and kissed us goodbye because her Lyft was pulling up.

We stood in the foyer, kind of immobile, for quite some time. Then Mark said he was going to walk the dogs, so I decided I'd put the laundry in and get dinner started. It was way later than our usual dinnertime, but the sudden loss of the last kid in the house, keeping us on a semi-regular eating schedule, was already starting to take effect. I set the table. I cooked dinner for approximately fifteen people, because that is what I was used to doing. Mark and I sat and ate, occasionally asking each other what we thought the kids were doing. I could feel a disturbance in the force but chalked it up to the unprecedented silence. Mark suggested we turn in early, since we had been running on no sleep for the past couple of days. But I knew what "turning in early" really meant. Maybe we could get into this empty nest thing.

So, I headed upstairs to start my "routine," which consists of the following steps: shower, brush my teeth, comb my hair, and apply thirty-five different antiaging creams that do absolutely nothing. Mark joined me in the bathroom to start his "routine," which is much less involved. He brushed his teeth and left the room. Usually, when I come to bed the lights are still on, and if they're not, Mark's cell phone light softly calls me home, like a lighthouse and a whaling vessel. But on this night, our first night alone in the empty nest, the lights were off, and the cell phone was dark. I attempted to reach the bed in the thick blackness but stepped on Chewie, who yelped. I hit the light switch and the soft glow of the light woke Mark, who apparently didn't want to "turn in early," but actually just wanted to go to bed.

"Turn that off!" he yelled, yes yelled, with aggression.

"I can't see the bed in the dark!" I yelled right back.

"Please. How many years have we lived here? If you don't know where the bed is by now, then you've got problems," he said, still yelling. This man who snores as loud as a jet airplane. This man who talks in his sleep but never says anything helpful. This man who has never gotten out of bed without turning on every light as bright as possible, no matter what the time. This man is taking issue with me turning on a light to find the bed, without killing my elderly dog?

"You're my fucking problem!" I screamed.

It suddenly dawned on me that we were in prime position to be THAT couple, the one that gets divorced as soon as the kids were out of the house. I grabbed my pillow with the satin pillowcase for antiaging with as much fanfare as I could muster and stormed out of the room. I slept in Lola's bedroom, which was much less comfortable, but at least I'd get a good night's sleep, instead of listening to the dulcet tones of jackhammer Consuelos. Plus, in an act of sheer genius, I left the dogs in our room, and let me tell you, that little Lena was still waking up to go potty at 5:00 a.m., so I think we know who won that round. The next two days were like a Mexican standoff of sorts, or at least half of one. Both of us being aggressively passive-aggressive in our ignoring one another. Both of us committed to NOT being the one to apologize, even though it was crystal clear that HE should be the one to beg for my forgiveness and shower me with flowers ... or at least empty the dishwasher for a change!

There are two kinds of dead in this world. There is the actual death of a person or thing that has passed away, and then there is dead-to-me-dead, which is way worse. Seldom has a body ever resurrected from the dead-to-me-dead. I feared Mark was headed toward the catacomb of no return. Even when he sauntered into the bedroom, wet and glistening from his workout, did I barely even bat an eyelash. Dead-to-me-dead men don't glisten, they sweat. Nor did I notice when he casually peeled off his soaking wet gym clothes and placed them in the laundry basket, then wrapped a towel around his waist, but around his lower waist, you know what I mean? I felt like saying, "You're wasting your time, Casper, I'm not even looking at your washboard abs and silky brown skin." And when he dropped that towel, glancing back at the mirror, to catch me looking at him, I waltzed out of the room because ghosts don't shower!

Imagine my surprise when the poltergeist suddenly appeared in the kitchen, freshly showered, smelling like soap and contrition. I continued my attempt to ignore the specter, but he somehow caught my eye with his electric smile. "Hey, let's not fight. We love each other. Let's be patient with each other. Okay?" murmured the presence.

Somehow, he must have possessed me because I heard myself saying, "Would you like to go to the beach tonight for sunset? Maybe take a baguette and some cheese? We haven't been to the beach all summer." As soon as I said it, I knew that Mark had risen from the dead.

I packed a small picnic basket with a tray table and some sort of fancy soft French cheese. Then I heated up a baguette and wrapped it in foil to keep it warm. Meanwhile, Mark put two beach chairs in the back of the Jeep and placed the dogs in their carriers, and off we went. We arrived at the beach just as the late summer sun was starting to set. It was a perfect night. The dogs curled up on the blanket I laid in front of us and fell asleep. We sat, soaking in the sultry summer air, while tearing off pieces of warm baguette, and spreading gobs of soft cheese on top. We relaxed into each other and discussed our future as parents who now had more freedom than we were used to. Where might we live? Where might we retire? Maybe we'll take long weekend trips Upstate? We wondered where Upstate was.

We gazed at the candy-colored sky, pondering our possibilities while listening to the sound of other people running after their small children. We smiled knowingly at each other. As the sun disappeared completely, we stayed and watched the stars light up the night sky. Witnessing the dazzling moon rise, as the ocean water gently lapped the coast, I realized that in the past, I had never taken the time to notice how serene it all was. How could I have missed all this beauty?

Then I was distracted by the sound of a father yelling to his young daughter, who was running away from him and getting too close to the beach bonfire. I watched that same father turn on his cell phone flashlight in a futile search for his daughter's tiny flip-flops. I watched his wife pack up the six buckets and twelve shovels and three beach chairs and two floats, and bags and bags and bags of snacks, and then strap a sleeping baby into a sling on her body. I realized that they had about eighteen more years before they would notice the beauty all around them, instead of the danger. I wanted to yell out to them and say, "I know the days are long, but the years are short, and they grow up, and are out of the nest in the blink of an eye, so don't blink."

But I didn't. Instead, I turned to Mark, who was grinning at me, and I already knew he was reading my mind. "How did we do that for so many years?" I asked, more in awe of that couple, than the memory of us.

"We just did," Mark answered.

"Do you miss it?" I asked.

Mark pulled me in close and said, "Are you kidding? Those guys are suckers! They're going to be dusting sand off their kids for the next three months." We both started laughing at all the collective memories we didn't make because we were too busy searching for flip-flops in the dark, and running after several kids at once, trying to prevent a potential beach tragedy.

"How about this beautiful night?" I said, still marveling at the peace and quiet.

Mark's eyes were focused on the night sky when he reminded me, "We've earned it, baby. This is just the beginning."

"Is that all there is?"

—PEGGY LEE

WHAT EPILOGUE IS THIS?

Something you've probably surmised by now, dear reader, is that I have a hard time ending things. Or rather, I have difficulty knowing how to begin the ending of things. You should have seen the lengths of these "short stories" before they were edited.

Are there succinct words to wrap up a collection of essays, or some lesson to be learned? Maybe James Patterson, at the very beginning of this book, was right.

A memoir would have been easier.

Okay, so maybe this is more of a personal addendum, or an afterword, rather than anything else.

Or maybe I'm just stalling.

I suppose I am hoping you'll eventually come to your senses and just put this book down.

I would, after all, feel more comfortable if you left first. Or if I left without you noticing. Actually, if I could make the book disappear after you've read it, that would be a great relief. This would spare my very fragile ego any hurt feelings your judgment might bring. Not yours specifically, as I know you're not judgmental, but someone's.

Anyone's.

Everyone's.

Not to mention the utter shock I experience every time I realize I still have feelings . . . and that they still have the ability to be hurt.

And even though I have built a fortress of self-deprecation, thicker than elephant skin around said feelings, somehow the dull buzz of my own internal doubt always finds a breech.

I tend to be an open book, turning my own pages for public consumption as a career choice. A studio extrovert, there to put on the razzle dazzle irreverently. I understand my assignment.

But the private me, the introverted, socially awkward me, would rather evaporate than tell the entire story, or go on a book tour.

Oh gosh, a book tour?

I hadn't even thought about the tour, which I know I will enjoy once I do it. But because I tend to ratchet up negative chatter in my head, it's the gearing up to do it that I find most arduous.

My proclivity to escape a gathering without the slightest detection is probably a self-defense mechanism. Born from years of crooked thinking or watching *The Invisible Man* one time too many. The old movie of course, not the really scary updated version.

I'm only telling you this in advance, in case we do meet in person, and you wonder why I'm perspiring like a beast of burden.

It's me. It's not you.

You have, after all, very kindly welcomed me into your home for decades. We've had coffee together, or whatever it is you drink in the morning, and perhaps even shared the morning headlines. You've witnessed my family expand, and then watched us grow up. Occasionally, you've introduced me to your families when we've bumped into each other, either in the studio audience or at a restaurant someplace. I've met adult women, with children of their own, named Hayley Vaughan after my character on *All My Children*. We've been together a long time! We've celebrated triumphs and mourned losses. And even though we mostly remained strangers, we actually have known each other.

Maybe these stories combined with what you already know, or thought you knew, will lend some small perspective or insight into what it took to get here and stay here. Because there have been times behind the scenes that were so unbearably severe and destabilizing that the thought of getting out of bed was insurmountable.

But not as insurmountable as the idea of not showing up.

And frankly, I owe a lot of that to you, because YOU, dear reader and viewer, have gotten me through the hard times whether you know it or not.

So maybe you have been reading my open book all along, or maybe you've read into it.

Perhaps you feel that a few chapters are missing, or a few loose ends need tying up, and that would be an astute observation. Sometimes certain things are better left unsaid.

Here, in this book, I've given you what I'm prepared to give. And what I think you are prepared to handle. After all, you wouldn't want to see a nightclub with the lights on, would you?

"They can't miss you if you don't leave" was sage advice I wasn't offered but overheard once.

But you know me, I'll still be here long after the store closes and the lights go on in the club. Somebody has to clean up.

So . . .

Hopefully you'll do me the favor this time. You'll leave first, okay?

Otherwise, we may be looking at a seven-volume collection of rambling personal essays, and NOBODY wants that. Especially not my now long-suffering editor, Carrie Thornton.

ACKNOWLEDGMENTS

Advanced apologies to anyone I forgot to thank, but know that it will haunt me for the rest of my life.

First and foremost, my endless gratitude to my mom and dad, Essie and Joe Ripa, who lead by example. Every good thing I am I owe to you. Your love, generosity, compassion, and work ethic are only matched by your fierce and unrelenting sense of humor. It's not lost on me all the sacrifices you made for your daughters and everyone else. And even though you probably kidnapped me from my birth mother, Cher, I forgive you. Thank you, Mom and Dad, for EVERYTHING!

To my in-laws, Camilla and Saul (Tony) Consuelos, thank you for your courage in leaving your homelands with three young kids for life in America. For raising Mark to be the embodiment of your profound, loving, familial spirit, and your boundless support and guidance. You welcomed me into your lives like I was your very own. Thanks, Mom and Dad! PS: Your secret about being in the CIA is safe with me.

To my hearts:

Michael, Lola, and Joaquin—my unending love, appreciation, and gratitude. You three have filled me with immeasurable pride and joy. You've impressively balanced being in the public eye, whether you liked it or not, while still maintaining your privacy, dignity, and normalcy. As individually talented, hardworking, and brilliant as you are, it is your kindness and altruism that fill my heart the most. Thanks guys, I hope this book doesn't cause you too much embarrassment. I think I showed great restraint.

To Linda, Adriana, Mike, and Kelly, thank you for raising the greatest nieces and nephews this aunt could wish for.

And to Alec, Sergio, Maddie, Isa, Gabi, Gianna, Luci, and Gigli, you're all so uniquely gifted and lovely. I simply adore spending time with you. It remains my privilege to be your number one favorite aunt. ;)

To my non–blood related siblings:

Gretchen and Willie Randolph, and Tenisha, Chantre, Andre, and Ciara. Thank you for all the laughs, meals, ball games, parties, and fights over who is going to pay the check.

Albert Bianchini and Kyle Barisich, whether at work or play, you two show up. Every special person day at school, and every single important life event. I can't wait to repay the favor someday. Hint hint.

To Jason Sellards, you read my earliest words and gave me the best feedback. Watching you write your memoir was my guide.

To the women responsible for my professional life:

Profound gratitude to Felicia Minei Behr, the EP of *All My Children*. Thank you for gambling on a newcomer. Angela Shapiro-Mathes, aka my BOSS, you have given me too many opportunities to list, not to mention your guidance, insight, and laughter, even when nothing was funny. Joanna Johnson, you created *Hope and Faith* and provided me with my favorite job to date. To my literary agent (I HAVE A LITERARY AGENT!), Cait Hoyt—WOW! And Andy, thank you for keeping me on deadline-ish.

To my editor, Carrie Thornton, I'm eternally grateful for the two years of our lives we'll never get back, but if I ever try to do this again, please kill me.

And finally, every once in a while a person comes along who sets the bar so high, both professionally and personally, they raise everyone in their radius and beyond. Debra O'Connell, YOU ARE THE HARDEST WORKING MAN IN SHOW BUSINESS! You're a fearless leader, a tireless mentor, and if rumors are true, a clone. But beyond all of that, you're an extraordinary wife and mother, and I believe the only executive at Disney to survive a drive-by shooting. I love you more than words.

To my team who are also like family:

Jason Weinberg and Bryan Lourd, thank you for the never-ending love, support, and guidance. We reverse-engineered the entire friend/client blueprint. (If there is one.) Jason, you FaceTiming me while standing next to your famous clientele got me through the grind of thesaurus-ing synonyms for words like "insanity" and "horseshit." Bryan, you Jedi mind-tricked me into thinking I could write to begin with. Thank you for spell-checking my copy edits. We have walked through many fires together, and speaking of fires . . . Thank you, Matthew Hiltzik, for always having your hatchet and hose at the ready.

The inner sanctum:

To Andy Cohen and Anderson Cooper, the stalwarts. Andy, you encouraged me to start journaling again in case I ever wanted to write a book. Anderson, I will never be able to properly repay you and Benjamin Maisani for a lifetime of favors, late-night dances, and endless giggles.

To Faith Ford, Ted McGinley, and RJ Wagner, I'm so grateful to have had the opportunity to share the soundstage with you three. What a gift.

To Jerry O'Connell, you are in a class by yourself in the friend department.

To David Muir, you are the backbone and moral compass I need sometimes.

To Barry Sonnenfeld and Susan (Sweetie) Ringo, the New Year's Eve maestros. Barry, I will never be able to tell a story, make a martini, or leg wrestle like you.

To the Perskys for all the years of Shelter Island picnics, peppermint ice cream, meatloaf, and stories.

To Jon and Lizzie Tisch, thank you for pretending not to notice when I spill things on your white carpet.

To Leo Gomez for getting me there.

To Rachael Harris, Nastaran Dibai, Sahra Jaamac, Lucy Liu, Cartwright Lee, Ellen Barkin, Carrie Ann Inaba, Elsa Collins, Monica Mangin, Isaac Calpito, Jeffrey O'Brecht, Jess Tubbs, Ian Sherman, Arlene Stewart, and Daniel Arias, who all had to listen to me agonize over writing this book.

The OG's:

Scott Silber, my first friend.

Dondré Whitfield, as an author yourself, you knew to do wellness checks on me.

Eva LaRue, Sarah Michelle Gellar, Finola Hughes, Ariel Kochi, Claudia Bell, Pam Newman, Walt Willey, Richard Esposito, it's always like no time has passed, even when a lot has.

The miracle workers:

Makeup—Kristofer Buckle, thank you for decades of friendship. You know how to make the most of me, and everyone else!

Hair—Ryan Trygstad, thank you for this cover, and all the covers!

Hair—Vanessa Alcala for all the early mornings.

Fitness—Anna Kaiser, easily the person I spend the most

time with, for body and mind. Anysia Kelly and Blaire Buchanan, Anna's trusted protégés.

Photographer—Miller Mobley for always capturing the image perfectly, and fast!

Nutrition—Dr. Daryl Gioffre for your endless quest to get me off sugar.

Longevity—Dr. Erika Schwartz, only if you want to live long and feel good.

For restoration from the neck up—Dr. David Rosenberg, providing works of art!

For the neck down—I'm still searching for the one, reach out if you know somebody.

Cosmetic Dermatology—Dr. Robert Anolik and Dr. Roy Geronemus, for resurfacing and freezing.

Cosmetic Dentistry—Dr. Marc Lowenberg, somehow keeping my teeth white in spite of all the coffee.

Ophthalmologist—Dr. Samuel Guillory, for attempting to save my eyesight.

The village:

To Michael Gelman, even though looking at you is like staring into the sun, I sure do appreciate your ability to keep the crazy train on the tracks all these years. When something looks easy, it rarely is.

To Ryan Seacrest, the boy wonder! And Alfred, his humble manservant. Thank you for switching coasts and coming to the dark side in record time. Working with you is no work at all, and vacationing with you, especially at one of your many subterranean estates, is absolute ecstasy.

To Art Moore, the gentlest of gentlemen. You live up to your name. No matter how much time I have with you, I always want more. Thank you.

To the *Live!* staff —The ones who really do all the work:

Chad Matthews, Flody Suarez, Brian Chapman, Déjà Vu, Angie Riley, Christine Composto, Cindy MacDonald, Dana Dodge, David Mullen, Edward Connolly, Esther Pak, Delores Spruell Jackson, Diane D'Agostino, Donna Bass, Elyssa Shapiro, Jan Schillay, Jim Niebler, Jason Francisco, John Ogle, Joni Cohen Zlotowitz, Kelly Burkhard, Kristen Osborne, Lauren McTague, Laurie Ciaffaglione, Lori Schulweis, Michael Fagin, Michelle Champagne, Monique Bobbitt, Scott Eason, Bill Cabral, Andrea Lizcano, Seth Gronquist, Ashley Lewis, Beau Hart, Caroline Schlobohm, and Shira Kaplan.

Special shoutouts:

To Kal Penn, thank you for normalizing my self-loathing during my writing process. I feel seen. And Gary Janetti, thank you for NOT CANCELING!

To the entourage:

Audrey Slater, who would have thought all those years ago in Physique 57 would lead to this? You read this book before anyone and laughed at all the right parts.

Lauren Travaglione, my one-woman chief of staff. Your quiet professional demeanor, loyalty, and stoicism are not touted often enough. You carry the workload of ten people, and you've got the thumbs to prove it. Lauren, I simply cannot imagine my life without you and your family in it. We are the Lucy and Ethel of backstage, only I'm Lucy of course. *Thank you* is not a big enough form of gratitude. I love you.

In a category all his own:

Mark,

You have always been the one. From the moment I saw your photo, I just knew we would go through life hand in hand. Awkwardly of course, due to our incompatible arm lengths, but still. We have created an incredible life together and I don't take a single second for granted. You have given me everything. In return, I give you my heart and soul, and these words on the page.

ABOUT THE AUTHOR

KELLY RIPA is one of the most powerful voices in media, with a diverse body of work both on and off the camera. A household name for more than two decades with a career at ABC spanning more than thirty years, Ripa has welcomed viewers with her sharp wit every morning as the host of the award-winning *Live!* franchise. Having established *Live!* as a major destination for entertainers, politicians, athletes, and other cultural icons during her stint as host, Ripa has been honored with six Daytime Emmy Awards for Outstanding Talk Show Host and fifteen Daytime Emmy nominations for Outstanding Entertainment Talk Show.

In 2007, Ripa and her husband, Mark Consuelos, ventured into the development side of entertainment when they began their New York City–based production company, Milojo Productions. Milojo produces and creates content across multiple platforms, working with Bravo, Logo, VH1, E!, CMT, HGTV, WeTV, TLC, Oxygen, ABC Signature, Hulu, and Discovery. Additionally, Milojo produced the Emmy-nominated documentary *The Streak* for ESPN and the critically acclaimed documentary *Off the Rez* for TLC.

Ripa lives in New York City with her husband, and together the couple have three children.